40 Years
in the
Wilderness

40 Years in the Wilderness

Inside Israel's West Bank Settlements

Josh Freedman Berthoud
& Seth Freedman

Five Leaves Publications
www.fiveleaves.co.uk

Forty Years in the Wilderness
by Josh Freedman Berthoud and Seth Freedman

Published in 2010
by Five Leaves Publications,
PO Box 8786, Nottingham NG1 9AW
www.fiveleaves.co.uk

ISBN: 978 1 905512 90 4

Designed by Four Sheets Design and Print
Printed in Great Britain

*to our
grandparents*

Contents

Prologue   5

Introduction   9

2007

One: Kedumim *From Rocks to Riches*   19

Two: Mitzpeh Yeriho *Far From the Calming Crowd*   65

Three: Kfar Adumim *Spreading the Word*   93

Four: Efrat *Normalisation*   126

Five: Karnei Shomron *Jews Versus Israelis*   163

Six: Ariel *City State*   197

Seven: Disengagement *Give and Take*   219

2009

Eight: East Jerusalem *The Lie of the Land*   235

Nine: Modi'in Ilit and Bil'in *Two Sides of the Wall*   263

Ten: Hebron *Doing Davka*   273

Eleven: The South Hebron Hills *Above the Law*   290

Twelve: Facing Facts *One Man's War on the Settlements*   311

Epilogue: The Settlement Freeze *Settlers Out in the Cold?*   331

Endnotes   341

Prologue

Boarding the bus at Jerusalem's central station felt like the start of any journey across Israel. Ethereal women, swathed in robes and headscarves, swaddling babies and balancing shopping under their arms; middle-aged Slavs with world-weary faces; bookish scholars with beards down to their chests, groomed into triangular points through years of constant tugging; lithe, tanned young women in tight jeans, flashing their midriffs ... all pushing and jostling their way down the bus in search of a seat in which to collapse and sleep their way through the next couple of hours.

In fact the only difference was that the windows of the bus were reinforced with bullet proof glass, a pertinent reminder that the number 148 bus might be a standard route, but this was far from a routine journey.

As the bus drew away from the dark shelter and into the dazzling Jerusalem sunshine, we took in the faces of our companions joining us on the journey from the moderate, secular centre into the reputed heartlands of Israeli right wing fanaticism. To our left sat a young religious man, dressed in the standard garb – not the black hats and coats of the *Haredi* Jews, but a subtly different uniform – that of the National Religious movement, the body at the heart of Israel's West Bank settlement programme. Like his *Haredi* counterparts, he sported a long beard, but his clothing was rather more relaxed. Loose-fitting navy trousers unsuited to the grubby pale blue shirt above them were set off by a notably unfashionable combination of socks and sandals covering his feet. Where his shirt spilled out over his waist, long, knotted *tzitzit* [symbolic strings] streamed out over the seat and became entangled in anything they touched. Atop his head sat the familiar large, knitted *kippah* [skullcap] as worn by all those of his tribe, and in his hands he held the *siddur* [prayerbook] from which he prayed intently, silently poring over every word, his thoughts a world away from the two *hiloni* [secular] English cousins who sat to his right, examining him so attentively.

And there on his bag were the marks of the battle that had scarred the country a few years previously. Colour meant everything in the summer when Sharon ploughed on with his proposed evacuation of Gaza and parts of the West Bank. Those in support of the evacuation of Israel's settlers tied blue ribbons to everything, whilst those who opposed the move, with all their pious might, wore orange – and flocks of orange clad demonstrators streamed through the streets of the Holy Land. Sharon won that battle but then gave up the fight, suffering a massive stroke in January 2006, leaving the country in a confused limbo. As a result, the issue is far from concluded and the orange fire still burns brightly in the settlers' hearts; protesters regularly march to Homesh – one of the dismantled West Bank settlements – to demand its reconstruction.

Knotted tightly to the man's bag was an orange ribbon, grubby with age and somewhat lacklustre – though its very presence confirmed the divide that has only become further entrenched in the period following the *hitnatkut* [Disengagement]. This orange ribbon was the most familiar and potent symbol of the place we were preparing to enter: the mark of the nationalist, religious, right wing settler movement. It was also a badge we sought to move beyond, in order to transcend the division of blue and orange, black and white, and discover just who these notorious settlers were.

Bullet proof glass is not easy to see through and on our way through Israeli-occupied East Jerusalem, it added a certain distance between us and the reality outside, shrouding the crowds of people gathered around the sun-bleached white stones of the city in an other-worldly haze. As the bus began to chug slowly up the hills away from the city, the land opened out and parched yellow mountains glanced brightly into the bus with a shocking glare. The mountainsides were dry and cracked and frequently barren, but for scrubby bushes that forced their way up through the thirsty earth. As the people faded away, save for the handfuls of religious nationalists at the stone bus stops, they were replaced with large boulders scattered across the pastel mountains.

But soon a settlement arose – signs of Jewish life in the Israeli occupied suburbs of East Jerusalem – built away from any older residences, either Arab or Jewish. Rows and rows of houses sat perched a few metres from the road, running along the edge of the shallow valley that faced back towards Jerusalem. They were newly built, rich and comfortable, each with a matching red sloped roof and each seeming to be the carbon copy of the next. Lush green date palms grew amongst the blooming settlement.

Beyond this small town was a Palestinian village. Squat, grey houses sat close to the ground and spread organically into the streets and alleys that ran winding through the village. Ramshackle buildings built of stone seemed to blend into the ground beneath them – now rising up from the earth, now crumbling back into it. Dusty grey paths ran undirected between the houses. But there were richer Arab villages too, similar to the Israeli towns – save for the people who moved there.

The road ploughed on, snaking through the carved rock; gorged into the mountainside. Silver-green leaves shimmered from the branches of olive trees, rooted deep into the surrounding hills. Some of the groves seemed wild, others less so, banked up the hills in grey stone terraces. Then other small Israeli settlements appeared, distinguishable by their familiar red roofs.

The bus drove on, shepherding its Israeli flock into the safety of their heavily-guarded communities, away from the Arabs, both rich and poor, towards the heartlands of Jewish settlement in the West Bank – and into one of the most contentious patches of land in the Middle East.

8

Introduction

"Why are you writing a book about us?"

From the Yemeni man in the pizza shop, to the 19-year-old soldier on guard duty, to the mayor of the town grilling us in her living room, this was the first question on everyone's lips when they made our acquaintance.

We came to the *Shtachim* [literally, the Territories] to meet the people behind the stereotype; the ordinary folk who have, for whatever reason, eschewed setting up home elsewhere in Israel and come to dwell on the other side of the Green Line (the 1949 Armistice Lines following the Israeli-Arab war of 1948, which marked the border between Israel and Jordan until 1967 and have been widely recognised as the border between Israel and the Palestinian Territories ever since). Although international law maintains that Israel's settlements are illegal, due to their being constructed on occupied land, successive Israeli governments have paid little heed to world opinion during their occupation of the land captured in '67. Settlements have been actively promoted by the state over the years, and hundreds of thousands of Israelis have heeded the call, despite the uncertain future and legal status of the townships and cities dotted around the West Bank. There are now over 300,000 Israeli settlers in the West Bank and a further 195,000 in Israeli-occupied East Jerusalem.

To the outside world, settlers are lawbreakers and are often seen in a homogenous light: religious zealots with a Bible in one hand and an Uzi in the other, hate in their hearts and God on their side. But Israeli ambiguity over the status of the settlements has resulted in a wide range of people moving to the West Bank. Once the preserve of extremists only, the normalisation of city settlements like

Maaleh Adumim now means that all kinds of Israelis call the West Bank home.

There are to be found, of course, the nationalistic religious extremists described above, but there are also those who moved to *Yehuda* and *Shomron* [Judea and Samaria: the Biblical names that Israel uses for the two regions of the West Bank] for reasons entirely detached from religion and war. Ariel, for example, is a mini-city "packed full of Russians", according to one *sabra* [Israeli-born] settler we interviewed. The residents are there largely for economic reasons: the subsidies provided by the government, including income tax breaks, lower rates for businesses operating from the region, subsidised educational costs, cheap housing and other related benefits.

The low cost of living played a significant part in persuading immigrants from the former Soviet Union to set up home in Ariel, and has helped bolster the populations of settlements throughout the West Bank. Such residents are

Maaleh Adumim

not concerned with the contentious politics of the region, but are simply looking for somewhere cheap and comfortable to call home. Others, such as the Ultra-Orthodox residents of Modi'in Ilit, are equally unconcerned with politics and have moved to a settlement which can provide them with a homogenous Ultra-Orthodox bubble, away from the corruption and temptation of the religiously diverse Israeli cities. Countless other settlers fall somewhere between the various camps.

We began our trip in Kedumim. The first settlement to be set up in the Shomron region, it has mushroomed into a crowded town of over 7,000 residents. On the face of it, Kedumim appears to be a religious settlement but scratch the surface and the cracks start to appear. The town has the same problems as any modern-day suburb. Bored with the rigidity of Orthodox living, some of the youth have rebelled, begun to break the Sabbath laws, and now escape to the coastal cities of Netanya and Tel Aviv for nights on the town. Some of the residents talk in militant terms about the continuing war of expansion, while others consider what it would be like to leave the settlement in search of a quiet life.

We met two Ethiopian girls who came to Israel on Operation Shlomo, the government-sponsored airlift from Addis Ababa, and who are at boarding school in the West Bank. "After all the hardship our families went through to get to Israel," said Yafa, "with people dying on the trek through Sudan, and so on – why would we want to give any part of this land back?" She complained about racism against the Ethiopian community from other Jews in Israel, but was quick to assert that "I'll never have Arab friends – all Arabs are just too frightening".

We broke bread with settlers who aren't religious, but whose Zionist beliefs have led them to believe that their mere presence in the *Shtachim* is what fortifies the borders and protects the country. "People in Tel Aviv see settlers as the ones creating the problems," said one young army captain we interviewed. "But I see settlers as the true patriots. Settlers keep the war away from the main cities of Israel."

And so it went on, during research visits spanning a two year timeframe. Our initial foray was timed to coincide with the fortieth anniversary of the Six Day War, when we spent the summer in the region, conducting research and writing a series of articles for *The Guardian*, providing readers with a real-time picture of life behind the Green Line, some of which fed into the material for this book. We returned sporadically over the course of the next eighteen months, before returning to the West Bank for the spring of 2009, bringing our research up to date and finding out how the situation had progressed during the political upheavals of the preceding year and a half. During the course of our trip, we encountered the entire spectrum of opinion of those who live in the *Shtachim*, and by doing so added colour to a region that is easily viewed in black and white.

As two Jewish cousins from north-west London, who have grown up on a diet of Zionism and solidarity with our co-religionists in the Holy Land, this trip was a living history lesson. It was our way of finding out the mindset and mentality of those whose entire raison d'etre is based on the victory of 1967, as well as those who came to live here more by chance than for any idealistic goal. It was a way to open our eyes, and the eyes of those who read our work, to the consequences of the Six Day War for those Israelis on the ground whose every waking moment is shaped by the war's outcome.

Warnings from secular Israelis inside the Green Line had been forthcoming and frequent, upon hearing of our plan to travel extensively throughout the settlements. "Are you crazy?!" they exclaimed, "You don't understand how dangerous it is to go to these places. They are not safe. People are killed there all the time." One of Israeli society's many stark divides also tended to surface at this point, when our *hiloni* advisers railed against the *datim* [religious people] who are famous for living beyond the

Green Line. "They are crazy too. They are all religious there. Extremely. They believe they are fighting God's battles."

In fact, according to a 2002 survey conducted by the Israeli anti-settlement movement Peace Now, just over half of all West Bank settlers identify themselves as religious[1]. Nevertheless, the point still stands: the Israeli *hiloni* majority feel that the West Bank settlers are a different people from themselves – a zealous, isolated minority, holding the country to ransom over ancient landscapes and archaic battles. This journey was mired in politics and vitriol before it had begun. Ours, then, was an attempt to demystify the myths; to debunk the rumours and uncover a sense of day-to-day life in these most contentious of lands. Our aim was to delve deeply and diligently into the dichotomy that sits at the centre of Israel's political quagmire. Because no problem can be solved before it is truly understood.

We were aided in our task by a combination of our religious upbringings and our close ties to Israel. On our twice-yearly family visits to Israel, we were exposed to the settlement enterprise first-hand, thanks to relatives of ours having set up home in the well-heeled settlement of Elkana. We always knew there was something controversial about the location of their home by comparison to the majority of Israeli towns and cities, yet on the surface their lifestyle and location seemed fairly typical of the Israeli experience. The children played the same games as their peers the other side of the Green Line; their parents worked in similar fields to other Israelis we knew; their home seemed as safe as any other in the Holy Land – but there was no escaping the underlying tension endemic to their choice of community, all the more so the older and wiser we became.

By the time we made the decision to embark on our journey, we had both spent lengthy periods of time up close and personal with the various facets of Israeli society, feeling on our necks the chill of the political winds

13

which swirled around the country year in, year out. Seth had spent 15 months in a combat unit of the IDF, following his emigration to Israel in 2004; Josh had lived for several months in Tel Aviv and Jerusalem, learning Hebrew in a university programme and getting to know the country and its residents, warts and all.

We were motivated to conduct our research by what we viewed as a dearth of informative material on life in the settlements and the mindsets of those dwelling within their fortified borders. Plenty of books and articles had been written detailing the history of the decades-old occupation of the West Bank, which had begun during the Six Day War of 1967, but precious little appeared forthcoming about the people behind the headlines.

Since we were co-religionists of the settlers we would be interviewing, and since we spoke their language, shared their cultural idiosyncrasies and empathised with their feelings of Jewish identity, we were well-placed to overcome the obstacles often thrown up in the path of foreign correspondents and journalists with little personal connection to the places from which they were reporting.

At first, we used our own list of friends and family to get a foot in the door and make acquaintance with settlers at the start of our journey; very soon, however, our hosts on various settlements lent a hand and passed on details of fellow settlers in neighbouring *yeshuvim* [settlements] – a process which greatly expedited our research and put at ease those we were to interview along the way. Most of the interviews were attended by both authors and so the vast majority of this book is written in the first person plural. However, on the few occasions when only one or other of us was present, the text is written in the first person singular, with a footnote explaining who is writing.

Despite ready cooperation from most, not all settlers who heard of our trip were willing either to help or trust us during our travels. Within days of setting out, we saw an indication of what we might soon be up against:

"Beware the Freedman cousins" warned one paranoid settler who felt our intentions to research the settlement enterprise to be unwelcome attention for an often notoriously shy segment of Israeli society. He posted his alert on a settler website, in the hope that others would heed his advice not to cooperate with our project; in the event, we were barely hampered in our quest to investigate life behind the Green Line.

Only in Hebron – a bastion of ultra-shadowy, ultra-religious and ultra-nationalist settlers – did we come up against any real hurdles, with the community's spokesman point-blank refusing either to help or host us. Even then, we were able to speak freely with several individual settlers, soldiers and shopkeepers alike in the city, all of whom seemed content to talk at length about their experiences of living in such a contentious part of the region.

We ran the gamut of settlements, both in terms of location and lifestyle: we traversed the length and breadth of the West Bank, and met everyone from die-hard secularists to dyed-in-the-wool religious zealots, all of whose tales were worth a public airing – and, upon reflection, the whole was even greater than the sum of the parts. By meeting such diverse individuals and being allowed unparalleled access to their home and work lives, we came away with an accurate and rounded view of life in the settlements, and in the process were able to put the wider Israeli political picture into a far clearer context: how the settlers relate to their co-nationalists and their co-religionists and how they interact with their Palestinian neighbours; how their views have been shaped by history and how their ideologies have shaped the region in turn.

Love them or hate them, settlements are at the heart of the regional conflict, all the more so in the wake of President Obama's ascendancy to the White House and Prime Minister Netanyahu's return to the helm of Israeli politics, and the resulting pressure the former has applied to the latter's steering of the Israeli ship. By conducting our research either side of the political upheavals in Israel and America, we have captured a snapshot of a particularly turbulent episode in Israel's history: one which many hope – and many fear – will shape the destinies of the Israeli and Palestinian peoples for centuries to come.

2007

Chapter One
Kedumim:
From rocks to riches

Simple folk

As we drew through the manned gate at the entrance of the *yeshuv*, the deserted streets showed that the Sabbath was almost upon its residents, who spent the final few hours making frantic last-minute preparations for the festivities that lay ahead.

It was no different for our host. Having thought she'd be putting us up in an empty house, Yehudit – the mother of the household – had found out in the morning that three of her kids, plus their spouses and children, would be descending on the familial home for Shabbat.

Varying degrees of orthodoxy were evident in the family, based on the clothing they wore. Yehudit was clad in a knee-length dress with trousers on underneath; her husband Aryeh was decked out in knitted *kippah*, vest and shorts while one of their daughters bounded into the kitchen in trousers and a t-shirt.

At this point, Amit – a son-in-law – stumbled out of a bedroom, dressed in *kippah*, pyjama trousers and wife-beater vest, and rubbed his eyes confusedly. Once our presence was explained, he sat down and filled us in on his background. He was twenty-eight, and had worked for Internal Security for the last six years, although was currently resisting their calls for him to spend a few years working for them overseas. Making a cutting action across his throat, he said "Any more than two weeks out of Israel, and I'm dying". He told us that he's a "man of the land", and that he'd never consider making *yerida* [moving "down" from Israel]. The father of the family's two blond grandchildren – Ori and Reut – he lives on another settlement, Bruchin, not far from Petach Tikva in Israel proper.

He grew up in Petach Tikva, and feels just as safe living in the West Bank as he ever did there. "People in *chul* [outside Israel] imagine life in the *Shtachim* as being like an action movie, but in reality there were six or seven killed in Petach Tikva during the intifada, and none in Bruchin, touch wood."

Yehudit agreed with her son-in-law. "People on the other side of the Green Line like to think it's more dangerous over here, because it helps them feel more secure in the places they live in. To feel safe in their hearts, it's good for them to say 'look over there – it's far more dangerous than our cities', even if the statistics don't back up the claim".

The only time that she felt scared was after the mayor's son-in-law was murdered, along with his grandfather and parents, in nearby Elon Moreh six years ago. Even the suicide bombing at the entrance to Kedumim eighteen months ago didn't scare her as much, regardless of the fact that it was on her doorstep, because the Elon Moreh massacre took place inside the family home. "That was when we put these up," she said sadly, pointing at the metal bars that cover each window of the house. "When you are in your car, you can decide who you give a lift to, but when a terrorist breaks into your house? That's when you lose control," she says quietly, still visibly shaken by the memory of the attack.

Grandchildren swarmed around the house, galloping through the lounge and out into the garden, fuelled by the cake and orange squash that Yehudit fed them whenever they swung by the kitchen for a pit stop. Once outside, they made full use of the elaborate tree house and climbing frame that Aryeh erected for them a few years ago, babbling away to one another in excitement at the prospect of an entire weekend playing together in their grandparents' home. Aryeh and Yehudit gazed adoringly at them from the living room window, all the while quizzing their children about how each grandchild was faring at school, how their health was, and all the other requisite questions doting grandparents must ask to reassure themselves. Four of their five children were married, and their youngest – Shaked – got engaged that week, to the delight of her siblings and parents.

Leaving the women to tend to the children, we headed off with the men to welcome in Shabbat at the local *shul* [synagogue]. There were several prayer groups throughout the *yeshuv* and we stopped off at a Yemeni congregation *minyan* [prayer service] on the way to *daven mincha* [evening prayers], then walked fifty yards to "Mishkan Meir", the main *shul* of the *yeshuv*. A proud white structure, with grand pillars and impeccable whitewashed walls, it held around two hundred men inside, as well as scores of women in the ladies' gallery upstairs.

The Edlises had three seats in the front row of the *shul* – they were original members of the *yeshuv*, and were treated accordingly. We sat with Tomer, one of the sons-in-law, who lives with his wife and three children in Modi'in. He had earlier claimed that he was not as religious as the others – and it showed. He barely prayed, choosing instead to whisper about the various members of the congregation. A lawyer specialising in conveyancing, his closely shaved head and fashionable shirt were reminiscent of the Tel Aviv yuppies, especially when he pulled up his shirt sleeve deliberately to reveal a flash, expensive-looking watch.

Like any Tel Aviv slicker, Tomer used the opportunity to show off his English – unlike the other family members who spoke only in Hebrew. He leaned in conspiratorially to discuss the rabbi. "He's very much to the right of the map, and in a minute he will speak from the *bimah* [pulpit]. He always mixes *divrei torah* [religious sermons] with politics, and some of the people don't like him to. But he does it anyway."

After a rousing selection of *nusach Carlebach* [a tradition of joyful, happy-clappy singing] tunes for *Kabbalat Shabbat* [Sabbath prayers], the rabbi lived up to his billing. He linked the weak leaders who followed in Moses' wake with the weak Israeli leaders of today, who he said have not lived up to the strong rulers who led the country to victory in 1967.

On the way out, Seth asked Aryeh why the rabbi talks about politics when the community doesn't like it, and was told "he might talk, but no one listens." In this sense, the bickering at the Mishkan Meir congregation appeared no different from that of the Northwest London communities we grew up in – rabbis always rub some of their flock up the wrong way, and there is always something going on at the *shul* that pits one section of the *kehila* (community)against the other. However, when sitting in the heart of the West Bank listening to a rabbi laying into the incumbent government for not being strong enough against their enemies, there seemed something far less benign about the scene. *Shul* politics are, by their nature, primarily concerned with parochial issues, so the Kedumim rabbi could hardly be faulted for getting hot under the collar about a subject so close to the settlers' hearts. At the same time, casting an eye around the *shul* and seeing the array of pistols tucked into waistbands and M16s slung over shoulders, it was alarming to see how close to home the war is in both a physical and mental sense – hence the rabbi's incendiary words carried far more weight than those of a mild-mannered minister in Hendon or Hampstead.

Walking home for dinner, everyone approached Aryeh to wish him *mazeltov* [congratulations] on the engagement of Shaked, his youngest daughter, to a boy from the *yeshuv*. "When we get married, Meir and I will first live in Jerusalem, but we want to live in Yesha [acronym for Judea and Samaria – The West Bank] as soon as we can," Shaked said assuredly on the way home.

Shaked was an ardent nationalist. For her two year spell in the army, she taught Zionist history to groups of soldiers from the Former Soviet Union who are serving in the Israeli Defence Forces [IDF] whilst undergoing conversion to Judaism. They are in Israel by way of the right of return law that allows anyone with one Jewish grandparent to immigrate – but if their mother isn't Jewish, they are offered the opportunity to convert at the same time as serving in the army.

"I told them 'if you don't want to be Jewish, then don't stay in Israel'", said Shaked. "I told them that this is a country for Jews, and it was obvious that many of them had only moved here for the *sal klita* [money and benefits available to new immigrants]".

"In my lessons I would teach them that Jews are hated around the world, and that the world is happy to be rid of the Jews once and for all. I explained to them that Israel is the first place just for Jews, where we can be ourselves without fear." Yehudit joined in, telling us that her parents were Holocaust survivors, and she never wants such a tragedy to befall the Jews again. "The *Shoah* [Holocaust] wasn't a million years ago," she reminded us. "It's still fresh in our minds."

The Holocaust remains a trump card for a large section of world Jewry, when it comes to the argument about Israel's right to exist and stand strong against its foes. Shaked and Yehudit's views proved no exception, and the fact that the Shoah impacted so heavily on their immediate family means they speak with conviction when they talk about the absolute necessity of Israel to be a haven to which Jews can flee, were anything similar ever to occur again.

At the house we gathered in the lounge as the women made the last-minute dinner preparations. Tomer declared loudly that "I'm very left wing", to which the others scoffed and made derisory noises – Aryeh included. Aryeh then said "don't worry boys, tomorrow Daniella will press 'reset' in your heads and you'll understand the right wing view". He was referring to Kedumim's mayor, Daniella Weiss, who had agreed to meet with us to discuss the history of the *yeshuv*. A well-known and powerful figure in the settlement movement, Daniella was integral to Kedumim's success. Tomer laughed at the mention of her name, "once you've met her, you'll understand why I'm left wing".

The conversation at dinner itself was free and easy. No politics – just family banter and tales from their respective lives. Tomer discussed property prices at length, eliciting a heated debate amongst the family, who weren't too other-worldly to discuss the real world at the Friday night table. There was talk about the youth on the *yeshuv*, some of whom were turning into "*punkistim*" and breaking Shabbat, wearing secular clothes, and sneaking off to party in Netanya whenever they got the chance. Aryeh, hearing all this, interrupted to sing the praises of the rest of the *yeshuv* children, holding them up as stellar examples of passionate Bnei Akiva [the main national religious youth movement] youth, who epitomise devotion to the Zionist cause.

Over lunch the next day, talk centred on the row that had erupted at *shul*, politics and religion colliding once again, as is common in Israel. Apparently a man who had *yahrzeit* [the anniversary of a relative's death] had led the service and, when it came to the prayer for the State, he had intentionally skipped the prayer for the health of the government. The rabbi – "who is equally right wing, remember," said Tomer – had interrupted the *chazzan* [cantor] and said the missing prayer himself, saying that "this is not the way to protest". It seems that the prayer in question is regularly the cause of some concern, with many of the congregation leaving the room whenever it is read in full, to protest against the government they feel has betrayed them with the Disengagement from Gaza.

Tomer said that he had been very right wing himself when growing up – "my two brothers and I used to row all the time with our left wing dad" – but now he takes his father's view, politically speaking. He grew up in a very *dati* family in Netanya, doing the Hesder programme during the army, whereby he spent five years alternating between a tank unit and HaKotel *Yeshiva* [religious study]. "When I was thirty, I took off my *kippah*," he said, "but we still keep Shabbat at home and raise the children to do likewise".

Tomer said that his politics aren't an issue with the Edlis family – "*Mah pitom!* [no way!] We all respect each other". However, when he used to come to Kedumim in the build up to Disengagement, his left wing bumper stickers were regularly torn off his car by disgruntled locals.

After lunch, Aryeh brought out a bagful of ice lollies for his grandchildren, and was at pains to point out to everyone the Arabic writing on the packages. They were kosher (made by Strauss, the Israeli firm), but he wanted us to see that he'd taken advantage of the cheap prices in the Arab village nearby by purchasing the food there. Yehudit told me that Aryeh "is a friend to many of them. Simple folk have a *kesher* [connection] between themselves; it's only the extremists who cause trouble". By portraying themselves as the "simple folk", the family distanced themselves from the radicals who, in their eyes, are the ones behind the perpetuation of the conflict. However, to many residents of Israel proper, as well as those in the outside world, the Edlises' choice of address is precisely why they themselves are labelled extremists and blamed for the continuation of the struggle between the two nations. Sitting at the Shabbat table, watching the Edlises interact with one another as happily as any family in the world, yet all the while residing on some of the planet's most disputed land, it is easy to see how one man's moderate is the next man's fundamentalist.

Pioneers

Perched on the edge of firm, padded armchairs, we respond to Daniella Weiss's questions with the trepidation that her fixed gaze and thick-set frame demand: Who are we? What do we want? What is the purpose of our book? Does Yehudit know us personally, or are we merely friends of friends? In short, how far can we be trusted?

It may be Shabbat afternoon, the one day when Kedumim's tireless Mayor is free to sit and chat, but Daniella Weiss is very much at work. Pioneering settler; fevered advocate of the "Whole Land of Israel" and an original member of the first group to settle the Shomron [the Hebrew name for the northern region of the West Bank] Daniella is in her element, well used to narrating the story that has come to define her existence. She sits back in her armchair, neatly clasps her hands and tilts her head, dark eyes beneath a bright white headscarf, glistening in recollection of her own personal legend...

"In 1967, Israel was gripped by a miracle. The country that was only just passed its Bar Mitzvah was conquering new lands. The whole world knew it was a miracle."

Just as the miracle had gripped her in 1967, it grips her again now, as her dominant, foreboding figure is overcome by a palpable change – her eyes wet and alive, but fixed somewhere over our shoulders as she recounts the near-far memories of 40 years ago.

Only the religious moved quickly, claims Daniella, acting on the miracle that they had been given. Gush Etzion, Hebron – the religious activists were keen to consolidate the new lands that God had generously gifted to the Jewish people. But the nation at large was complacent, apparently unappreciative of the opportunities that God had bestowed unto the Jewish people to "return to their ancient homeland". Daniella, too, was not as active as she had wished.

"It was not until the Yom Kippur War [in 1973] that I woke up to the importance of the land. It was like God shook me and said 'Look at what you have conquered! Wake up and settle! Take it, it's yours!' This was the ancient Biblical home of Joshua, of Moses. Now we needed to settle. The Yom Kippur War showed the danger of wasting time."

So Daniella joined the movement dedicated to settling Shomron. A small group of protesters – a few hundred at most – came to a place called Sebastia, amongst the mountains near where Kedumim now stands and began their sustained attempt to turn governmental ambivalence to their advantage.

In Daniella's telling it was a perpetual struggle between an ambiguous, pusillanimous government and a zealous group of religious activists. The activists may have had God on their side, but according to Daniella, they had little else. "The hills were black," she recounts, pointing to her long, dark skirt emphatically concealing her legs from sight. "There was no light. No water. We had nothing."

The group slept out in the naked hills, amongst the ruins of the Ottoman-era Sebastia train station, in the freezing cold of winter. Rabbis with large crocheted *kippot* and bushy beards, young children, women swaddling babes – all camped out against the night and sang songs and cooked food by day.

"We were strange people," recalls Daniella. And so they seemed to the rest of Israel. "'Who are these strange hallucinating people?' they would ask. 'What are they doing? Biblical hills? There's nothing there!'" Daniella smiles faintly in her recollection of the people's disbelief, a hint of triumph in her eyes as if to say 'they never thought we'd get this far'.

But success was not without struggle. The Sebastia group was staying out without the consent of the government and the army was dispatched to bring an abrupt end to their "hallucinating" antics.

But they soon returned, singing and dancing, into the bosom of the bare hills. And again the army evicted them. Again they returned... And again they were removed... Eight times in total, the infatuates prostrated themselves at the foothills of God's mountains, expressing a fevered love for both the earth below and the heaven above, that were perceived to unite at this small patch of land between Jordan and Israel.

Despite their strange appearance, Daniella describes how the protesters' passion and determination impressed many Israeli academics and politicians. Visits from various dignitaries at once legitimised the group's actions in the eyes of many, whilst giving the euphoric muddle an extra shot in the arm to fuel their fever.

International support gave Daniella and her crowd further confidence. When The UN debated the 'Zionism = Racism' motion, Jewish officials from the US and Britain came to Israel to express solidarity with the Jewish state. They also came to Sebastia, and Daniella read this visit correctly – influential representatives of the international Jewish community were proclaiming that the West Bank was a natural and integral part of Israel, indistinguishable in importance from Tel Aviv or Haifa. The protesters gathered courage.

The fervour had a profound impact on visiting journalists and according to Daniella one such writer, from the Israeli broadsheet *Haaretz*, wrote of the protesters, "In spite of everything, maybe there's something in them". Dignitaries and now intellectuals: Daniella and her tribe were duly bolstered; their hallucinations were taking shape.

Pulled along by the weight of her own narrative, Daniella unveils the next chapter of her adventure with barely a pause for breath. The next dignitary to visit Sebastia was Shimon Peres but he offered little in the way of support. Alighting from his helicopter, he addressed the group, telling them to pack up and leave. Daniella, who was from the unremarkable Tel Aviv suburb of Ramat Gan, had been told to go home. Patience with the settlers, it seemed, was running out.

Daniella fixes our gaze, as she narrates what could have been the stillbirth of the protesters' love affair with God's naked hills. "Rabbis sat on the floor and wept," she recalls. "They couldn't leave again." Daniella rests, mournful, then draws strength from what she is about to retell. "But somehow we found the strength to stand up and join hands with one another and sing. *Am Yisrael Hai!* – The people of Israel live! Over and over again we sang those words. Those three words became our anthem. The people of Israel live! For three hours we sang."

This mantra, resounding as an incantation throughout the valley, seems to have worked its magic. With palpable pride, Daniella describes how the very next day, Shimon Peres signed a compromise with the settler representatives, including her husband, another of the motors within the settling machine: the group could stay. "The government would provide supplies for thirty families. They thought they'd be able to control us, to keep us in place and watch over us. They thought we'd grow tired and go back to Tel Aviv... This was the start of Kedumim."

Looking at Daniella Weiss, it's incredible to think that the government thought her and her kind capable of backing down. She still exudes the same fervent faith in her ideals and her beliefs appear to be most alive when they are locked in a struggle with a conflicting power.

But at Sebastia, the settler movement, which by the end of 2009 amounted to almost half a million Israelis living over the Green Line, was spearheaded by just a few hundred enraptured protesters, sodden and singing in a dilapidated railway station. That the left wing government chose to pander to the movement rather than to nip it in the bud either speaks of incomprehensible weakness, or, more likely, of a reluctance to give up the land which had a profound historical resonance for many Jews. However, in Daniella's telling, it was an indisputable victory for the religious pioneers at Sebastia over their own government.

The struggle continues today. Daniella tells of the protests she still attends religiously, every time the government threaten to "give away" more land. And she is critical of those who don't come to help, generally from the large, secular settlements such as Ma'ale Adumim and Ariel. "The religious lead the way – we're the ones who fight the battle. Everyone else is complacent."

When the government threatened to withdraw from the Golan, they boarded buses to Jerusalem to protest. Daniella even insisted that her daughter who was nine months pregnant join her on the demonstration – "even if it meant she would have the baby on the bus". Why? "Because this is the Holy Land and Jews must never be evicted."

In Sinai too, Daniella boasts, the people of Kedumim performed well. When Israel withdrew its settlements from the region in 1982, forty of Kedumim's eighty families were there, demonstrating against Israel's contribution to peace with Egypt.

"I have been in jail in Jerusalem for my protests. I am used to the battle."

And she brings the battle into her home too. As we are preparing to leave, two guests come to visit and her husband begins to talk to them in hushed tones. "Be quiet until I've finished speaking!" Daniella snaps, and resumes her narrative. "Yes captain," replies her husband meekly, and sits quietly until she's done.

In other ways, the fight has changed since Daniella first took up the cause. In a rare, fleeting mention of the Arabs (who have remained largely absent from her narrative, as though the hills were as uninhabited as they were black) Daniella tells how, five years ago, a Palestinian terrorist burst into her son-in law's house and opened fire on his family as they sat at the dinner table, killing him, along with his parents and grandfather. But for a woman whose very existence is shaped by struggle, each tragedy along with each victory seems only to strengthen her resolve to settle God's land for God's people.

With her talk of the ancient homeland, Daniella has flung us back in time, far beyond 1975 and the embryo of the settlement project, to a time when the Israelites dwelt throughout Judea and Samaria; the Biblical Jewish world, which, after a 2000 year blip, has been seamlessly restored, according to God's will.

As we leave the shadows of her home for the bright streaks of sunshine splashing across the ancient mountains, the air infused with the scent of jasmine and birds of paradise, Daniella's world stays with us for a few minutes as we head home. But then the Muezzin's call to prayer resounds throughout the valley, piercing through the heat, reminding us of the reality of this "ancient Jewish land". The land it seems, wasn't so much unloved for 2000 years – but rather it enjoyed the attentions of another lover.

And now the first lover has returned to take charge, reciting vows and promises of affection from a bygone era; the neatly paved roads of the settlement jealously cling to the mountains and cement the other lover from sight. But the Muezzin's piercing call insists that out of sight is far from out of mind – and that Daniella's battle for the land is very much alive.

The good old days

However, according to Shoshanna, friend and neighbour of the Edlises and one of the first residents of Kedumim, the relationship between Jews and Palestinians in the West Bank wasn't always one of enmity and division. A typical *sabra*, Shoshanna has no time for pleasantries, but had agreed to let us stay in her house at a moment's notice and is happy to sit and reflect on her deepest thoughts and feelings within minutes of meeting – "provided you Englishmen don't keep saying thank you."

As we sit sipping cold water and eating cakes in Shoshanna's garden, surrounded by figs, kumquats and pomegranates swelling on the overhanging branches, the no-nonsense statistician fills us in on the changes that have taken place during her time in Kedumim.

Shoshanna's main motivation for settling in the West Bank was strategic. Gesturing behind her house, the short but imposing *Ashkenazi* [Jews of Central and

Eastern European descent] matriarch indicates the commanding view, largely obscured by the greenery blooming throughout her garden. "You can see the sea from here," she insists, emphasising that Israel's security depends on the control of the mountain heights and the retention of aerial superiority.

But despite her desire for Israeli sovereignty to extend over land conquered from Jordan in the '67 war, Shoshanna wished for a peaceful interaction with her Palestinian neighbours. In her telling, the Palestinian residents had been exploited and subjected to a harsh standard of living under Jordanian rule. Thus when the Israelis took over, the Palestinian villagers were initially grateful to the new occupying power.

"We gave them water, electricity, doctors and dentists and they were happy. We had a good relationship with each other."

And Shoshanna insists that this is what the settlers wanted – Israeli sovereignty but one which included a harmonious interaction with the native inhabitants of the West Bank. Her telling fits with Ariyeh's recollections, in which Jews and Arabs of the West Bank initially got along well with one another. Shoshanna continues, "I learnt Arabic when I arrived and they learnt Hebrew. It was important that we all got along in this place."

Shoshanna seems to have recognised that "this place" was in fact different from Israel itself, and her desire to learn Arabic suggests that she was prepared to adapt herself to suit her new environment. "I don't hate Arabs," she adds as an afterthought, responding to the unspoken but oft-repeated allegation that settlers are inherently racist. Then, as though fighting down those who make the allegations, Shoshanna warms to her theme, "The left wingers are racist!", she riles. "They hate the Arabs. They want to pull out of Judea and Shomron, put up a big wall and keep the Arabs away." Shoshanna, on the other hand, speaks fondly of a time when Jews and Arabs lived together – separation is not something she believes in.

Nevertheless, the interaction had to be on her terms – the land, and thus all of its Palestinian inhabitants, must remain under Israeli sovereignty. And she seems surprised that the Palestinians were not prepared to play by her rules. The rise of Palestinian nationalism dismays her and she sees it as coming hand in hand with the growth of Islamic fundamentalism. In her outlook, it seems that the Arabs of the West Bank ought to have been pleased at being liberated from Jordanian oppression and grateful for Israel's provision of services. That they "became" free-thinking Palestinians with their own nationalistic aspirations was not part of the script.

The Oslo Accord of 1993 was when it all began to go wrong. "They formed an army and we gave them weapons, then they just turned them against Israel and started killing us." Shoshanna emphasises the change that she perceives to have taken place from one generation of Palestinians to the next, when she speaks of an "Arab friend" whom she quizzed on the future of the West Bank. "If we were to give back the land," she asked him, "would the Palestinians still try to kill Israel?" According to Shoshanna, the man affirmed her worst fears. "He said yes. Not that he would do it, but the new generation – the young terrorists – would try to destroy Israel." A change had taken place before Shoshanna's eyes – the compliant, amenable natives had given way to a new generation of radical separatists – and Israelis were no longer welcome in the West Bank.

But despite the terrorist threat, Shoshanna feels safe in Kedumim – as much here as anywhere else in the world. A strengthened resolve in her convictions, which are now predicated on the need to stay put in order to prevent all out war, means that Shoshanna no longer enjoys the good relations she once enjoyed with her Arab neighbours.

A strong, determined woman, with short, brusque sentences and a steely conviction, Shoshanna's mind appears to be made up. In her 60s, it's too late for her to change now, and facts from the world around her are bent to fit her own telling. Thus, for her, the left wingers of Israel are separatists, with an innate hatred of Arabs, while the new generation of Palestinians are ungrateful for the benevolent colonial rule that Israel has administered.

Future events, too, must prove Shoshanna's world assessment correct. Talking of the spread of Islamic terror, she claims that the world – particularly Europe – doesn't understand the severity of the situation. "I wish they'd just bomb the Eiffel Tower," she says decidedly, "then the world would wake up to what's going on." Her vision of a peaceful Israeli rule shattered, Shoshanna's conviction has become hard and resolute and she now bangs the world's round holes with her square pegs, adamant she'll make them fit her own outlook.

As she clears away our drinks and takes the remaining cakes back into her quiet home, her stern glower subsides for a moment or two, suggesting a compassion that has grown weary and tired with the world and its population that has refused to behave as it should. And apart from the few hundred homes that sit amongst hers on the mountainside, Shoshanna's seems a very isolated world indeed.

The settlement

The adults of the household spend Shabbat afternoon sleeping, so it seems an appropriate time to walk around Kedumim. It takes less than five minutes to reach the perimeter of the *yeshuv*, at a point which looks down over the main road and across to the Arab village on the next hill. There is no fence and no sign of security patrols either, which seems strange – but not to the residents. One man tells us that "weak people live behind walls", assuring us that the lack of a fence actually acts as a deterrent to would-be attackers. "They'll look at us living here with open borders, and think 'Oh, the *yeshuvnikim* must be strong after all'. Having no fence reduces the chance of terror against us," he assures us. "Terrorists find a way in, wall or no wall, so if by having no wall we at least make them scared of us, that has to be better." Another passer-by explains it differently – "We want to keep building outwards," he says. "Any kind of wall or fence would restrict our growth, and imply that we have claims to only a finite amount of the surrounding area."

The *yeshuv* has few cottage industries, which reflects the reluctance of manufacturers and businesses to open plants in the region as a whole. According to Yehudit, as the government might yet end up "kicking us out", the multinationals won't take the risk of investing money setting up plants in the region, thus the residents are forced to commute inside the Green Line to work. However, says Yehudit, if the government said the settlers could stay here for a minimum of, say, fifty years, then "big business would be here in a flash".

We pass a vast hothouse where tropical plants are grown and shipped out for selling, and then come across a couple of barns of chickens. The long-haired religious youth who tends the fowl said that the reason the chickens are near-silent was that "I feed them whenever they're hungry, so they're ok". He seems indifferent to their plight at being crammed into tiny cages for the length of their lives, having decided that as long as they had enough to eat, all was well in their world.

His nonchalance is reminiscent of the reactions of those Israelis who reassure themselves that as long as the Palestinians are not starving, there's no need to spend time improving their lot. The fact that the Palestinians are by and large penned into hamlets and not afforded the liberty to move freely from place to place is of scant concern to people unwilling to put themselves in the Palestinians' shoes and think about how they'd react under similar conditions.

To one side of the entrance to the *yeshuv*, a signpost reading 'army base' points up an adjoining lane, where trees stand fifty feet high, scores of white storks circling, nesting in their branches. We tentatively approach the front gate of the base, taking care not to make any sudden movements and to keep our hands away from our pockets. A girl decked out in full combat gear shouts to us from the sentry post next to the gate, and we introduce ourselves and our mission, and she says we can talk to her, "but first of all, don't move another step closer", proving she was still a long way from trusting us.

Fifteen minutes later, and we are getting on like a house on fire. Tami, nineteen, is doing "as much service as boys do" – a proud little fighter, who can't believe two Englishmen would be writing a book about the area, let alone wandering around such dangerous territory in so brazen a fashion. "It's ok, I was in Nahal [an IDF infantry unit] for fifteen months, so I know the dangers," Seth tells her. "Well, if you were in Nahal, then you're even more stupid," she laughs. "You should know that you shouldn't be out here alone."

To the average Israeli, especially to those who've served in the West Bank, the region is strictly off-limits to anyone but the foolish or reckless. Even though the statistics prove that cities in Israel proper are far more dangerous than the West Bank in terms of Palestinian terror, there is a stigma attached to roaming around the Territories that strikes fear into the hearts of Israelis and thus impedes any chance of interaction with the locals to discover that there are plenty of moderates amongst them who wish them no harm at all. IDF officers do a good job scaremongering amongst their charges, as Seth found during his own service, and warnings administered to impressionable eighteen year old recruits remain seared into the consciousness long after they've returned to civilian life.

Tami tells us to go back to the *yeshuv*, "because you could be attacked by people in cars", pointing at the green-plated vehicles speeding past on the main road. When asked why she thought there was no fence round the *yeshuv*, she shrugs and says "the security wall must be doing its job".

Save for a nonchalant tortoise ambling along the road, the streets of the *yeshuv* are deserted, with most of the residents opting to spend Shabbat resting indoors. On the main road, nearly every car or truck going by is Palestinian. There are very few private cars – in the main it's taxis, *sheruts* [shared taxis] and lorries. The guard on the front gate has little to do. Having no cars to search and no people to interrogate means his afternoon can be whiled away as peacefully as those he is employed to protect.

Not far from the army base, there stands a plaque for those leaving the *yeshuv*. On it is inscribed *tefilat ha derech* – the prayer for a safe journey. Across the road, as though to emphasise the need for faith, stands a memorial to four Kedumim residents who were killed when a terrorist detonated their car on 30th March 2006.

The story goes that a 24 year old Palestinian from the El Bureij refugee camp near Hebron had disguised himself as an Orthodox Jew and caught a lift with the Kedumim residents, from one of the hundreds of hitching posts scattered across the West Bank. When the car approached the settlement entrance, he detonated the device, killing all four passengers, along with himself.

The memorial stands at the sight of the explosion, paying tribute to the lives of Reut Feldman (20), Shaked Lasker (16) and Helena and Raphael Halevy (60). Debris from the destroyed vehicle is strewn rudely before a bed of dazzling flowers, attesting to the cause of their deaths.

There is an inscription, too: "The earth shall not cover their blood". Just as the flowers are prevented from growing over the ruins of the car, the blood stains the earth. The deaths of these victims have become central to the struggle that has consumed this piece of land.

The memorial then offers a means of overcoming the pain; a viable way to turn the personal healing process outwards, towards the wider community. "Building the land brings comfort and makes you stronger," the slogan proclaims.

Thus the deaths of these Kedumim residents become another stage in the building and settling of the West Bank. Settlers have given their lives to the cause – the land has been earned through spilt blood: remember the blood and build. Enmity, pain, hatred and tragedy are preserved and used as the foundation for more settlements.

And so the cycle continues.

Creating facts

We learnt more about the perpetual conflict on our second meeting with Daniella. If on Shabbat, the day of rest, she had seemed energetic and driven, then Daniella was in true battle mode as she sat at her desk on a working day. Despite incessant phone calls, Daniella remained unnervingly focussed on her story, displaying the undying determination that makes her one of the settler movement's most powerful assets.

"I feel I'm part of a historical drama," states Daniella boldly, fixing our gaze in full command of her office, her world. "You see the established thing – hundreds of communities and so on and so forth – and then you hear that we started in a tent, with no modern facilities. For you, it's like 'wow!'"

She has a point. The disparity between then and now is indeed impressive. Mindful of the few hundred protesters on the rain-soaked hills of 1975, Daniella picks up a small, laser pen and aims it incisively at pinpoints on a huge aerial map of the Kedumim environs, hung on a wall beside her desk.

"When we came here, we found a very primitive area. A lot of the land of Judea and Samaria – something like two thirds – one and a half million acres was rocks. Rocks, rocks, rocks, rocks, all over. No trees, no bush, no flowers."

"Primitive" land – that is, a land begging for cultivation; an apparent extension of the old Zionist adage "a land without people, for a people without land." Although, of course, this time the people in question already had a land. And again the land had a people, though for Daniella the united assault of the Arab nations in the Six Day War justified Israel's appropriation of Jordanian state land for Israeli development.

"One of the backbones of the settler movement, according to the guidance of Rabbi Kook, was that we could only build on rocks – not on people's private land... Now as there was a lot of rocky land, the settlers, including me, settled on the rocks."

As Daniella's laser pen indicates on another wall map, that land is now littered with Israeli settlements. From rocks to riches, the settlement enterprise has covered vast amounts of ground with people like Daniella in charge. However, somewhere along the line the guidance of Rabbi Kook has gone unheeded, because according to official Israeli Civil Administration data obtained by Peace Now over 32% of land in all Israeli settlements is private, mostly Palestinian land, while in Kedumim itself that figure is as high as 47.64%.[2] If Daniella is aware of this fact, she chooses not to mention it.

So precisely what is motivating her in this mission? What is the over-arching meaning of this project?

"I feel that it means we're part of the Bible. It's a spiritual experience."

And this is key to understanding Daniella's raison d'etre. Not only is this God's land and the Jewish people its rightful heirs, but the settlement movement is fulfilling ancient Biblical roles; acting according to a pre-written Biblical script in which all events are prescribed and all meaning pre-established.

The future, too, is hinted at, just as Messianic redemption is alluded to within the Bible. On the wall behind Daniella's desk hangs a familiar looking yet disorientating landscape, dominated by an unrecognisable marble structure in the foreground. After a few seconds it becomes apparent that this is the imagined Jerusalem of the future – complete with a rebuilt Temple where the Dome of the Rock now stands[3]. It is an emphatic illustration of Daniella's vision, which is apparently one step closer to being realised now that the Jewish people have returned to Judea and Samaria.

So where exactly does this leave the Palestinians, to whom Daniella continually refers as "the Arabs". Daniella is characteristically swift to outline her predictions, prescribed in the Bible and re-enacted in the 21st century:

"The proper order of things in the land of Israel is like this. First of all, in the entire Promised Land, including Greater Israel, there should be one sovereignty: the Israeli sovereignty. Jacob is Israel, Israel is Jacob, Israel is Jewish. I don't want to mix terms, so I specify. Now, according to the rules specified by Joshua, there are three options offered to the different people who live in this Promised Land. One option is to accept Israeli sovereignty – to be citizens in Greater Israel in return for perfect, complete loyalty to the state of Israel and its values. The second option is for those who feel that they can't accept Jewish sovereignty. They will have to choose by themselves to go anywhere in the world they want – the US, France, England, Egypt, Jordan... well, not necessarily Jordan, because that too is part of Greater Israel. The third choice, if they do not accept, is to fight. And we will fight back. And our only choice is to have the upper hand.

"If we don't pose these three options clearly, there will be an ongoing clash. Sometimes a battle, sometimes a war, but an ongoing clash. That's what's going on now – and that's why it seems to be endless."

Daniella's uncompromising attitude has, in recent years, led her towards conflict even with those within the settler movement. Following the Disengagement from Gaza and parts of the West Bank, Yesha [the settlers' council for Judea, Shomron and, formerly, Gaza] have been on the receiving end of the Kedumim mayor's scorn.

"Yesha brought about the catastrophe in Gush Katif [the Jewish settlement in Gaza] by going hand in hand with the army and the government. And the number one reason for the failure was that the leaders of Yesha thought that holding on to Gaza and Shomron meant to tear apart Israeli society."

But for Daniella, the threat of dividing the country was secondary to giving up land that she believes is indisputably Jewish. Or, to put it another way, the land itself is central to the unity of the Jewish people:

"There was an inability of people in leading positions to understand that devotion to the land was our role – and not to care about the fragmentation of Israeli society. Ahad Ha'am[4] said that it's not Jews that keep the Sabbath, it's the Sabbath that keeps the Jews. The activists say the same about keeping the land of Israel. I believe that the stronger we hold to the land, the more we will be a strong, united nation."

And according to Daniella, the people of Israel appreciate this dedication, even if they don't agree with her objectives – indeed she has been literally saluted on Tel Aviv streets.

"I represent something... this belief that we came here to stay for good. Whoever represents this gives life to the people who sit comfortably in the pubs."

And not just in Tel Aviv, but in London and New York too. Daniella sees her resilience as benefiting Jews the world over. Settlers, to her mind, are the pioneers on the front line, guaranteeing the safety of those back home. And she berates the attitude of those content to live in material comfort:

"If you ask me, I'd say the biggest threat to the present generation is immense growth of materialistic and technological offerings, and altogether it creates an illusion of comfort, affluence and relaxation: I can relax – I have all the food that I need, the comforts, pleasures... all in a box. Yet, what protects us as human beings – and the people of Israel even more – is that, thank God, we are created with body and soul. And so the soul is yearning. And as you surround yourself with material things there is something inside that wants to burst."

Daniella portrays the settlers as the body most prepared to reject the material world and act according to the dictates of the collective soul of the Jewish people. Their actions serve as a light to Jews whilst ensuring the unity and safety of the Jewish people. That the majority of Israeli Jews supported the Disengagement is beside the point. For Daniella, they were clearly wrong; the "disaster" of Gush Katif and the continuing rocket fire has proved the settlers right. From Tel Aviv to New York to London, Daniella asks the Jewish people to appreciate the role settlers play in guaranteeing the safety and unity of the Jewish people. With no trace of irony, Daniella portrays settlers as protectors of world Jewry.

But even as Daniella emphasises Jewish unity, cracks appear when she talks of the protests against the settlements. Stressing each word with a strong, dogged bark, Daniella berates her critics. "In Haifa and Tel Aviv, they took over Arab property. But the settler movement wasn't allowed to touch private property."

As if to lend weight to her argument, Daniella glimpses something on her computer screen. Anti-settlement activists are protesting in Hebron and the settlers' counter protest criticises the double standards of the Israeli left. Daniella reads their placards aloud,

"You see what it says there!" She exclaims, triumphantly, "The *kibbutzim* are built on occupied land! Don't tell us we are on occupied land!"

And so we have come full circle. Israel was originally held up as the solution to all the Jews' problems. But in elevating the status of the settlers as the defenders of the state; in stressing their moral superiority and alleging that the unity of the Jewish people is dependent on their activity, Israel itself is relegated to a spiritually and idealistically inferior entity: The Occupied Territories become the true Israel, the settlers the true patriots.

And then the legitimacy of Israel itself is called into question. The Israeli state is built on occupied land; "made Arab refugees of Haifa, Tel Aviv and Ramle, [whereas settlers] weren't allowed to touch Arab property." The message is clear: settlements are more legitimate than Israel itself. Israel, it seems, is expendable, at least as far as a moral argument is concerned, in order to justify the settlers' presence.

The critics of the settlements, the middle of the road Israelis, are dismissed with the same vehemence that they use to deride the settlers – and the unity of the Jewish people suddenly looks far less assured than Daniella would have us believe.

Through the looking glass

Driving down to the bottom of Kedumim, Ariyeh takes us to where it all began, back in 1975, to the army base where the first families lived while the government resisted their calls for expansion. Yehudit and Ariyeh had visited the families then, as they slept in the cold tents, children freezing in the soldiers' barracks. Yehudit had thought they were crazy. But Ariyeh now proudly explains how the wily settlers had smuggled plank after plank of wood into the tents, below the radar of the army and the government – until one day several wooden huts sprang up, surprising everyone: thus the first walls of Kedumim were built.

It was soon after this that the government's thirty caravans arrived and the next time the Edlises came to visit, it was to spend a bright, summery Shabbat with their friend, the bus driver of Kedumim. The moment they arrived, they fell in love with the place and decided to stay.

Ariyeh takes us to see the caravans that were home to Kedumim's first residents, including the Edlis family –

one or two still stand on the original site as a monument to the way things were, large sheets of glass replacing walls so that visitors can peer into the cramped dwellings and learn how the first settlers of Shomron lived. We look in on the small, boxlike rooms, divided by flimsy partitions, which used to house whole families. Ariyeh indicates the bunk beds in one room, roughly eight by eight foot, which accommodated their three children, all of whom were under the age of five.

But Ariyeh and Yehudit were young too, both in their twenties, and Yehudit remembers being "optimistic, motivated and excited" about the challenges that lay in store. With limited electricity and water, Ariyeh explains with a wink how "farting kept us warm" in the cold winter nights. Food was cooked and served in the shared dining room and all thirty families ate their meals together. By day, the adults commuted to work as normal.

Ariyeh recalls those early days fondly. For him, as for the rest of the settlers, they were pioneers embarking on a new adventure in the name of the state of Israel – just like those early Jewish pioneers upon whose hard work and vision the state of Israel was founded. No doubt this feeling was bolstered by the journalists and reporters who visited the settlers repeatedly, as intrigued by the settlers' determination as they were by the development of events. As Yehudit describes, they "knew they were doing something special."

We get back in the car and drive a little way up the hill to the site which held the settlement's first prefab houses, as Kedumim began to dig its heels into the West Bank. Ariyeh walks us around the scores of cuboid houses (known as *ashkubiot*), hardly bigger than the caravans themselves, which still house the settlement's new arrivals, along with those who do not have the money to move on.

Over the years, various owners have built small porches of MDF and corrugated iron, tacked onto the front of the concrete blocks; others have laid tarmac from the path to their units, cementing their residence into the fabric of the settlement community. Nevertheless, the rows of "houses" all comprise the same essential building blocks – identical prefab cuboids containing a lounge and a kitchen, adjoined with a doorway to a block consisting of two bedrooms. More bedroom blocks were assigned to those young families with large numbers of children that still fill this small, transitory and poor neighbourhood.

We head up the hill to trace the path of Kedumim's growth through the late Seventies and early Eighties. The settlement's expansion is restricted to our left by a Palestinian-owned olive grove, which is unfenced and comes right up to the road's edge. At harvest time, the farmers have to coordinate with the army to ensure that they are allowed to pick their fruit in peace, because "there are crazy people everywhere", admits Ariyeh, somewhat dismissively.

Kedumim's spread up the mountainside was rapid. Families took out loans from one of the few banks that would finance them, each family serving as a guarantor for another. Land was divvied up, allocated by drawing lots and an architect was drafted in, who came up with three different designs from which each family selected their home. These three homes were then cloned throughout the first neighbourhoods of Kedumim, each family finally receiving a permanent plot of land, a solid home, a neat garden and a view of the stunning mountains over which Israel now ruled.

Ariyeh and Yehudit – now with four children – left their *ashkubia* in 1981 and moved into their newly built home, where they still live. Once the stones of this permanent abode were laid, Yehudit felt they were there for good.

Ariyeh drives us along the broad, tree-lined streets, passing the kindergarten where Yehudit works and the school for disadvantaged kids along the way and we head up the next hill towards Kedumim North.

And there, amongst more tiny caravans bursting with women and young children, who lack the money to build their own homes, sits the nerve centre of Kedumim's security – a roomful of screens showing every minute detail of the settlement and the surrounding land. The room is staffed by private security guards, residents of the settlement and girls brought to Kedumim for their *sherut leumi* [compulsory national service] placement.[5]

Introducing us to the team, Ariyeh asks one of the girls to show us how the cameras work – "show us where Daniella's sitting" he smiles, though he isn't joking, as we discover when the girl obediently moves the lever in front of her to scan across the mountains and zoom onto the window of Daniella Weiss's office, several miles away. All day long, the girls sit and turn the cameras, which are stacked discreetly atop well-positioned towers, scanning the settlement for potential intruders. In the corner of the room, a stash of M16s and sniper rifles provide uncompromising back-up. Kedumim might not have a fence, but this settlement has come a long way since it was just a few caravans on a hill and it is far from unprotected.

Having just driven from the 1970s to the present day, our next trip is like taking a step back in time. Ariyeh takes the car through Kedumim North – a more recent extension to the settlement, stretching over the adjacent mountain top – and then turns onto a side road, heading towards the steep, barren mountain slope. The road quickly becomes a rudimentary black path; sticky tarmac sweating in the sun, uneven and barely wider than a single car. Thus the black snake slithers awkwardly through rocks and brittle brush, crawling steeply up a bare mountain, a couple of miles from Kedumim itself.

This is Har Hemed, a hilltop outpost, illegal even according to Israeli law. But as Ariyeh points out, his car wobbling and shuddering over the bumpy road, Har Hemed has a deliberately ambiguous identity. "Is this illegal?" he asks, genuinely bemused. "I mean, the government says so.

But look over there." We follow his gaze to a series of electricity pylons extending from Kedumim to the top of the mountain. "You see – the government provides electricity and water. So is it illegal or not? I don't know."

Of course, Ariyeh is not stupid. No doubt he is aware that this outpost is illegal even in the eyes of the Israeli government that approves internationally contested settlement programmes. But his question highlights the governments' duplicity in the settlements it condemns – opposing their expansion in words, but facilitating their survival in actions. With water, warmth and light, communities blossom. As Ariyeh has just shown us, Kedumim itself was once just a few caravans on a hill.

The newest addition to Kedumim, the small collection of shabby caravans and flimsy tin shacks blowing precariously in the wind is far removed from the luxury and modernity of the Edlises' part of town. Roughly fifteen caravans sit side by side, lonely, with their owners out at work. A couple of hundred metres away a solitary soldier stands sentry, guarding the parched mountain top. He looks hot and thoroughly bored.

In front of the soldier are several cramped, corrugated iron shacks that apparently house more families. Beside these are two more shacks, smaller still. A goat emerges from one, as though to emphasise the desperate living conditions of the human beings dwelling next door.

The narrow black path stretches on to a handful of *ashkubiot*, centred around a makeshift children's playground. In an attempt to add character to the uniformity of their flat-packed patch of paradise, some of the residents have painted butterflies and rainbows onto the caravans' dreary white walls. One or two prefab units have faux-stone masonry plastered to their façades, aiming for the semblance of a home built with care and attention – except that the tiling remains unfinished, and large square gaps reveal iron trellising screwed into the bare walls beneath. The overall effect is stark and depressing, yet the signs of flourishing family life, the

47

provisions of water and electricity and the precedent set by settlements throughout the West Bank suggest that the residents of this currently "illegal" outpost have a lot to look forward to.

As we drive back home, Ariyeh explains that the settlements are intentionally stretched as far as possible across adjacent mountains, in a string-like formation, to ensure that the settlement secures all the land between for its own development. Children from established settlements frequently pioneer their own outpost near to the original, which, over time, consolidates its place, receives water and electricity until it becomes accepted as a suburb of its parent settlement and eventually gives birth to an outpost of its own. Other patches of land in the area, which remain unfarmed by Palestinians, are earmarked for future development. "See that land there?" asks Ariyeh as we pass an empty strip between two mountains. "If no one claims that in the next ten years, we'll build there too." Given that Palestinians are prevented from coming near the settlement, it somehow seems likely that the land will go unclaimed.

According to Ariyeh's daughter, Shaked, it is not only the Jews that have spread over the West Bank's mountains. She describes how the Palestinian villages that surround Kedumim have "exploded in size" since she was a young girl. "Soon they will be stronger here than we are. That's why we need to stay here and have as many children as we can."

Shaked's description is reminiscent of a tribal society in which neighbouring peoples raise many children in order to ensure their future rule over the region. Aerial superiority is important, too. Ariyeh indicates Arab villages on mountains higher than Kedumim and claims that they "rule" over the Jewish settlement, whereas Kedumim "rules" over the Arab villages below. Governments, armies and modern warfare are overlooked. This is tribal warfare; numbers and height are everything.

Indeed, two rival Biblical tribes is just how Ariyeh refers to the Israelis and the Palestinians of the West Bank. "It's like Jacob and Esau[6]. Jews and Arabs may again be able to live side by side in relative calm, but they will never be at peace."

As Ariyeh drives us out of the settlement and through a tiny Palestinian hamlet a mile or so from Kedumim, he points out an olive press where they make oil. Then there is the falafel stand in Kedumim which is manned by a large relic of a Jew, dark, Middle Eastern and bushy-bearded. Behind the ramshackle eating area is a ruin from the time of Bar Kokhba – nothing ornate or fanciful, but the remnants of a Jewish olive press. High in the mountains, away from big cities and modern life, the ancient memories and parallels are intoxicating, enduring like the stone relics set deep in the mountainside. And they have had their effect on people like Ariyeh.

Parking the car in front of the house, the veteran settler shows how an ancient, Biblical precedent also offers a grim glimpse of things to come – individual agency giving way to an inescapable cycle of pre-scribed events: "It is written that the children of Jacob and Esau will always fight. We simply have to make sure that we are stronger than them. That's the only way we can rule. We have to make them fear us."

Welcome to the neighbourhood

We make our way to the meeting place, which is a modern three-storey building in the middle of large, beautifully-tended gardens. Walking in, we are met by the sight of three teenage Ethiopian girls dancing to Rihanna in the gym, before the door is hurriedly shut by one of their friends.

Daniella and Ayelet are doing their jobs as part of their *sherut leumi*. They are *madrichot* [leaders] of a boarding programme to help the studies of 135 girls, all bar one being of Ethiopian descent. The one, Zoya, is Ukrainian, the last surviving member of the FSU school which had been set up to mirror the Ethiopian model. All of her classmates had fallen foul of the strict rules of the *pnimia* [dormitories] and been kicked out in disgrace, but Zoya had stayed straight, and opted to stay on with the 134 Ethiopian girls when her compatriots had left.

Established by Kedumim resident Menashem Moshe, the programme, part of Kedumim's all-girl high school, is for Ethiopian girls between the age of thirteen and eighteen, who come from home environments where they're unlikely to complete their studies. The school was set up twelve years ago to allow girls serious about their education to escape the crime, drugs and bad influences rife in the poorer towns of Israel – with formidable success, it seems. The girls study by day with *yeshuv* children in the main building of the school across the road, then come back to their dorms to continue working in the evenings.

The girls are allowed home most weekends, and travel to and from the *yeshuv* in bullet proof buses, "but none of them are concerned about the security situation", according to Ayelet. Eleven *madrichot* live on the campus with them, and give them extra-curricular assistance, whilst the school teachers are available in the evenings to help them with their studies. It is meant to be a religious school – all of the girls are dressed modestly, and there is no contact with boys – "but in practice they do what they want, by and large," says Daniella.

When we ask whether the girls have any contact with their Arab peers over the hill, Ayelet says "of course not – they're dangerous". She goes on to opine that "I've never heard of anyone just giving up land to others, and I especially don't understand it here when this land is meant for Jews." What about Israeli Arabs? "Well, they can live here," says Daniella, "but only because we're charitable enough to let them."

The *madrichot* don't discuss politics with the girls, instead they leave them to make up their own minds

50

about the conflict. Most of the girls were born in Ethiopia, and came to Israel during Operation Shlomo[7], in 1991. The school started with twenty or thirty pupils, and grows every year due to its reputation and popularity.

The girls' days are full from morning till night. There are after-school activities, as well as evening classes for girls keen to study more – and most of them are. The girls are here by choice, so there is a strong work ethic amongst them. They are not allowed to leave the *yeshuv* without parental permission, "but most of them find some excuse or other to visit the doctor in Kfar Saba when they want a day off," Ayelet assures us.

Speaking to Daniella and Ayelet on the way out of the dining room, we learn that the ultimate aim of the *pnimia* is to change Israelis' perception of Ethiopians. "If more of our girls end up at universities," says Daniella, "then people will think better of the Ethiopian community, and it will influence the government to help us more." As it is, "none of the parties help us, and many of the girls are scared that no matter how hard they study, or how well they do in their exams, they'll encounter racism as soon as they leave, and not be able to get on in life."

Some of the students want to leave Israel, according to Ayelet. "They're angry at the State, and want to go to the US, Europe – or even back to Ethiopia." Many of them came to Israel with Dick Whittington-type dreams, "believing Jerusalem was made of gold, and even that there was still a *Mishkan* [temple] standing there". They were raised on tradition that taught them that they were the only Jews left in the world, and that Israel was empty and waiting for them to arrive – "so it was a big shock to come here and find out that it was full of Jews who weren't welcoming to them at all".

After lunch, we meet with two of the students – Mazal Itzhak and Yafa Melese, both nearly eighteen and in their final year at the *pnimia*. They had come to Israel with their families in 1991 during Operation Shlomo, and live in the same building in the small, poor town of Kiryat Ikaron, near Rehovot. Their families didn't know one another back in Ethiopia – Mazal is from Gonda and Yafa from near Ambova – but the girls became close friends whilst growing up in Israel. They are dressed in modest clothes – skirts and long-sleeved shirts – and are both perfectly at ease talking to us about their backgrounds and experiences at the *pnimia*.

Mazal tells us that she couldn't carry on at "regular school, because there was no way for me to travel there every day, and all the nearby schools were too secular for me." She made the decision to come to the *pnimia* three years ago, and – "even though it was so hard at the start to be away from my family" – she doesn't regret it for a minute. "They don't just teach us schoolwork, they build us for life," she says. "It helps us to stay religious, and helps us succeed in the outside world." When she finishes her studies at the end of the school year, she will spend one or two years doing *sherut leumi*, then go to university to study teaching or design.

Yafa thinks it is vital to have a school such as this, where Ethiopians live together, separated from the "*pharangiot*" [non-Ethiopians]. "If you bring *pharangiot* into a class of Ethiopians, the level of the Ethiopians' learning falls," she tells us. "It's because Ethiopians need special attention from the teachers which *pharangiot* don't require. Ethiopians don't have anyone at home who can help them with their maths, English, and so on. Our parents aren't equipped to assist us with our studies at all."

The *pnimia* recognises this, and has a team of *madrichot* and teachers on hand to aid the girls in their after-school studies whenever they request it. "The next generation of Ethiopians won't need a system like this," says Mazal, "since we'll be the parents, and we'll have all the tools to help our kids."

The girls still have non-Ethiopian friends, since they learn with the *yeshuv* children by day in the main school in Kedumim. "It's good to mix with them," says Yafa,

52

"because we get to teach them about our culture. On Chag Hasig [Ethiopian holiday to celebrate their mass immigration to Israel], we gave talks to our classmates and explained to them the history of the Ethiopian Jews."

Discussing racism against the Ethiopian community, Mazal asserts that "if the state itself were racist, they wouldn't have brought us here in the first place." There is still a lot of racism amongst individuals, but she doesn't think it's specifically aimed at Ethiopians. "There's racism everywhere," she says. "Against Filipinos[8], and against Yemeni Jews – although we seem to have replaced the Yemeni these days. You can either worry about it all the time or not – you have to make the choice."

Yafa tells us that she feels fortunate to have been accepted onto the *pnimia*, especially when she sees how some of her childhood friends have ended up back in Kiryat Ikaron. "One girl I was very close to is now really straying from the path", she says sadly. "She smokes, drinks, doesn't do any work – but she refuses to come here because she doesn't want to live away from home."

Neither of them worry about the security situation in the *Shtachim* – "we don't watch TV, so we don't worry about what is said on the news," said Mazal. "It doesn't feel like we're on a settlement here, instead it just feels like a quiet place to work, out in the countryside."

The girls are both adamant when asked whether they would sanction returning the West Bank to the Palestinians. "I'd never give away any of this land," declares Mazal, eliciting a similar response from Yafa, "We went through such hardship to get to Israel, with people dying on the trek through Sudan, so we are too attached to the land of Israel to give any of it away."

Both girls are politically active, and took part in protests against the Disengagement of Gush Katif in 2005. Mazal states that "of course land-for-peace doesn't work – just look at what's happening in Sderot." In the future, she would happily live in the *Shtachim*, "assuming that my husband doesn't mind."

Regardless of the threat from Palestinian terrorists, Mazal still feels safer here than in the city. "Here, it is only Arabs that cause problems, whereas in the city, even Jews might attack you – the city is far more scary."

Staying on the theme of fear and loathing, Yafa interjects, announcing that "I'm scared of all the Arabs". So what would she say if someone told her they were scared of all Ethiopians? "I'd laugh at them," she says, the irony apparently lost on her.

"The image we have of Arabs is the problem," says Mazal. "For example, the other day there was an Arab worker fixing the roof at school, and he had two *shomrim* [security guards] standing next to him the whole time. That made us think he must be dangerous." She concedes that there must be "some good Arabs", but says that the impression they get of "bad Arabs outweighs any impression of the good". With no contact between the girls and Arab students of the same age, it appears that the only Arabs they will come across whilst on Kedumim will always be surrounded by armed guards. Thus their stereotypes of dangerous Arabs are reinforced.

Guardians of Eden

One afternoon, the settlement held a fun-run in honour of a boy from Kedumim killed in battle in Lebanon eleven years ago. Ishai Shachtar, who was born and raised on the *yeshuv*, was a sergeant in a Nahal brigade when he fell in battle, and every year the youth of Kedumim run the length of the settlement to commemorate his passing. We went with Miryam, who is the secretary of the school as well as the future mother-in-law of Shaked Edlis. She came here in 1979 and lives here with her husband Yisroel and their children. When we met at her house, Yisroel was excited to quiz us about the book, telling us "it's vital to do *hasbara* [PR] for Israel", and that we should get the settlers' story out to as many people as possible.

We drove alongside the running children, until Yisroel spotted the fallen soldier Ishai's father jogging slowly along, and jumped out of the car to join him for the final mile. Yisroel's pistol bounced precariously in his waist band as he ran with his friend, and we drove off to the finish line and parked up. An entire Golani platoon was there, in shorts, t-shirts and with M16s slung across their backs, and they gulped down water as they rested from the run. Even though Ishai had been a Nahal boy, the Golanis' presence as army representatives went down well amongst the hundred or so *yeshuvniks* who had gathered to cheer their children on. The kids were decked out in orange t-shirts emblazoned with Ishai's name – the orange was, of course, in honour of the anti-Disengagement movement, which shows no sign of waning support in these parts. It's important for the children to do fun-runs like this, according to Miryam, "since it gives them a connection to the land of Kedumim itself". Her reasoning echoed the words of Daniella Weiss: "marching through the West Bank kept the settlers' spirits alive, when they saw the land they were demanding to live in".

The memorial culminated in a park which Miryam said was "donated by lovers of Israel in the States". Daniella Weiss spoke to the crowd from a dais, before morphing from mayor to dustman and helping to clean up the scores of ice cream wrappers blowing around in the breeze. We helped her clean-up operation, then accepted a lift back, during which she told us that a new neighbourhood in Kedumim has been named Mizpe Ishai in the soldier's honour. She also complained about the hardship of running the settlement – "I work fifteen to eighteen hours a day," she sighed. "I'm the mayor, so what can I do?"

Daniella thrives on her image as a selfless warrior, toiling from morning till night on behalf of her constituents and the land itself. Wedding herself to the struggle, her tireless efforts are the ultimate proof of her love for Greater Israel.

***

Later that evening, Aryeh and Yehudit called us to watch a programme on the fortieth anniversary of the Six Day War. A state TV broadcast, a studio debate between two young religious settlers and a *Haaretz* columnist saw both sides lay into one another with barely-concealed hate. There followed a documentary on Hebron, which began with an interview with the instantly recognisable Yehuda Shaul of Breaking the Silence (an activist group dedicated to exposing army and settler misconduct in the West Bank).

As we watched images of Yehuda chatting to Palestinians in Hebron, Yehudit exclaimed "I just don't believe it!" "I know," Ariyeh replied. "He's a Jew, yet he's helping the Palestinians." As we watched, Aryeh and Yehudit both tried to educate us on Hebron's history, reinforcing the severity of the city's 1929 massacre of 67 Jews by Arab residents. "Why did it happen on that day? They had the opportunity... Arabs always want to kill us, to expel us, and that day they had the chance to."

As the camera turned to film two Peace Now women near the Cave of Machpela, Aryeh began to curse them – "*Nevaylot* [bastards]" – before Yehudit told him to watch his mouth in front of his guests. She then told us that "you have to remember that only three percent of all of Hebron was given to the Jews. The TV only ever film two roads when they're showing Hebron, so you get the impression that the whole place is Jewish, but that's just not true."

However, when confronted with images of venomous twelve year old settler children threatening a cameraman with rocks and sticks, she turned back into the kindly grandmother, tutting, "Oy, it's terrible that they act like that," and shaking her head sadly. Again we saw the two-way pull present in Yehudit's mind, a woman whose dedication to fulfilling what she perceives to be God's will is unquestionable but who, at the same time, can't bring herself to support the crimes carried out in God's name.

56

***

Later that night we went out on patrol with the *yeshuv* security team. Arriving in a burst of flashing orange light, they picked us up from the house and made room for us to squeeze onto the back seat of the Jeep The three men were at the start of a ten hour shift, and passed the time passionately arguing about football in the vein of bored soldiers and security guards the length and breadth of Israel.

We drove up and down the winding roads of the *yeshuv*, then paid a brief visit to the hilltop of Har Hemed. As a final flourish, they took us to see a vineyard planted at the edge of Kedumim, so that they could tell us the prophetic story attached to its history. The most religious of the three boys told us the tale, as we looked out over the vines bathed in the glow of the orange light on the roof of the Jeep

"It says in *Neviim* [Book of Prophets] that vineyards and flowers will grow in the Shomron region, even though the land is so unyielding and hard to cultivate," he told us. "Some years back, a man from Kedumim took it upon himself to test out the prophecy, so he planted this vineyard and named it after the brother of a famous rabbi in Israel. And look at it now," he said, spreading his arms out grandly over the rows of fruit. "It came true, just like the *Tanach* [Bible] said it would."

This was yet another nod towards the Biblical aspect of settling the region, like Aryeh's Esau and Jacob or Daniella's claim to "feel like I'm part of an unfolding Bible story". The boy who told us the story of the vineyard didn't consider that his Arab neighbours had contributed to the successful coming-to-pass of the prophecy, even though they had been growing olives on the same hills for years. Still, as far as he was concerned, "it is only thanks to the kindness of the settlers and the army that they are allowed to harvest their olives at all".

As good as it gets

Yehiel is a slim, dark-skinned, balding man in his forties. Nightly he stacks pizzas into the wood-fired oven of his small, neon-lit take away, wearing a large, knitted *kippah* and grubby white T-shirt that matches the walls around him. When the pizzas are ready, he removes and slices them for the assortment of Russian soldiers; Iraqi policemen; Ethiopian students and religious *sabra* kids who enter in dribs and drabs to stock up on greasy food and cola.

Having remained gruff and detached for our first couple of visits, in typical Israeli fashion Yehiel suddenly bursts into life on our third visit, eager to sit and chat with us as though he has known us for years. "You've caught me at a time when I'm full of spirit," he explains. And so we take a beer – Yehiel brings his syrupy black coffee – and we head through the mosquito-netted door to the sticky plastic chairs outside, that constitute the terrace Chez Yehiel.

"I like this place," asserts our host, leaning back in his chair and spreading his shoulders, confidently. "Some settlements have one view and one direction. But others are open, free. Like Kedumim. But the people are religious and ideological, too."

For Yehiel, this is undoubtedly a good thing, in the face of what he perceives to be a general apathy and ideological malaise running through the rest of the country. The problem, it seems, runs from the top down.

"There are no Zionists any more. None of the leaders think about the state of Israel. There was a time when Ben Gurion was prepared to go and live in a tent in the desert for the sake of the country, but since Begin there's been no ideology, no direction... Plus they're all corrupt – they don't just want their big salaries, but backhanders all the time."

A familiar complaint in Israel nowadays, Yehiel's disaffection reflects a general mistrust of leaders – particularly apparent amongst the settler communities who feel that their last great advocate, Ariel Sharon, sold them out with his withdrawal from Gaza and West Bank settlements around Homesh. This lack of leadership impacts on the people and Yehiel waves his arms as he laments the apathy of the Israeli public.

"The people are tired. There's no power with them any more. They don't have the energy for revolution – they should be taking to the streets, but they're not motivated. They're no longer interested in politics."

So would he be going to Homesh next week, to protest against the government's decision to evacuate its residents almost two years ago? Yehiel shrugs and his eyes glaze over. "Uh," he says dismissively. "I doubt it."

Yehiel might be as unwilling as his compatriots to take his views to the streets, but in the comfort of his own pizza parlour, he is at pains to explain why he totally opposes Israeli withdrawal from the West Bank or the Golan. He is convinced that the Arabs don't want peace.

"My parents come from Yemen. My parents are Arabian Jews – I know Arabs. You're from England? So you know English people. I could tell you I know Germans – I'd say 'they're nice, polite and gentlemanly', but then a German would tell me 'no, they're strong – I know, because I'm German.' Fine, he'd be right... Well I know Arabs. And believe me, they don't know how to compromise."

He indicates our box of half-eaten pizza, sitting on the table.

"If you were to tell me this was yours and I said it was mine, and we both insisted and couldn't agree, then I'd say 'tell you what, let's share it...' But not the Arabs. They don't know how to share. They don't know how to compromise. So there will never be peace, because they don't know how to compromise with Israel."

It is hard to argue with Yehiel's assertion that he is better placed to "know Arabs", given that he was born to and raised by Yemenites, but his Jewish Israeli identity has always placed him in opposition to the Arabs that his parents left south of Saudi. Yehiel describes how even as Jews in Yemen, his parents felt different to the Arabs there. "Arabs all owned horses, but Jews were allowed donkeys only."

And Yehiel is keen to assert his difference from the Arabs he knows so well:

"They're not a modern people. They kill one another for breaking rules; they live completely by religion. Their mums are happy when their son kills someone in the name of God. They're ostentatious. They're show-offs. They speed around in fast cars, always trying to act the big man..."

At this point, it is hard not to think of Israeli kids up and down the country, or indeed young men from any corner of the globe. But Yehiel is warming to his theme.

"They'd kill their neighbour if he sold his land to a Jew! What kind of people do that?! Jews wouldn't do it. Sure, they might ostracise him. Maybe put a sign up shaming the man in public, but they wouldn't kill him! And the only way they'll change is through education; with TV, the internet, radio – so, slowly, they might change. But for now they're closed-minded and stubborn. They think their way is the only way."

Perhaps sensing our scepticism, Yehiel challenges us to find out for ourselves.

"You don't believe me? So don't take my word for it. Go to Gaza and speak to them, see what you think. But if you're too scared to go to Gaza as journalists, then there you go – you've proved my point." [At this point, BBC correspondent Alan Johnston is being held captive by Hamas militants in Gaza, following his kidnap on 12th March 2007.]

So what's to be done in the face of an enemy that won't compromise? "The only thing is to be strong. The only time Israel has commanded the respect of the world – and of the Arabs too – is when it's been strong with the Arabs. For example 1967."

But what about Israel's bloody nose in the Yom Kippur War? Surely that stalemate paved the way for Israel's first official peace deal with an Arab state — precisely because Egypt felt it had gained enough strength over Israel to be able to compromise. But for Yehiel, whose entire upbringing has been shaped by war, the Egypt peace treaty is little to get excited about.

"It's not peace. It's a cold war."

But surely a cold war's better than a hot one?

"Not so. Egyptians fund terror attacks against our country, but because we're at peace, we can't do anything about it."

Yehiel swirls the dregs of his coffee around his small glass and then places it emphatically back on the table, looking to us for a response. "Welcome to the Middle East" his faint smile seems to suggest.

So is this really all there is, for a man like Yehiel? Is he really so jaded, so steeped in conflict, so untrusting of the "enemy"? What does the future hold with no leaders and a disinterested public? How can life be improved for everyone?

"It can't. This is it. This is the improved life. Every neighbourhood has bomb shelters. Many have them in their own homes. With Hitler we didn't have that — but now we do. The only answer is to stand strong against the Arabs and if things get bad, we've always got the shelters to protect us. That's life."

Yehiel starts to clear the table as we sit, somewhat drained by yet another bleak outlook on the future. It's getting late and Yehiel takes the chilli and oregano shakers back indoors and begins to lock up shop. As he turns out the lights, ready for sleep before doing it all over again, we wonder how he can simply resign himself to the prospect of damage limitation in the face of an ongoing conflict. It seems a thoroughly depressing way to live one's life.

But Yehiel just smiles. "Don't worry. You learn to live with it. And if you don't, there's always prozac. Three pills a day, and you'll be fine."

***

Yehudit had offered to give us a lift to Tel Aviv, in keeping with her unconditional hospitality. As we passed through the gate, and onto the road shared between Israeli and Palestinian vehicles, Yehudit whispered the prayer for a safe journey under her breath, the words etched, through habit and necessity, onto her heart.

We passed through small Arab "villages" – shops and houses stretched along the main road, clutters of Hebrew signs amongst the Arabic, clamouring for the attention of a clientèle that have long since taken their business elsewhere. Groups of Arab men sat outside the open fronted cafés; others debated the fault of broken engines in dimly lit garages as we zipped past, en route from Israel's outpost to the mainland itself.

To the left, the larger town of Qalqilya sprawled into the distance. To the right, a towering section of the separation barrier loomed, at this point an impenetrable wall of giant concrete slabs and imposing grey watchtowers driving through the land, coiling around Palestinian houses, until it came to an abrupt end. This section of the wall had not yet been built.

Yehudit still didn't know whether Kedumim will be inside or outside the wall, as the route is currently under negotiation. If Kedumim is to be included, it would mean diverging from the Green Line and annexing a huge section of Palestinian land to Israel.

But for Yehudit, if the wall is sealed at this point and Kedumim is left outside, it would be a lethal blow for her home town. Not that she's concerned about the security the wall might provide. Indeed Yehudit is quite dismissive of the wall's purpose and effectiveness altogether and feels quite safe in her home town. But her concern is that if the wall isolates Kedumim, then the settlement has no future. The current residents would stay, she claims, but no one else would move there. ("What Israeli in their right mind would move outside the wall?") Which, of course, means that all the properties would lose their value, and she and her husband would be unable to move. Thus the Edlises would be stuck outside Israel, after having dedicated the last thirty years to ensuring that the West Bank becomes an inseparable part of the Jewish state.

But all of this is assuming that the government doesn't decide on further withdrawals. The current view seems to be that after the "disaster" of Gush Katif, and the subsequent barrage of rocket attacks from Gaza into Israel, the government is, for the time being, reluctant to evacuate any more settlements. Nevertheless, Sharon's actions in Gaza set a precedent, and though she thinks Israel would be committing suicide to give the Palestinians such a strategic outlook over Israel's centre, Yehudit admits that she now thinks it's a real possibility that her family might one day be told to leave Kedumim.

So what would she do?

"I'd leave," she states simply. "I don't want war – I'm old, I want a good life. Ariyeh's more ideological than I am. But even he would leave, if it came down to it."

But Yehudit remains hopeful for her future, depending as it does upon the West Bank settlements. Indeed she hopes for a return to the climate in which Jews and Arabs get along once more, their children coming together in joint activities and the adults sharing in each others' parties, weddings and religious festivals. So it was once upon a time, so should it be again – though of course this would all have to happen under the umbrella of Israeli sovereignty.

But as we pass the wall and approach a heavily guarded checkpoint, our yellow licence plates waved swiftly into Israel, leaving the green plates behind, it is obvious that even Yehudit doesn't believe her dreams of reviving bygone harmony. The future might be unknown, but it seems to leave little room for hope.

And yet, on a daily basis, life carries on as normal for Yehudit, who lets us out at a major junction – her heading off to her course in puppet therapy, which she uses with the special needs kids at the kindergarten, and us in a different direction. And within forty minutes of leaving Kedumim, we're back in the heart of Tel Aviv.

Chapter Two
Mitzpeh Yeriho:
Far from the calming crowd ·

American pie

A battered, blue Dodge van pulled to the curb in Jerusalem's Anglo-dominated German Colony and a middle-aged American woman in thick glasses and blue headscarf waved to us from behind the wheel. The rear door rolled open, bags of shopping bursting onto the street as a young, red-headed boy flapped to catch them. Clambering over the shopping, we squeezed into the van and sat down, clutching our bulky bags to our chests as we cast our eyes around the many faces that peered out from amongst the groceries and pieces of furniture packed into the car.

Esther, the driver and mother of the family, introduced us to the many pairs of eyes staring bemusedly in our direction. The red-haired, or rather strawberry blond child, who sat behind Esther, with a face not dissimilar to that of Prince Harry, was Ruven, Esther's second son. Ruven's T-shirt and boyish face belied the fact that he was several months into his spell of service with the IDF. A very different face sat to Ruven's left – a *Haredi* man, with black beard, black hat and white shirt, dark eyes barely smiling behind his glasses. This was Nosson, the husband of Esther's daughter, Miriam, who sat on the seat behind, in demure, dark dress, emblematic of her Ultra-Orthodox customs. She clutched her eldest daughter, blonde-haired toddler Elisheva, whilst strapped into a baby seat beside her was the newest addition to the family, another daughter, Rivka.

Esther spoke in a tight, slightly muffled Brooklyn accent as she turned the car around and headed towards her home in the Judean settlement of Mitzpeh Yeriho.

"It's a good thing you called when you did. I always come into Jerusalem before Shabbos to do the big shop. They've just built a major supermarket close by the *yeshuv* – plus a huge bowling alley – but it's cheaper to get all the groceries in Jerusalem."

At just half an hour's drive from Mizpeh Yeriho, it is also convenient to shop there and Esther combined the stockpiling of food, nappies and household goods with the collection of her daughter and grandchildren. Nosson, Miriam and the two girls were moving out of their Jerusalem flat and preparing to head back to Brooklyn – hence the items of furniture piled in amongst the ice cream and washing powder.

As we drove out of the Jerusalem traffic and into a long tunnel, bored through the hillside, city life suddenly receded as we re-emerged from beneath the ground, heading down, down, into a parched lunar landscape of beige and bleached hills, ruffled, like gathered velvet.

The open windows drew billows of hot, dry air through the car, baking us like spuds in a fan oven, as we ran down towards the Jordan Valley and the Dead Sea, over which Esther's remote settlement sat in waiting.

There were no signs of life on the deserted sandy mountains that spanned for miles on either side, until occasional Bedouin villages sprang up – flimsy tin shacks leaning into each other for support; a few possessions spread amongst the outer spaces, where specks of men stood until they flashed past into the distance as the Dodge van sped on.

"We don't have any contact with them," said Esther, of the Bedouin, "except for when they steal stuff from the *yeshuv*."

Esther was born in Brooklyn then moved to New Jersey as a child where she married a man called Arthur and gave birth to six children ("six for the six million"). She eventually decided to move her reluctant family to Israel in 1996. Esther nodded through the windscreen, beginning to talk rapidly, as Ruven stretched forward to change the radio station.

"All of this is so different from New Jersey. There everything's green, everywhere you look. But here, it's desert for miles. But it's not dead, like people think. There's a lot of colour and beauty in the detail – lots of flowers, lots of life. I often go out for walks and take photos. I'll show you later.

"And you can get a lot more for your money here – a much bigger house – even if they did rip us off when they built it. But there aren't many English speakers. Maybe 10%. And my *Ivrit* [Hebrew] is no good which makes it hard to fit in. If I'd have known then about some of the more Anglo *yeshuvim*, I'd have chosen somewhere else But I didn't. Still, the view here's beautiful and that's why I chose it. Have you heard about the view from Mitzpeh Yeriho?'"

As we neared the *yeshuv*, the road was in the process of being widened, large machinery hacking away at the dusty mountain slopes.

"They were developing this road before but they stopped two years ago, when they were talking about giving the land away. But now they're building it again. I don't know why they would start again if they're still thinking of giving us away."

Having driven downhill since leaving Jerusalem, the van then turned off the main road and started a shallow ascent along a rough slip road, up towards Mitzpeh Yeriho. We passed a quiet security post, apparently unmanned; the entrance rather more dilapidated than the approach to Kedumim.

The *yeshuv* was home to approximately 300 *dati leumi* [nationalist religious] families, largely comprised of Sephardi and Ashkenazi Israelis and a few Americans. Strict orthodoxy was evident amongst the children we passed playing in the street, the boys in large crocheted *kippot* and trailing *tzitzit*; long skirts and sleeves de rigueur for the girls. The married women of Mitzpeh

Yeriho were required to cover their heads within the *yeshuv*.

Neat, modern homes were dotted on either side of the tree-lined road through the small *yeshuv*, the perimeter of which was visible behind houses on several sides as we drove. The houses themselves were unremarkable; markedly poorer than many of those we had seen in Elkana, though still comfortable enough to house the hordes of children teeming through the streets.

Pulling up outside Esther's imposing, boxlike house, we caught a glimpse of the view for which the *yeshuv* is renowned; creamy brown mountains folding like cake mixture off into the distance, melting into one another as a slowly setting sun dragged shadow across the sleek contours of the dry land. White into beige into brown, the mountains tumbled down towards the Jordan Valley.

Getting out of the car, we met Nosson properly as Esther organised her children in unloading the car. He smiled and shook our hands – it becoming apparent that he was but 24, despite his black beard and two children. Known as John amongst his unreligious family, Nosson became increasingly *frum* [religious] in his late teens and since took on the Hebrew name of Nosson. Smoking a quick cigarette before heading inside, he chatted openly, proving himself to be rather more approachable than many members of the socially conservative, pious, Ultra-Orthodox communities.

Having finished his cigarette, we grabbed the remaining shopping bags and went inside to meet the family.

The dining/ living room area was even busier than the car, as various family members moved in and out of the kitchen unloading shopping, cooking, cleaning and getting ready for Shabbos. Arthur, Esther's husband and father of their six children, was there, large and sweaty in a grubby white T-shirt and out of breath from playing basketball with his son Sammy. Sammy, 23, was a growing replica of his dad, minus the grey beard and glasses.

Sammy and Ruven wore *kippot* and jeans, while their younger sisters, Aliza and Naomi wore long, casual skirts and long sleeve T-shirts, in the manner of Israel's modern Orthodox. Only Talia, 19, had followed her elder sister, Miriam, in settling into the Ultra-Orthodox *haredi* mould, her sombre uniform of full length grey skirt and blue shirt mirroring that of her sister.

There is a significant distinction between these two types of religiosity, with the ideologists driving Israel's settlement enterprise coming mostly from the *datim leumim*, rather than from the *haredim* [Ultra-Orthodox]. Whilst the modern orthodox that populate most of Israel's religious settlements often have four to six children per family, Esther estimated that her two *haredi* daughters would give birth to twelve to fourteen children each. And if they followed the trends of their new communities, they would also be unlikely to live on a settlement in the future – if they did so it would likely be for economic and not political reasons. Whilst the modern orthodox of the *datim leumim* see religion and the Biblical land of Israel as being inseparable, the Ultra-Orthodox *haredim*, on the whole, place no inherent value on the land; the coming of the messiah will liberate Israel – not mankind.

Whilst the *dati leumi* and the *haredim* are alike in their fastidious observance of the Jewish religion, their politics and lifestyles are worlds apart. Miriam and Talia might have lived amongst their *dati leumi* family for now, but *haredi* and *dati leumi* communities tend to be separate, and in the future Esther's daughters may well end up in an homogeneous Ultra-Orthodox community, far removed from the family home.

***

A burly man, Arthur bounds into the kitchen and swigs water from a bottle. He gives his son Ruven a bear hug and they catch up after Ruven's week in the army, Sammy chipping in with comments on his own time in the forces, designed to show his brother who's boss. They laugh and talk about baseball. In the kitchen, the effervescent daughters unload cola, cherryade, peanut butter and cookies into the packed cupboards. This is an American home; a New Jersey outpost in the Middle Eastern desert. Esther was surprised to find that instead of making her children feel Israeli, the move to Israel in fact made them more American. Even those with the most Jewish of names have American alternatives, remnants of who they were before they moved up to Israel, and elevated in religiosity: Esther is also known as Ellen, Ruven is Judd, Nosson – John.

The three-storey home is packed with people. With two parents, six children, one son-in-law, two grandchildren, an invalid aunt and her live-in carer – plus two guests – every room in the house is used twice over. The carer has her home in the bomb shelter; Aunt Helen is squeezed into the utilities room, her wardrobe a rail of clothes beside the freezer. Until Miriam and her family move back to America to be with Nosson's father, who has cancer, they will share a room with Elisheva, whilst baby Rivka sleeps in a cot in the bathroom.

In the living room, Ruven shows off a trick he's just learnt in the army. Fed up of eating tuna, the soldiers have mastered a way to spice up the food, reviving its appeal. Ruven opens the can, sticks a piece of tissue on top of the fish, so that it soaks up the oil, then sets the tissue alight: smoked tuna. The tissue goes up in flames and a steady bonfire burns in the middle of the living room, at which point Arthur points out it might have been a better idea if Ruven had played his game outside. Ruven puffs at the flames, fanning them until charred tissue floats around the room and the flames die down leaving a faint smell of toasted tuna flakes. Having failed to impress with his demonstration, Ruven grows bored and leaves the unappetising ashes, heading upstairs. We use the opportunity to give the family some space.

Up on the West Bank

Mitzpeh Yeriho is a small *yeshuv*. At its highest point, the settlement's only shop – a small convenience store – sits amid a medium car park, a few trees and a bus stop. From there, the *yeshuv* spreads a kilometre or so down a gentle slope, with the majority of the families living in the network of streets that fan out from the main road.

Near the shop there is a *yeshiva* [learning centre], in this case a small high school for religious boys. Alongside the school is a basketball court and a couple of hundred metres away a children's playground sits amidst a well kept green lawn, incongruously verdant against the parched dry heat. At the edge of the lawn, the *yeshuv* crumbles away – a stark drop marks the edge of Mitzpeh Yeriho as the land tumbles down a sheer cliff face to the valley below. A small fence prevents the children from running too far.

Beyond the fence, to the East, lies the astounding view for which the settlement is renowned. Mitzpeh means lookout, thus Mitzpeh Yeriho is named for its spectacular view over the Palestinian city of Jericho that lies sprawled out on the flats of the Jordan valley, four miles to the north east, on the left side of the panorama. To the right of Jericho, the Jordan Valley sweeps down to the Dead Sea, the northern tip of which is visible to our right, beyond the mountains that range from beneath our feet. That brilliant blue splash in the desert quickly dissolves from bright shocks of colour to a pastel, fading blue as it dissolves into sand and salty air, along the valley floor.

Directly beneath us, beyond the low, rolling hills, flows the Jordan River running left to right down the centre of the valley, the west bank of which gives the name to this most controversial patch of land. Barely visible beyond the river, the mountains of Jordan grow in the distance, shimmering and fading as they rise in the desert haze, and, before they reach their summit, they dissolve from sight altogether.

71

We head right along the perimeter of the *yeshuv*, the cliff's edge, and down a path along a mountain peninsula that juts from the settlement in towards the Jordan Valley. With the *yeshuv* a kilometre or so behind us, we turn back to see just how isolated the place is. Mitzpeh Yeriho sits alone on top of the hill, surrounded by dry, deserted mountains. The near side of the settlement is sealed off from the lower hills and the Jordan Valley by the impassable stone drop, whilst the short distance to Jericho is deceiving – miles of mountains, a vast drop in elevation and hostile relations combine to put the city shimmering on the desert floor effectively out of reach.

And all along the West Bank border those same bleached velvet mountains unfurl like the flabby rolls of a sleeping bear, towards the desert floor. Nothing disturbs the slumber, save for small signs of life tucked into the crevices of the hills: Bedouin camps, almost invisible along the contours of the ancient landscape.

We head back along the path, towards the *yeshuv*, and its newly built houses, tarmac roads and air conditioned cars. An SUV slips past, crowded with young children; a red-headed family refrigerated in a sealed box in the desert. It is an incongruous image, and part of the wider question of what effect such physical, social and national isolation have had on the residents of Mitzpeh Yeriho.

***

Friday night prayers were held in a bomb shelter close to the house. This was not the main service of the *yeshuv*, but rather the American community's alternative congregation, with up to fifty congregants singing and dancing in the Shabbat, in the small, cramped shelter.

White muslin hung from the walls and a white sheet formed a *mehitza* to separate the men's section from the women's. Arthur sat with Sammy at a table to the back of the room, as the prayers were sung from the *bimah* in the centre.

The *chazzan* (cantor) led the congregation in a monotonous chant at first, before reaching the more tuneful parts of the service and bursting into well-received song. He used melodies in the style of the late Rabbi Shlomo Carlebach who promoted song as a preferred method to achieve spirituality, and who was also one of the earliest settlement pioneers. The singing soon reached a deafening crescendo with each tune descending into la la las and Yiddisher rounds as Arthur turned the table before him into a mini drum kit.

More and more men stood up to join the *chazzan* singing and the group began to parade around the *bimah* and the small men's side of the room. The white sheeting, the smart dress and the joy of the occasion, along with the singing and the clapping created a real sense of celebration of the arrival of the Sabbath, as a tiny, gorgeous boy with long black *payyot* [earlocks] and huge brown eyes to match his dark skin, leaned from his father's shoulders to try to grab his *kippah*.

But beneath the young child's foot, a gun rested in his father's belt. Behind him in the procession another man had a gun lodged into his waistband, and another, and another. As the heads bobbed round the conga line, they revealed on the wall behind the same picture that Daniella Weiss proudly displayed in her office – the vision of the rebuilt temple. And the sanctity and purity of the white Sabbath being so joyfully welcomed in now felt trapped amongst the pistols, the politics and the pulsating military drum beat that rattled around the cramped walls of the small bomb shelter.

The sermon was delivered by a man called Levi, another American; young, and with a large bushy beard. The speech began with a quote from Meir Kahane, some words of wisdom from the assassinated leader of the banned extreme right political party Kach, which advocated the expulsion of all Arabs from Israel and a ban on sexual relations between Jews and non-Jews. Levi then went on to discuss why the Jews are the chosen people –

"*kaha*" [they just are] – and that response became a running theme throughout the rest of the sermon: why will we always fight Esau? *Kaha*. Why are the Palestinians firing rockets from Gaza? *Kaha*. That's how it is. Israel and Palestine are at war, *kaha*.

Levi linked the story of the day's *parsha* [reading from the Torah] with the current situation in Gaza, although without a great deal of success.

His attempt to compare Korach (the *parsha's* central figure) to the Ishmaelite tribe, and then further to the militants of Gaza was tenuous to say the least and, when we asked him to expound further on it after the service, his half-hearted shrug – "it doesn't matter" – indicated his own uncertainty about his words. However, in an environment where the residents live and breathe the language of war and conflict on a daily basis, it was almost incumbent on him to try to draw parallels between Biblical battles and today's struggle between Israel and her enemies.

Levi works in a shop in Jerusalem's Old City selling Judaica and spends his spare time raising money for a Kach school that spreads the word of Meir Kahane to its pupils. Levi also discusses the far right rabbi's teachings at a discussion group on Shabbat afternoons and works closely with the principal rabbi of the *yeshuv*, who is also a Kachnik, with the result that the banned political party's nationalistic policies have gained quite a hold on the residents of the *yeshuv*. An advertising trailer is parked near the grocery shop, on which a huge photo of Kahane is emblazoned, along with a phone number to donate to the numerous charitable causes that his followers carry out – which includes the funding of children's' activities and education.

Strangely, Mitzpeh Yeriho is not generally considered to be an extremist *yeshuv*, and upon hearing that the teachings of Meir Kahane (who is widely believed to have inspired Baruch Goldstein to massacre 29 Palestinians and wound a further 150 in a Hebron mosque) are being openly taught at synagogues of Mitzpeh Yeriho, many Israelis outside the isolated settlement are surprised to learn about what exists beneath its innocuous surface.

As we strolled home with Sammy and his father to join the rest of the family for lunch, our progress down the narrow path was slowed by Levi, big and stocky next to his short, middle-aged friend and another American man. The short man excitedly yapped a story to Levi, his small frame jumping eagerly as the cadence of his high voice rose and rose. Clearly this was his story of the week, and he was desperate to tell it.

Apparently the BBC had recently run a sports story in which a presenter had referred to Jerusalem as the capital of Israel and had later apologised for doing so. "Can you believe it?!!" the man panted, bouncing up to Levi like an under-walked Labrador. "They actually apologised!"

"I can believe that," Levi drawled, coolly.

"Yeah I mean I can believe it too," the short man said, in an apparent U-turn, and turned from the BBC to another pet hate. "Yeah and I bet what else will happen is like one day soon the UN will just like vote to dissolve Israel. Like an Arab state will propose it and then everyone will vote."

The short, yapping man looked to Levi for approval and gained it, inasmuch as Levi didn't disagree – and so he babbled on.

"Yeah they'll just vote and there'll only be like three countries on Israel's side and all the rest of the world will be against us and then they'll just dissolve the country."

Their misgivings about the way in which the world views the Zionist state was magnified by the lack of soothing voices of calm around them. From what we'd seen thus far, this community took one party line on the political situation, meaning there was no one to take an opposing view and suggest that perhaps things weren't as stacked against Israel as they would have themselves believe.

The group then went on to discuss Arab enmity, Israeli isolation and the root cause of it all – pure, unbridled anti-Semitism – until they reached the end of the path and dispersed into their respective houses for Shabbat dinner.

The conversation got back onto anti-Semitism whilst sat around the dinner table, which was covered with food: American sweet potato pie, BBQ chicken, mashed potato and coleslaw sitting happily alongside Israeli hummus and matbuha and Yiddisher challah and kuggel. As the family crowded around the table and helped themselves to the piles of food, Esther asked us what life was like for Jews in England. Was there much anti-Semitism?

When we told Esther that we had experienced very little anti-Semitism ourselves, she found it hard to believe, repeating the oft-heard charge that England is anti-Israeli and anti-Semitic. We reiterated our personal experiences.

"But aren't there lots of Arabs in London?" she asked, bemused.

We affirmed her suspicions but told her that in our own experiences, Jews and Muslims get along fairly well with one another on a day to day basis. This Esther found very hard to believe.

"The Jews and Muslims get along?!" she snorted and we nodded as people stared at us in disbelief. Eventually, once she had got her head round the idea, she conceded "that's good, I suppose", but her experiences of life in the West Bank made the idea of Jewish/Muslim harmony very hard to swallow.

After dessert, another American friend came to visit the family. According to Esther, many Americans had left the *yeshuv*, leaving just a small, close community behind. Many of them spoke poor Hebrew which made it all the more important for the group to stick together, as there was little else to do on the *yeshuv* other than socialising. Esther admitted that she found it hard to integrate. Not the most confident of women, she explained that this made her broken Hebrew seem worse than it really was, and as a result, the women on the *yeshuv* assumed that she simply couldn't speak to them. Over the years Esther had not made many friends. She admitted that her American/Israeli identity made her feel like an outsider in both Mitzpeh Yeriho and the States and that when she saw Jews visiting Israel from America, she resented them.

"They're here for two or three years in Jerusalem, rich and spoilt with their expensive *sheitels* [wigs worn by religious women, for modesty], smart clothes and Daddy's credit card. I want to tell them 'you're just a visitor, you don't live here, you don't know about the place.' We're the ones who have to live here."

Esther would have liked to have followed other American immigrants to more Anglo settlements but, lying outside the expected route of the separation barrier, the family home has little value and moving house is pretty much out of the question.

Esther kept busy with her art and photography. Having trained as an art teacher, she found that once she was on the settlement, there was little interest for her services: "either they don't have money, don't speak English or just don't care." So Esther settled for making challah cloths and wall hangings to fill her spare time and earn a bit of extra cash.

Their guest was also having difficulty finding work, though he lived in Jerusalem and not in Mitzpeh Yeriho. He was looking for work as a security guard, but thought he would have trouble getting a gun licence. "Maybe I'll just give them your address here," he said to Arthur, "then they'd give me a gun no problem."

However, according to Nosson, no one in Mitzpeh Yeriho really needed a gun, "but they all want them just to look cool", he said plainly.

As the family sat eating peanut butter cookies and ice cream, the conversation kept largely away from politics and religion and focused on news from back home. At one rather surreal moment, the whole table began humming the theme from Star Wars. Long after they had finished eating and the friend had left, the family sat together – Arthur, Ellen, Helen and Hadassa, Miriam and John, Sammy, Judd, Talia, Aliza and Naomi, with Elisheva running around as the dog howled in the corner – and played board games and laughed at Arthur's jokes and spent time together like any average suburban east coast American family.

An isolated household, on an isolated *yeshuv* in the wild West Bank, the family clearly depended greatly on one another's company.

Itchy fingers

On Saturday, the synagogue was once again packed with worshippers, clad in blue and white *tallitot* [prayer shawls] and swaying fervently in time with the prayers. The women's section was filling up by the time we arrived, with mothers and daughters taking the supplications equally as seriously as the men on the other side of the net curtain *mehitza.*

The dress code for the men was the standard settler outfit of chinos, sandals and untucked white shirts, and again the ostentatiously displayed handguns in the waistband, coupled with the thick, bomb-proof walls of the building and the airtight steel door of the *shul*, meant there was no escaping the entrenched, defensive atmosphere that even permeated the sanctity of Saturday morning prayers.

Arthur and his family had sponsored the *kiddush* [small meal of wine and cake after the service] after the service in honour of their baby granddaughter Rivkah, so that she would one day get married – the story being that a family friend had never married, and that was because she had never had a *kiddush* held for her. Just to be sure, Esther insisted that her granddaughter would have this *kiddush* – and the celebrants milled around happily as they toasted the health of the far-future couple.

The small, yapping man from the night before was in action again and had cornered an apparently disinterested congregant, delivering his now well-honed anecdote about the BBC and its hatred of Israel.

"So they apologised about calling Jerusalem the capital." He enthused, "I tell you, one day, the UN will vote and they'll dissolve Israel, just like that."

He continued in this vein for quite some time, his one member audience clearly so bored that he could barely dignify the energetic lecturer with facial expressions, let alone a verbal response. At least he *seemed* bored, until he fixed the yapper a stern, firm look and waited for him to grow quiet. And then he spoke.

"You ready for the war?" he asked, deadly serious.

"Which one?" replied the yapper, wagging his tail expectantly.

"The next one." Dramatic pause. "It's gonna be big."

The conversation then turned into a bubbling discussion of who was to feature in the next big war. All the major players were there, Iran, Syria, Israel, America – it was bound to happen and soon – and the warmongering continued with tangible enthusiasm. And again there was no calming voice in the small community to temper the violent sensationalism.

Expulsions and conversions

Esther is in good spirits at lunch, as is Aunt Helen's carer, Hadassa, who sits with everyone for the meal, very much a part of the family. The reason for the celebration is that Hadassa's son has just converted to Judaism.

Hadassa is a Marrano[9] from Colombia. During the Spanish Inquisition, most Jews were expelled from Spain for refusing to convert; others, however, converted to Christianity and so avoided expulsion. Marranos, or

Hidden Jews, are the descendants of those who converted but nevertheless continued to practise Jewish customs and maintain Jewish beliefs out of sight of the authorities. Over the generations and the ensuing centuries, as the Hidden Jews gradually assimilated into wider society, their Jewish practices decreased. Nevertheless, many Hidden Jews still remember their families going under ground to light candles on Friday night, long after the Spanish persecution of Jews had come to an end.

Hadassa is one of these people. She remembers her mother doing vigorous cleaning on Friday – in preparation for a long lost Sabbath – and washing her hands every morning, reflecting the Jewish ritual. "She has a Jewish *neshama* [soul]," says Esther.

Due to the centuries of assimilation, Hidden Jews are not considered to be technically Jewish, but when Haddassa came to Israel, she claims she felt a strong spiritual attachment to the land and the people and began to take on all of the Jewish beliefs and rituals. Though she speaks very little Hebrew, she knows all the *brahot* [blessings] and covers her head in public, like a religious Jew.

Her son's conversion ceremony had taken place in Colombia, along with ninety other Hidden Jews, and was conducted by a friend of Esther, a resident of Mitzpeh Yeriho, who originally hailed from Colombia himself. Now that they are converted, the ninety are preparing to remarry en masse, according to Jewish law.

Given that it would be hard to be Jewish in Colombia, as people are generally required to work on Shabbat, and the Jewish community is small, they are all intending to come and live in Israel. Or at least Hadassa calls it Israel: arrangements are being made for all ninety Colombian converts to come and live close to Hadassa and Esther, in neighbouring Ma'aleh Adumim, the burgeoning settlement that severs Jerusalem from the Palestinian cantons of the West Bank.

Conversation then moves on to those very Palestinians, with Esther revealing some worryingly entrenched views. She, along with many others we've met so far on our travels, has successfully managed to override any feelings of shame or embarrassment about her unabashed xenophobia towards her Arab neighbours. By contextualising her hate and convincing herself that it is permissible because of the nature of the conflict, she has managed to justify her feelings as acceptable in the circumstances. It is a battle of good versus evil. Jew versus Arab. "Jacob versus Esau". God versus the Devil.

In Mitzpeh Yeriho as in other religious settlements, many believe, with an unshakable conviction, that they are part of a Biblical narrative that has evolved over several thousand years, and is now being played out on the plains of Judea and Shomron where they make their home. They gaze out of their hilltop homes over the desert plains, the Biblical cities resplendent far below, and believe that it is their destiny to fight for the cause until their dying day.

"God told Abraham to settle the land of Israel, and that's what we're doing," explains Esther when asked why she'd made the move from New Jersey to the mountain range east of Jerusalem. "I came here when I was in my early twenties, and thought 'I just have to live here'. I never felt comfortable back home. I read in the Torah that this is where the Jews are supposed to be and I'm never going back."

The overriding 'holy war' element to her way of thinking appears to be the reason she is so happy to conflate the ethnicity of all Muslims into one homogeneous "Arab nation". This is apparent when, on being asked what she would do to bring peace to the region, she espouses the views of the late Meir Kahane, saying "I would pay the Arabs to leave and send them off to the Arab countries all around us. Israel is so small," she says, "and their lands are so big – I just don't understand why they want a piece of our country too".

When it is pointed out that the "Arab countries" have appeared reluctant to take in the refugees thus far, she cries "exactly – *that's* the problem! They don't want them!" her face betraying her confusion at this state of affairs. There is no hint of recognition in her eyes that the Palestinians are not, by definition, Jordanian, Syrian, Lebanese or even Egyptian. Instead she has them all down as "Arabs", who thus ought to be dealt with and aided by other Arabs – and certainly should not be the responsibility of the Jews.

She wasn't always like this, she tells us. "I was a liberal for the first forty-two years of my life," she says. "When I lived in the States, I didn't have an opinion on the Arabs at all. But when I moved here, and I heard all my neighbours saying 'I want to kill the Arabs – they're evil', I started thinking that there must be something in what they were saying. When the intifada broke out and the terror attacks hit Israel, I began to think that perhaps they were right."

However, a couple of years ago, she met Musa – an Israeli-Arab physiotherapist who helped treat Arthur's aunt who had suffered a broken hip – and her feelings towards "the Arabs" took another twist. "He was such a nice guy – well-educated, polite, a real gentleman. What the experience taught me was that everyone has to be judged individually – but the problem is that most Arabs aren't educated and can't get along with us."

That she could utter both halves of that non sequitur in the same breath is sobering enough, but worse is the fact that she is clearly confused as to her feelings towards the "other side", yet appears to be happy to err on the side of racism whilst she remains undecided.

"They're not all bad, but most of them do want to kill us unfortunately. And that's the problem. They just want to kill and hurt us and they don't want to live in peace. Musa was educated though – that's the difference. Israel needs to help to educate the Arabs. They teach their children hate, e.g. in their maths books they'll have sums like

82

'if three Jews are killed with nine bullets, how many bullets does it take to kill a Jew?' They hate us. They're taught to kill us.

"We don't teach that kind of hatred. Sure, maybe the kids hear it in the *yeshuv* – 'I hate Arabs', that sort of thing, 'I wish they'd all leave'. Or they might say they want to kill them all because the Arabs have done so much to the Jews – it's a natural reaction, to want to kill them all. But it's not taught in schools."

However the views of Meir Kahane, which Esther voices, *are* purportedly disseminated at the school for which Levi organises funds, and throughout the *yeshuv*. Lamenting the hatred nurtured at generic "Arab" schools and despite admitting that the loathing espoused by certain settlers does not help the situation, Esther seems reluctant to acknowledge the similarity between the mistrust learnt by certain Palestinian children and that absorbed by children on the *yeshuv*.

Nevertheless, Esther recognises that the children's respective upbringings entrench and aggravate the divide. Esther recalls entering an embroidery shop in the Arab quarter of Jerusalem's Old City and being treated kindly by one of the Arab women there, but when she told the other shop assistant where she lived, she "felt the hate from her. It was in the way she looked, but she had to act nice with me because she wanted my money."

According to Esther, the woman hated her because she was Israeli – and not because she lives in the West Bank and is thus a direct obstacle to the establishment of a national Palestinian homeland. Just as Esther was surprised to hear of Muslims and Jews co-existing in London, she simply views Jewish Israelis and Arabs as irreconcilable enemies.

"The prejudice can't be got over. When we come into contact, we already hate. We don't ever see each other, or mix, to prevent that."

So should Jews and Palestinians perhaps be mixing, at schools for example?

"Well we can't, because we wouldn't want to learn their religion and they wouldn't be interested in ours," states Esther, back at square one.

Esther is a woman who loves her children with all her heart and soul; who displays an equal devotion to the land of her forefathers; who has taken in her husband's elderly aunt to look after for her autumn years – yet who could dismiss "most Arabs" as casually as if she was discussing the weather; a woman who came here with "no opinion on the Arabs" but who now believes there "must be something in it" when all of her settler neighbours deride them as evil and call for them to be killed. And her story is by no means unique – and by no means exclusive to settlements. It is the same in closed, cut-off communities such as this the world over. The rulers of the roost suck in the weakest, chew them up for a year or two, then spit them out in their own mould – and in a walled-in environment such as Mitzpe Yericho, there is no one around to counter the hate.

***

Most of the family went to bed after lunch, making the most of the day of rest to catch up on their sleep and recharge the batteries before the week ahead. Seth followed suit and retired to Sammy's bedroom where he was staying, and marvelled at the military shrine to which he'd devoted one wall of his room. Sammy had served in a tank unit during his spell in uniform, and his tour of duty had evidently left some lasting impressions on his taste for interior design. Beneath posters of various tanks and APCs stood a display of a huge range of shells and bullets that he'd amassed during his time in the army. Most soldiers that Seth served with keep a few mementos from their national service, as did he, but Sammy's array of weaponry was on a different scale.

He had a collection of bullets arranged in order of size, from tiny dum-dums to armour-piercing Browning shells and even a mini-RPG, which fortunately appeared to be defused. Tank shells and spent grenades sat on another shelf of the stand, as well as a camouflage helmet, various pins and sets of dog-tags, and a heavy metal air gun propped against the wall. A complete fox skin completed the rather morbid collection.

A knock on the door ended Seth's wonderment at the miniature museum, and it was time to go back to *shul* for *mincha* [afternoon prayers]. The short service was followed by a *shiur* [lesson] led by Levi. The dozen or so men gathered around a long table with Levi at the head, grabbing handfuls of pretzels and crisps as they listened to his interpretation of the section of *Gemara* [a collection of holy texts] they were scheduled to study

One of the men slipped into a back room and returned clutching a bottle of lethal-looking alcohol, its potency confirmed by another of the group who gleefully declared "look, it's 190 proof, folks!" before pouring out shots for his friends. Emboldened by the powerful liquor, the men began to act like naughty schoolchildren and shouted out inane interruptions as Levi struggled to keep order. "I wouldn't even use it as toilet paper," crowed one man when Levi pointed to a picture of Shimon Peres that he was using as a prop – and so it continued for the duration of the session, Levi alternating between talk of Biblical warfare and 70s American rock bands.

His talk centred around the construction of the Temple by King Solomon, but quickly – and unsurprisingly – morphed into a more modern-day political discussion, akin to the sermon given earlier. According to Levi, "by Biblical reasoning Yigal Amir [Rabin's assassin] should be Israel's prime minister, since he who kills the leader becomes leader himself". This declaration prompted several of the group to shout out "I'd vote for him" without a trace of irony in their voices.

The entire proceedings were reminiscent of a secret Klan meeting – guns, alcohol, conspiracy theories, and paranoia all combining to imbue the participants with a sense of self-importance and righteousness cast adrift in a sea of oppression and misunderstanding. As their wives and children slept, the men got to act out their fantasies as soldiers in the last line of defence against an encroaching world that has no time for Israel or the Jews – a world that only understands the language of war and must be dealt with in kind.

The outpost

When we returned from the *shiur*, the family gathered and whiled away the remainder of Shabbat playing cards round the dining room table, whilst we headed out for a walk round the settlement. We were pointed by Esther in the direction of the *yeshuv*'s hilltop community, situated a mile away along a winding road snaking its way between the mountains.

We ambled along the deserted road, looking down into the valley below where Jericho lay sprawled out in the midst of an otherwise deserted landscape. Further out the Dead Sea sparkled in the afternoon sun, and beyond it the hills of Jordan rose up majestically, shrouded in part by the dust that hung low in the distance. We barely passed a soul as we trudged along, and the silence all around us bore testament to the utter remoteness of the *yeshuv*'s setting.

About two thirds of the way towards the hilltop, the burnt out hull of a car appeared at the bottom of an incredibly steep ravine, a reminder of the inherent dangers in forging an existence in such a precarious clime. As we rounded another corner, the first caravans of the satellite settlement appeared, perched atop the hillside looking out into the vast expanse beneath.

Our arrival was first noticed by a particularly agitated canine member of the hilltop community, who marked our every step with ever-louder barks of displeasure. He was soon joined in his chorus by two dogs further down the road, who lived in the garden of the most remote house in all of Mitzpe Yericho. The owner was a young man who'd grown up on the *yeshuv*, and decided to remain nearby in almost complete isolation on his own private hill.

The rest of the caravans were situated at the end of the road we were walking along, and appeared to be huddling together against the bitter wind blowing all around them. Most of the residents were sleeping indoors, and the few who we did encounter were hurrying back to *shul*, so we walked past the caravans and made our way to the viewpoint on the side of the hill and took in the panorama beneath us.

From this vantage position, we could see one or two other tiny hilltop *yeshuvim* dotted amongst the mountains between here and Jericho, but otherwise there were precious few signs of life. The occasional army patrol Jeep sped by, but the combination of it being Shabbat as well as such a remote part of the country meant the roads were barely in use.

As the sun set beyond the mountains, we watched the lights of Jericho switch on in unison, as the rest of the plain was blanketed by the rapidly approaching night. We headed back to our hosts at that point, back along the same road on which we'd arrived; an even more treacherous route now that the sun had disappeared.

***

We hitched a lift to nearby Ma'aleh Adumim with a headscarf-sporting woman who dropped us near the centre of town. Whilst physically close to the likes of Mitzpe Yericho and the other small *yeshuvim*, Ma'aleh Adumim is light years away in terms of modernity and creature comforts. Its vast size by comparison to the bulk of other settlements in the *Shtachim* means that it is, to all intents and purposes, essentially a small city rather than a remote outpost in the midst of the desert.

Other than the manned checkpoint on the outskirts of the town, Ma'aleh Adumim has been normalised and looks and feels like any other location inside Israel proper. An enormous shopping mall stands proudly on one side of the ring road, facing the country club and outdoor pool on the other side of the hill. Thousands of brand new homes are crammed together in uniform arrangements, and schools, libraries and other amenities are conveniently placed within walking distance of the main neighbourhoods.

Walking through a lush park in the town centre, the first thing to strike us was the normality of the place, given the unfamiliarity of the places we'd stayed in up until now. Youths decked out in typical Israeli fashion – jeans, trainers, vests and chains – gathered on one of the park's lawns, some baiting their vicious looking pit-bull puppies with plastic bottles whilst their friends cheered from the sidelines.

Most people we passed were decidedly *hiloni* – bare-headed men, alongside women in tight jeans and revealing tops – and a multitude of languages was being spoken. Amharic, Russian, French and English all competed with Hebrew as the most popular dialect, reflecting the diverse population of Ma'aleh Adumim.

The security fence that ran around the perimeter of the town was barely visible from the centre of town, and out of sight certainly translated into out of mind for those within its confines. The mall was heaving with schoolchildren who'd finished classes, as well as casual shoppers and diners packing the cafés, none of whom appeared any more concerned about their security than they would have in the heart of Tel Aviv or Jerusalem.

For all that is said about settlers being of a certain type, a glance around Ma'aleh Adumim's range of secular, non-political citizens shows just how far the settlement enterprise has come. The government's drive to offer cheap housing and convenient access to Jerusalem has paid off in drawing in the crowds. According to Esther,

"The government built Ma'aleh Adumim here to prevent the Arabs expanding into this area and they made it so enormous that it's too big for us to ever give back."

Too much has been invested in the town, as well as too many roots laid down by its residents, for it to be uprooted as easily as other, less permanent *yeshuvim* have been in the past. Ma'aleh Adumim has become simply a satellite town of Jerusalem, a salubrious suburb which is becoming as acceptable an address as any other in the eyes of a public who are happy to put affordability and convenience before ethics and politics.

Life on the edges

Back in Mitzpeh Yeriho, the isolation and remoteness of the place is all the more palpable after our visit to the city settlement of Ma'aleh Adumim; small, quiet, dusty and secluded, the Israeli equivalent of a one-horse town. The lack of work and a feeling of being cut off from Israel, despite its proximity to Jerusalem, lend weight to a general stifling atmosphere, a town that lives on its own news and introspection.

On the patio outside her home, Esther chats about how life has changed since being a young woman in New Jersey. From a non-religious family, it wasn't until the age of 19 that Esther went *Ba'al teshuva* [became religious]. But Esther was also adventurous and at 22 she headed off travelling, alone: "Not the sort of thing that *frum* girls do," she claims, doubting that any of her kids would follow in her footsteps: "they're not independent like I was."

Esther spent one month in England, two in France, Greece and Italy and another two in Israel – which is where she first developed her love of the land. But it wasn't until the age of 42 that she managed to persuade the rather more reluctant Arthur and children to swap their suburban American lives for life in the Holy Land.

"When I first arrived, I wanted to kiss the ground," Esther remembers. "It's the land that I love, the Land of Israel."

After a year and a half living in an absorption centre in Jerusalem, the family moved to Mizpeh Yeriho – Esther having fallen in love with the view. The size of the house they could afford here was a draw for the family – along with the open expanse of land that lay around their home. Esther wasn't compelled by a need to settle this particular patch of land – for her all of Israel was the same – and the West Bank was as much a part of Israel as any other.

Esther grows fruit trees to bring her closer to the land, for which she has a burning passion. On the inside of Esther's front door hangs a poster with a photograph of a barren Israeli landscape. Beneath the picture is printed a quote from the Torah in which God says that He has given Jacob all of the land of Israel to settle. It is clear where Esther gets her nationalism; her belief in the land of Israel for the Jewish nation.

"The government and the state of Israel mean nothing for me – it's the land that matters. I read the Torah and I see that this is where the Jewish people are supposed to be. But I feel distant from the Israeli government. I used to call myself a Zionist but I don't now; the government gave away the land."

Esther focuses on a perceived lack of Jewish education in Israeli schools that encourages Israelis to seemingly dissociate from their Jewish heritage.

"It's terrible that people don't learn about the *Tenach* [Torah, prophets and commentary] and Judaism – they lose their connection to the people and to the land. Israel becomes like any other place in the world. That's why people can give the land away. This is God's land. He gave it to the Jewish people. If there was Jewish education, people would know that they can't give it away. I only went to one protest against the Disengagement but it was 99.9% religious – because they're the ones who know we can't give away God's land."

Esther points to her own children – whom she has imbued with a religious, nationalistic education – and says that Sammy wants to go off and form his own hilltop settlement with his friends, thus putting his inherited love of the land into uncompromising action. But Esther claims that it was the Israelis that Sammy came into contact with during his army service that were the left wingers – the English speakers were on the right. "Sammy used to have arguments with the left wing Israelis in his unit. They all assumed settlers were trouble makers who hated Arabs," she claims.

Hearing Esther speak of her family's separation from the Israeli people, government and state, and her love for, first and foremost, a Jewish land for the Jewish people, we are reminded of a conversation with a secular Israeli UN worker in Jerusalem – on absolutely the opposite end of the spectrum from Esther – who also hinted at a growing divide between Jews and Israelis. "When will people start to see me as an Israeli citizen and not as a Jew?" she exclaimed. "I don't count myself as a Jew. I care about Israel, not about the Jewish state."

Hearing Esther describe the flipside of the coin, one is struck by the isolation that certain settlers are now starting to feel politically. Right or wrong, people like Esther apparently perceive Israel as a political entity that is losing touch with its Jewish identity. On the margins religiously, geographically and politically, Esther, with her love of Jewish land over the Israeli state, represents one side of a widening rift between those who want Israel to be a modern democracy that lives by international laws, and those who want it to be a Jewish state on *all* of the biblical Land of Israel. Such a rift warns of a potential undermining of the current political status quo, which attempts to bridge both of these extremes, by maintaining Israel as a modern democratic *Jewish* state.

Esther's outlook also echoes the views of other settlers who apparently feel the reins of control over the West Bank slowly slipping from their grasp.

***

When it was time to leave, we collected our bags and Esther, as generous with us as ever, offered us a lift back to Ma'aleh Adumim so that we could catch a bus to Jerusalem. She complained about friends of hers who had been stoned by Palestinians on the roads in the West Bank – though she emphasised that this particular region had always been very quiet: no bullet-proof buses in this region. Esther reiterated her belief that Palestinians were not educated enough and that they needed to be brought up to date, but judging from what we had heard from Levi and other Kach supporters, many in Mitzpeh Yeriho needed education just as badly as any stone-throwing Palestinian.

Leaving Esther was sad, inasmuch as to her mind, the world was a truly upsetting place. Right or wrong, she honestly believed that the Jews were trying their hardest to live in peace in the West Bank – a Biblical land in which they have every right to live. Palestinians are Arabs, so why should they need their own state? And if they want to live in the West Bank – which is indisputably Israel – then why must they continually attack and kill peaceful Jewish citizens? In her view, things will only get worse, too – the Jews cannot escape persecution. And to top it all off, it was the settlers who got the blame for everything.

No matter how distant this was from our own beliefs and from those of most others in Israel, let alone the wider world, this was a view that Esther lived and breathed in her detached community of Mitzpeh Yeriho. Only her family and the desert landscape seemed to make her life enjoyable as she dreamed of living closer to people she could talk to, and despaired of the condition of the Jewish people, bound to live forever in enmity and pain.

Chapter Three
Kfar Adumim:
Spreading the word

The hitchhikers' guide

Hitchhiking in the West Bank is a routine affair, with bands of hippy-looking religious kids flooding every major crossroad in the West Bank. Indeed it is so routine that there is seldom any chit chat along the way, as the driver ferries his passengers from one settlement to another. So when a tall, bushy bearded religious man stops his rusting estate at the *trampiada* [hitching post] and beckons for us to get in, we reckon on another swift, silent ride. But the openness of our driver, Ben Yeshai, proves to be the perfect introduction to the settlement of Kfar Adumim, just 15km from Mitzpeh Yeriho.

Ben Yeshai and his son

Friendly and inquisitive, Ben Yeshai is eager to get to know his passengers. Upon hearing that we are from England, he reveals that his mother grew up in the distinctly un-Jewish town of Windsor, which explains his flawless English. She had moved to Israel, alone, at the age of eighteen, becoming increasingly religious, before eventually meeting and marrying Ben Yeshai's father, an Orthodox Jew from Yemen. Just as Ben Yeshai has inherited his English from his mother, his looks come from his father: dark skinned, with dark brown eyes and curly black hair, beard and twisted *payyot*. He is tall too, his long limbs folded and wedged untidily into the cramped driving seat. Behind Ben Yeshai sits his physical antithesis – a tiny blond boy, with fair skin and wispy *payyot* tucked behind his ears. This is Ben Yeshai's son, Shlomo.

Announcing that we've never been to Kfar Adumim before, Ben Yeshai excitedly explains the principles behind the *yeshuv* that is situated just a few hills away from Jerusalem's East side; part of a ring of settlements that effectively binds the whole of Jerusalem to Israel. Kfar Adumim, along with its Siamese twin Allon, was established as a mixed settlement for religious and non-religious Jews. In a state in which the divide between *hilonim* and *datim* is stark and inflexible, to have the two living side by side in mixed neighbourhoods is an unusual undertaking.

According to Moshe Amir, one of the founding members of the *yeshuv*, the settlement is deliberately intended to increase understanding and cooperation between religious and non-religious residents. The idea is that both communities live together "like one big family". The harmony is protected by a constitution which strikes a balance between the religious dictates of the observant residents and the secular requirements of the non-believers. For example, the residents may drive inside the settlement on Shabbat, which is forbidden according to Jewish law, but not in front of the synagogue. The swimming pool is open on Shabbat, but is closed on religious festivals. New members are vetted and interviewed to determine their tolerance of the lifestyles of the "other side" and it takes a majority of 75% of the residents to change the constitution.

Religious and secular children study together in the same schools until they are fourteen and, according to Moshe, parents are happy with this arrangement as they see that the kids are "not changing too much" from the way they have been brought up. "It works," says Moshe proudly.

Ben Yeshai shares Moshe's pride as he chats with heartfelt sincerity and gangly gesticulations along the slip road into Kfar Adumim.

"It's a good system. The most important thing for my son is that he will grow up to be a good man. Sure, it's important that he knows the Torah, that he understands Judaism, but most important of all is that he will be a *mensch* [a good man]. I'm now wondering whether to send him to a separate religious school, so that he has a good level of Jewish education. But he's learning tolerance living here. Some of the girls walk around the *yeshuv* in short skirts, and vest tops with no covering – and sure it upsets me. I mean they could at least wear T-shirts. But then that's what this place is all about. It teaches me to be tolerant; to be more understanding."

As we arrive in Kfar Adumim – where we have arranged to meet Anat, a *madriha* [leader] at the settlement's *midrasha* [study centre] – Ben Yeshai first insists that we come to his home for a drink. This is not merely politeness, nor is it an anxious insistence that we honour him with our presence; instead it is a simple assumption that, having come to Ben Yeshai's town, we will be in need of refreshments and he would love to provide them.

But first he takes a cardboard box from his boot and takes us to meet his baby chickens. Within minutes we're squatting in a tiny hutch, having flapping chicks shoved into our hands, so that we can get to know the animals.

"Hold them by the legs," insists Ben Yeshai, "That way they won't fly out of your hands."

He then opens the cardboard box and releases a dozen baby quails and for a while they stand stunned amongst the chicks, who look equally shocked at the presence of the new arrivals. The chicks swarm to the fence and the quails stand rooted to the spot, panic in the eyes of every bird. But slowly, tentatively they approach one another and begin the slow process of getting used to living together.

Ben Yeshai takes a bird and holds its head, drawing a thick finger across its tiny slip of a throat.

"Here's where we slit their throat for *shehita* [Kosher animal slaughter]. I'm a *shohet* [Kosher butcher]. I'm also a *mohel* [circumciser]."

Thankfully, he doesn't offer to demonstrate that too.

"Now you hold it again," says Ben Yeshai, thrusting another quail towards us.

"It's important that you get to know the land, that you feel it and understand it. Too many people these days don't even know where their food comes from. That's why I keep my own animals and grow my own vegetables. The Arabs – they know and understand the land well. We Jews need to start getting closer to the land again."

On leaving the hutch, Ben Yeshai notices a gap at the bottom of one of side and finds a large rock to block up the hole. Ben Yeshai's farming project is far from sophisticated at this stage; he is clearly still finding his own way back towards the land.

His home, too, reflects the gradual spread over the land of the West Bank – it is another caravan, the start of a new growth of Israeli life across the Green Line. Ben Yeshai's is a medium sized trailer, and we head through to the ample kitchen/dining/living compartment where Ben Yeshai asks his wife to put on extra vegetarian schnitzels for his two guests: "you will eat with us, won't you?"

We sit and eat schnitzels and salad off plastic plates, as Ben Yeshai's wife, a porcelain-faced American woman, feeds their restless eighteen month old son, Daniel. In the small sleeping area next door, their middle child, Noga, sits playing with her toys, before running in to her parents, her piercing green eyes sparkling as she playfully shows off her teddy bear to the visitors. Whilst Shlomo is quiet and serious like his mother, Noga shines with her father's effortless grace.

Ben Yeshai heads to the blender to make smoothies, commandeering one of us to chop home-grown carrots as the other reads a book to Shlomo. It is a children's book, which graphically depicts the persecution of Russian Jews at the hands of the Cossacks. Shlomo explains that it is only through the Jews' faith in God and their observance of prayer and ritual that they are delivered from being skewered on the Russians' bayonets. With pictures to illustrate the bite-sized information that is conveyed in children's language, the book is a bizarre history lesson, and one that is designed to elicit faith in God, a sense of Jewish victimhood and a mistrust of foreign nations in equal measure. "You live in England?" asks Shlomo, wide-eyed. "Is it true that there are *Christians* living there?"

Unsure of the result of his carrot and date smoothies, Ben Yeshai approaches, pressing us to taste them. "I thought I'd try something new," he explains, "but they're a bit strange."

He chats to us about our book, convinced that we are doing a service for Israel by representing life as we find it in the West Bank. Excited by the project, he recommends that we attend spiritual, religious *yeshuvim* where members volunteer to farm the land and share the produce. Much as he loves the unity of Kfar Adumim and the lack of divide between religious and secular residents, he claims there are no "simple folk" living here.

"It's a more expensive settlement than many of the others. You only really get the top thirty percent of society, in terms of wealth."

Nevertheless, Ben Yeshai and his wife share their modest caravan with their four small children – all of whom sleep in one tiny room.

As we get ready to go, Ben Yeshai bear hugs us both as though he's known us for years, then provides us with his email address and the promise of friends all over Israel, seeming every bit the *mensch* that he wants his children to be.

There was only one thing that Ben Yeshai said that jarred with the man we found – he who gave a lift to strangers, brought them into his house, fed and looked after them and treated them like his own family; the man whose primary goal in life was to raise his boy to be a *mensch*. That one thing was his mention of a left wing that spends its time "loving the Arabs" too much. This one rogue sentence soured Ben Yeshai's lips and other than his choice of address was the only hint that he gave of the impenetrable divide that permeates the West Bank.

A few weeks later, in a bar in Tel Aviv, Josh mentioned to a friend of a friend that he had been to Kfar Adumim and was immediately asked if he had met Ben Yeshai. It seemed our host had made as strong an impression on Josh's interlocutor as he had on us. Josh replied that he had indeed met him, and the friend went on to tell him the story of Ben Yeshai's younger brother, Gavriel, who had been a student at a Yeshiva in Hebron. On the 27th of December 2002, Gavriel, who Ben Yeshai says would "go to any length to help others", agreed to a friend's request to swap shifts serving dinner to the other students. After the starters, Gavriel went to the kitchen to begin serving the main course, when two Palestinian terrorists burst in and began letting off rounds of M16 fire. In what the Israeli papers described as "A Night of Blood", Gavriel was shot eight times in the chest, and died along with two of his fellow students. He was just seventeen years old.

Teaching the facts

As well as its dedication to its policy of being a mixed *yeshuv*, Kfar Adumim also boasts another unique feature in its *mechina* and *midrasha* facilities. The *mechina* is a seminary focusing on pre-army teens, imbuing them with the necessary study and social skills to "go on to top positions in the military", according to Anat, one of the programme's recruitment staff. A former IDF spokeswoman, she is currently completing a psychology degree at the Hebrew University in Jerusalem, before beginning a Masters the following year in Bar Ilan University, Tel Aviv. She is an alumnus of the *midrasha* at Kfar Adumim, which is a study retreat where students can delve into a wide range of academic subjects. "We study Dante, classics, Mishna, Gemarra, Nietzsche..." Mirit, one of the current batch of students, explains breathlessly over the 'rum-less mojitos' she serves us.

As part of the *midrasha* staff, Anat lives in a house belonging to the *yeshuv*, with stunning views over the desert valley laid out like a canopy beneath the hills of Kfar Adumim. Swinging in a love-seat facing the mountains in the distance, Anat talks about the natural beauty all around us, steering clear of the political situation, so as not to spoil the tranquil imagery she was conjuring up on our behalf. When the subject does eventually come up, she says she is "left wing – but only if you *have* to categorise me as anything". As far as she's concerned, Kfar Adumim's existence "doesn't displace anyone – even Bedouin – and thus living here doesn't feel like being in the *Shtachim*". Indeed, according to the Civil Administration data collated by Peace Now, Kfra Adumim contains one of the smallest percentages of private land of all the settlements, at 3.87%[10], although it is of course part of the land claimed by the Palestinians for their future state. Citing the academic boycott of Israel being discussed by various British trade unions, Anat says she feels her country is unfairly singled out by the world for criticism: "They could boycott the USA or Russia," and she feels that the double standards are, in part, due to anti-Semitism: "It used to drive me mad when I was serving in the [IDF] Spokesman's Unit."

Anat walks us to the dining hall to eat with some of the other students. The *midrasha*'s mini-campus is a mixture of caravans and stone buildings, set back from the rest of the settlement: this is the students' domain, and they study, sleep and socialise here, wrapped up in their own world, far from the madding crowd. We eat 'omelette quiche' and lasagne with five twenty-somethings, all of whom quiz us on our work, all of whom speak in glowing and gushing terms about the *midrasha* and its effect on their lives.

We are to sleep in their midst, in one of the caravans, and as the evening winds down we spend time talking to the students about their hopes and dreams, the intimacy of the setting swiftly breaking down barriers that may have stayed standing longer had we met in more cosmopolitan environs. There is a cultish zeal about some of our interlocutors; almost as though they have come to see the *midrasha* as an elixir of life, wanting to spread the word of its power far and wide for others to experience the miracle too.

Kfar Adumim's is by no means the only *midrasha* in the West Bank; many settlements have set up schools and study retreats for residents of Israel proper, and the students attend in their hundreds. The intentions of the settlers are noble enough – wanting to provide a quiet environment in the countryside conducive to study – but, at the same time, there appears to be a marketing ploy going on beneath the surface.

Ya'akov, a long-haired, post-army Israeli with dreams of India and Laos, has spent the last four months studying philosophy, religious texts and other material in Kfar Adumim. He had no connection to the *Shtachim* before taking up his place at the school, yet is now seeking to extend his stay on the settlement well past July, when the study programme ends.

He spends most of his free time swimming with his dog down at the *wadi* [gorge] near the school and his love of nature, combined with the tranquillity of the surroundings, means that he can see himself spending another six months living and working in Kfar Adumim. Politics plays no part in his desire to stay and that is just what is so alarming about his decision to remain.

Through a combination of accessibility to the West Bank and stimulating activities once they arrive, the students are left with the impression of life in the *Shtachim* as no less appealing than English students might find a similar retreat in the rolling hills of Devon. There is no talk amongst the attendees of fear of attack, nor any politicised polemics about whether the land should be retained by Israel – instead, they are entirely normalised to the area during their four-month sojourn there.

As we found earlier in our tour, a similar situation exists in the *midrasha* at Kedumim where again the intention is nothing short of laudable, but at the same time, throwing the girls into the heart of the conflict has effects other than just providing them with better schooling. Yafa and Mazal, the two Ethiopian girls with whom we spoke, saw life in the *Shtachim* as entirely normal, having adopted the same anti-Arab prejudices as their hosts on the *yeshuv*, and declaring their intention to live in the West Bank during their adult lives.

This is what happens when the settlement doors are thrown open to the rest of Israel. Youths who would otherwise have little or no connection to the political situation find themselves drawn in, exposed to the minutiae of life behind the Green Line, and – in many cases – are put in the mould of settlers-to-be.

The settlement enterprise thrives on the illusion of normality and, to all intents and purposes, much of what these students experience in the *Shtachim* is normal – on the surface at least. However, the peaceful atmosphere in which they study, or the still waters of the *wadis* in which they swim, can be easily branded trompes l'oeil when it comes to the wider implications of living on such contested land. But, as long as all looks rosy to the influx of wide-eyed students who flock to the region, they are easily conditioned to see the area exactly how the settlers want them to see it: just another part of the state of Israel, and a part that is as integral to the country's make-up as Jerusalem and Tel Aviv.

Pictures of paradise

We head over to Nofei Prat, a religious satellite settlement of Kfar Adumim, where we visit Sara [not her real name], a young Englishwoman who emigrated to Israel a few years earlier. After completing her national service (doing voluntary work rather than military duties, as is the way for many religious women), she moved to Kfar Adumim from Jerusalem to get away from "smoking weed all day" – except she then discovered one of her neighbours in the *yeshuv* "blazes all day long – I can't escape it...", she smiles.

Married, with a baby son, Elhanan, she was drawn to this *yeshuv* in particular as her best friend already lived here, on the next hill along to Sara's neighbourhood. Sara is decked out in a curious combination of headscarf and tracksuit trousers; the headscarf denoting her religious modesty, the trousers a nod to her semi-secular ways. Sara told us that "the dress code is changing", noting that girls can get away with more liberal interpretations of the rules governing their attire than ever before.

Her apartment is on the ground floor of a new stone building, and the interior boasts a huge television, as well as the other mod-cons that she might have expected to own had she remained in northwest London. To all intents and purposes, her life is not far removed from that of her peers back home: the comforts and trappings of life in Kfar Adumim easing her transition into her adopted country.

Tamar, Sara's American best friend, turns up with her husband Moshe, their two toddler sons trailing in their wake. Tamar's get-up resembles Sara's: trousers and a headscarf, while Moshe, who is also from the States, is decked out in a cut-necked army T-shirt with a matching hat (the Nahal infantry insignia is emblazoned proudly on both items). Moshe's long blond hair and wispy goatee seem out of place in the conservative, modern Orthodox setting of Sara's West Hill community, but his style is par for the course where he and Tamar live, up on the "ecological outpost" on Hill 468, a steep twenty minutes' walk away from Sara's house. They live with seven other families on the windswept hilltop, where they are committed to a system of recycling water, growing their own vegetables, working the land, and generally living as ecologically soundly as possible. Whilst Hill 468 is amongst over 100 illegal outposts that Israel has pledged to demolish in keeping with its road map commitments, Moshe is "sure" that the government will declare their community legal "sooner or later".

Moshe invites us to visit him at home later that day and after lunch at the local falafel stand, we set off for the long, uphill march towards his isolated encampment. Outposts are always strange places: there is a Russian-doll aspect to them, since it is one thing to be cut off from Israel proper in a settlement, quite another to then be cut off from the mothership *yeshuv* itself by withdrawing even further into the wilderness. Consequently, outpost life is only for the hardiest – and most extreme – amongst the settler faithful. Hill 468 is no exception.

Once we have ascended the almost inaccessibly steep incline, we are greeted by the sight of seven caravans, a water tower, and very little else – save for an obsolete and out-of-commission mammoth machine gun sat perched on the hillside, its sights forever trained on a point in the middle distance. "It's for the kids to play with," explains Moshe. "We were going to paint it with flowers, but we never quite got round to it..." He leans in conspiratorially and tells us that "Jordan control the area [around Kfar Adumim]", and that therefore the region is kept safe via

"Jordanian connections – I don't know how they do it, but they do". He seems to think that the Palestinians would-n't eschew violence of their own accord, and that – since there has been little trouble for the settlers in recent years – therefore someone else must be pulling the strings to keep the natives in line.

Moshe and his family have lived on the hilltop for three and a half years, eking out an existence in what appear to be fairly inhospitable conditions – if not on the part of the Palestinians, then certainly on the part of Mother Nature. The earth is tough and dry, the wind whips its way round the hilltop in never-ending circles, yet Moshe is undeterred in his quest. He is talking to us at the same time as working furiously on his latest carpentry project: he and his shirtless friend Josh are sawing up wood and piecing it together to form a store room and a shade for Moshe's porch. The two of them could be anywhere – their baggy trousers and crooked smiles no different from their rustic peers in England, America or Europe – but the ever-present pistol in Moshe's waistband signifies the price they pay for their seemingly idyllic existence.

For now, however, Moshe is only concerned about the baby trees he's planted in the front garden; he's wrapped them in cloth and constantly waters them, fretting about their wellbeing like a farmer worrying about newborn lambs: "I'm not sure they'll make it," he frowns in concern. Eventually, he takes us into his car-avan, which is an homage to clutter and confusion, but Moshe at least is able to circumnavigate the mess with ease. On the wall are certificates declaring his having passed courses in aromatherapy and reflexology, hang-ing above shelves crammed with 'Lessons in *Tanya*' and other religious tomes. Children's toys vie for space with bottles of whisky, cutlery, ceramic bric-a-brac and other sundry items – this is home for him and his three dependants, and not only does he love his lot, he sees his role as vital to protect the natural beauty of the area. "If we weren't here, millions of houses would be built all over the hill, ruining both the nature and the view," he explains.

He's building a two-room extension at the back of the house, constructed entirely from used car tyres, and has constructed a concrete recycling pit for glass packaging (his love of beer ensuring that the pit runneth over with green-hued bottles). We realise that, to now, his only stated motivation for living in Kfar Adumim is ecologically-based; where does he stand, we ask, on the more common settler ideology of maintaining a Jewish presence in Judea and Samaria? "Don't get me wrong," he replies. "I do believe [also] that we should hold onto the land, but I came to the hilltop to set up an eco community, one which forces me to get friendly with my neighbours and live amongst real Israelis [and not just have American friends]. I would not be as happy if I lived on the other side of the Green Line, because there I wouldn't be able to afford to live near Jerusalem, as I can here." As with countless other families, cheap land and government subsidies have played a large part in his decision to set up home in the *Shtachim*.

He is clearly extremely dexterous and talented at building, Seth tells him, having seen the fruit of his labour all around his caravan and garden. "We all are up here," he replies. "You have to be – you can't just call out a plumber when you live somewhere like this..." The group of families on 468 are planning to expand the hilltop, he says, "but not in a way that will ruin the view, so we'll only build on one side of the hill, and even then only in a way which will be below the line of sight from the peak".

Moshe loves the fact that religious and secular families live together in Kfar Adumim, since it means that the children of the *yeshuv* are not ostracised if they choose to switch sides as they grow up – he was cast out of his home community in the US for just such a 'sin', he says. After we bid him goodbye, we walk past the other caravans alongside his, noting the motley collection of artwork adorning the outer walls: abstract oil paintings, Che Guevara iconography, and Jewish leitmotifs. Flanked by radical left wing imagery, the right wing nationalists paint an incongruous picture, grafting yet another patch of land to the Jewish state as they plough their somewhat lonely furrow towards their vision of a better, brighter, eco-friendly future.

***

On Friday, we take Ya'akov's advice and meander down the hill to Wadi Qelt, where he likes to go every day to swim, walk and meditate on life. Since it is the start of the weekend, the *wadi* is crammed full of fellow Israelis with similarly leisurely intentions: the water is full of bathers; others sit on the rocks or the grass, many playing guitars and recorders as they offer musical thanks to the gods for the opportunity to relax in such awe-inspiring surroundings. Considering the largely dry and dusty desert environment in which we are located, the *wadi*'s lush topography is indeed a tropical oasis. The gorge snakes its way between miles of stark cliff-face, and we set off through the shin-deep water to take in the sights for ourselves. Small fish nip at our heels below the surface; dragonflies hover round us curiously as we half-walk, half-splash the course of the *wadi*.

When we get back to the bathing pool, we find Ya'akov clad only in y-fronts, his long, dark hair soaked through, a glint of pure joy in his eyes. He's "making up" with his dog "after our argument" – apparently they'd fallen out after Ya'akov made her go into an underwater tunnel, "she got scared, then got angry with me, but now she's forgiven me", he explains. Later he tells us he'd "rather have a dog as a friend than a friend who acts like a dog", which seems a reasonable policy. Two soldiers guard the bathers, since the *wadi* has seen its fair share of trouble – two girls were killed here ten years ago, and the memory lingers on; despite many daytrippers having relegated it to the back of their minds, they can't ignore that the contentious politics of the area mean they have to remain forever on their guard.

Talking to God

As the sun began to set on Friday evening, we walked with a couple of dozen students up a small, dusty path, not far from the cluster of caravans that made up the *midrasha*, towards the top of a hill which levelled into a majestic lookout over the dry desert mountains east of Jerusalem. We had come to welcome the arrival of Shabbat and, as the sun glowed orange and then red, slipping away behind the darkening hilltops, the Holy City shimmered before us, its lights accompanying the faint stars that were hesitantly populating the heavens above.

The lookout was carved from the side of a mountain and featured two concentric semi circles of flat yellow boulders which formed a kind of private amphitheatre in which we could sit and overlook the valley beneath, and the Palestinian villages and Jerusalem beyond. The basic, permanent structure was built as a memorial to the rabbi of the *midrasha*'s wife, who had died of cancer four years previously. A flat carved tablet at the front of the dugout commemorated her life, while a few small pebbles placed on top of the tablet spoke of recent, more personal recollections of her passing. Behind us, to the edge of the amphitheatre, stood two lone trees, stubby and wooden and almost cartoonlike in their barrenness, their crooked branches reaching out to heaven in a tearful embrace. In the bark of one, a simple phrase had been carved one lonely night. "I love you."

Facing west to Jerusalem to welcome the spirit bride of Shabbat, students joined arms in small groups while others stood off to the side, alone, swaying in the hot evening wind that blew over the mountains, as they sang the tunes of the Sabbath and offered the inaugural prayers. Long after the harmonising had finished they stood on, swaying in the dark silence; Jerusalem and the stars above the only lights to be seen.

At dinner that evening, the entire group of students, as well as teachers and guests, congregated for a communal meal; thirty people or so sat around large, flimsy school dinner tables, hummus and salad and chicken and rice piled up on plates between them. Conversation was characterised by a strong sense of camaraderie after everyone had stood up to introduce themselves, and there was free and easy interaction between friends and strangers alike.

The bridging of divides that typifies life on the mixed *datil hiloni* settlement of Kfar Adumim extended to the conversations occurring all around us as we dipped challah in the heaps of hummus on our paper plates. Religious and secular, left and right, extremist and moderate were all here, locked in fervent but respectful discussion about all manner of issues, and it was surprising to find that of all things Jewish settlement in the West Bank itself was openly contested here, even as the students studied and stayed in occupied lands. Most of those who supported the establishment of a Palestinian state either thought of this Jerusalem satellite settlement as too much a part of the national consensus to be considered occupied land, or thought they'd only worry about the significance of their presence here as and when the time came to return the land.

As we tucked into our main courses of roast chicken and potatoes (and Tivall veggie schnitzels for the vegetarians), a typical debate fired up over the future of Israel and how to deal with its widely feared "demographic problem". Beginning with an entreaty to Josh, a fellow Jew, to move to Israel, the 22 year old girl to his left, Galit, worried that if people like him don't come from the Diaspora to live in Israel, in nine years time the Arab population of Israel will outnumber that of the Jews and the Jewish state will cease to be. Apparently including the two and a half million

Palestinians living in the West bank in her statistic, Galit's definition of Israel was clearly the settlers' dream of a Greater Israel. Galit recognised the predicament of wanting to have her cake and eat it and wondered aloud about how Israel could keep the West Bank, without upsetting the country's ethnic demographic. The answer, it transpired, was further division.

"We need to build a big fence to keep the Arabs to their own areas," said Galit, without a flicker of shame in her large, dark eyes. "The problem is that at the moment they can move all around and there can be intermarriage. They need to be separated out of Israel."

Overhearing this alarming bit of problem solving, Liat, to my right, erupted with indignation.

"The wall doesn't help anything. I grew up near Abu Ghosh on the other side of Jerusalem, with Arabs all around me. I had many Arab friends – Palestinians and Israeli Arabs alike. I didn't even think who was Arab and who was a Jew, we'd play together and go to each other's houses. We even learnt Taekwondo together. Now the wall is separating Arab communities from one another and on top of that there's no money for them because they can't travel around to find work."

Josh asked Liat how her friendships have fared since the erection of the wall.

"There's no relation now. We no longer see one another."

"The Intifada did that." Galit spits, bitterly.

"That too," admits Liat. "That too."

With the right winger on Josh's left and the leftie to his right, the debate rose around him as Galit began to lay into Liat about her degree of commitment to Israel as the Jewish state.

"So if you grew up with no distinction between Jew and Arab and you're not religious, how do you feel attached to Israel?"

"It's my home," Liat replied. "It's where I was born. My family are from here, my culture, my people. Of course the Jewish state is important to me."

"But you don't believe in Judaism. What's a Jewish state to you? It could be anywhere."

"It doesn't matter where it is, it's the idea that's important. But it's here – and this is where I'm from, so this is the place I'm attached to. But just because it's a Jewish state doesn't mean there has to be division between Jews and Arabs."

Galit ate a couple of mouthfuls of chicken in sullen silence and Liat used the opportunity to move away, apparently riled at the accusation of disloyalty just levelled at her. She blended in with a group of hippyish friends, nose rings sparkling through waves of black, frizzy hair, as Galit, in her religiously long sleeves and skirt, remained removed from the others to Josh's right. She continued with her dogmatic appraisal of Israel's problems, serving to emphasise the gulf that apparently existed between herself and some of her more laid back fellow students. Highly strung and jittery, she contrasted her love of Israel with her hatred of everywhere else in the world, though she admitted that she'd only left Israel once in her life ("I went to Spain, but I hated it. I couldn't stand being away from Israel. I found I couldn't breathe.")

With rigid gesticulation and nervous eyes that belied the hardness of her words, Galit went on to describe the death of the left wing in Israel, which she related to the moral vacuity of the secular population, "They have nothing to believe in. Nothing inside them. No direction. No soul."

A religious girl herself, Galit's faith in God extended to a belief that divine intervention will solve Israel's political troubles and overcome the fearful demographic problem she had outlined earlier, allowing a Greater Israel to exist with a significant Jewish majority:

"Sixty years ago, there wasn't even a state of Israel – and then the miracle happened. There are always miracles. Something will come up."

A lesson in loyalty

Following an uncomfortable night's sleep in the airless caravan, we arose to find the mountains of Kfar Adumim already crackling under the sweltering sun. We crunched along the dusty path that ran beside the row of ramshackle caravans; *midrasha* students sitting lazily on the steps of their digs, chatting, smoking, relaxing, and continued to the dining hall where we sought the respite of solid walls from the permeating waves of heat.

A handful of students milled around the kitchen, making preparations for lunch, which would follow the completion of morning prayers by those at the more religious end of the *midrasha*'s spectrum. Oren was there; a guest of one of the students, and an admirer of Robert McKee, with dreams of being a writer. Unwilling to become too entangled in the process of making salad, Oren approached us – two good-humoured eyes smirking between wild, frizzy curls that had escaped his long pony tail – and pulled up a chair, addressing us in near perfect English. He'd been travelling recently, he began, and met a lot of Englishmen, like ourselves. Initially he had thought he'd like them, for some reason assuming he'd dislike the French, but after a few conversations he soon found the opposite to be the case.

"I didn't meet a single Englishman I liked because every one was critical of Israel," he complained. "They all had a perfectly logical and reasonable argument about why Israelis were bad and Palestinians were good and yet not one of them knew what the fuck they were talking about. No, not you guys – you're Jewish, that's different – I mean the English. Why do they think they know what they're talking about? They should mind their own business. I mean look at them – the UK goes around the world killing people, building an empire, raping and looting and they have the nerve to tell Israel how to behave?! They won't fix their own problems, but they want to change

Israel? Look, I've never met a single Scot who calls himself British, only the English. They just love controlling people!"

Leant back in his chair, his head cocked to one side, Oren wore an ironical smile, exuding a sense of injustice laced with confidence.

"I feel like they've let us down, the British. They used to be on our side. They owned Israel, they gave us the land and supported us and now they're trying to tell us what to do. Still, it's not like America is any different. They're not our friend either, I mean they had the arms embargo until the 60s or 70s. So why are they friends with us now? They're using us. They want a strong ally here – and they're grooming Egypt so that they can go with them, just in case we slip up.

"So there's no such thing as a friendly country. Powerful countries just want Israel to do as they say so that they can remain in control. But let me tell you – *no one* can tell us what to do. We won this land. This is a Jewish country – our country – and now we'll look after it ourselves. They say 'do what the Palestinians want and we'll look after you', but they didn't look after the Jews before. The US and the UK knew about the [concentration] camps; they had planes fly over and photograph them, but they didn't do anything about it. Well now Israel can look after the Jewish people. We don't need help. We'll do it however we can.

"It's a very Jewish thing to lie low, keep your head down and avoid trouble," said Oren, demonstrating his point by curling forward, tucking his head into his lap so that his frizzy pony tail covered his knees. "They give you a slap – so you keep your head down and don't respond."

Oren sat back up and straightened his hair, before spreading his legs, leaning forward with his hands placed squarely on his knees and fixing us a stare with his piercing blue eyes,

"But now we look after ourselves. We've got our own country and if anyone fucks with the Jews, they know they'll get what's coming. No one can look after us – you didn't look after us then and you won't look after us now. Thank you very much. Or *fuck* you very much."

He maintained eye contact in the aftermath of his polemic, in a fixed pause that underlined his words. Then he turned his attentions to Diaspora Jews.

"Foreign Jews should be getting more involved. Israel looks after them; the least they can do is look after us, too. Personally, I don't care about Israel. I care about the Jewish people. This is their state. I live a hard life in Israel so that the Jews who live outside have a refuge, a country that will stand up for them. Meanwhile, they live a rich life – the least they can do is give money to support Israel."

The idea of Israel serving as a refuge for world Jewry in the event of another Holocaust is an oft-repeated argument, one that has come to supersede all others when it comes to explaining why the Jewish state must survive. Aside from drowning out other, less sensational arguments in favour of Israel's continued existence, the statement also tends to overlook the argument, popular amongst those who oppose the notion of a Jewish state, that for many Jews, particularly those in Arab countries, Israel's creation in fact catalysed a deterioration in those Jews' safety and well being, as anti-Semitism rose dramatically. For Oren, though, this was a price worth paying.

"There may be some Jews who had it better before the creation of the state of Israel, but there were more who had it worse. Israel is the only thing preventing another Holocaust. Life got worse for some Jews, but the good outweighs the bad – and those who got it bad can come to Israel anyway, where we don't need to rely on the grace of any other country. Where we can look after ourselves."

Again, that determined look, with the wry smile; his right hand jabbing towards the floor in support of his assertions, "This is a Jewish country. *That's* what counts. I'm a Jew. Not an Israeli. There have only been sixty

113

years of Israelis, but there have been Jews for thousands. It's the Jewish state that's the important bit – and if the Arabs don't want to live in a Jewish state, they can leave!"

With Oren's final point ringing through the air, a new arrival to the room, and student of the *midrasha* felt compelled to respond.

"How can you say that? The Arabs pay their taxes to this country and they don't get shit! Just look at East Jerusalem. Israel is a democracy – it's about time it gave people their rights. There should be equal rights for everyone – not more talk of making people leave. It's not fair that the Jews rule over the Arabs like this. It's not right."

Apparently self conscious at having his attention drawn to just how far his thesis had progressed, Oren opted for arguing with the newcomer's facts, rather than defending his own argument, claiming that East Jerusalem's Arabs don't pay taxes at all, although his opponent was adamant that they do... but before they had a chance to resolve the disagreement, they were silenced by the *midrasha*'s only Ultra-Orthodox resident, who stood poised with a *siddur* and a cup of *Kiddush* wine: the room was packed full of students, and it was time to say the prayers before lunch.

Firm foundations

After lunch, the students dispersed into small groups and set off for various residents' homes in the settlement – households that had agreed to act as surrogate families for the students, for the duration of their stay. Josh accompanied Yoel, a slight, precise student with frameless glasses, a neat goatee and pony tail, to a house around ten minutes' walk away from the *midrasha*. An intelligent and incisive 25 year old of Hungarian and Argentinian parentage, Yoel had sat in the caravan the night before, perched cross legged on the sofa as he had spoken in perfect American English about his reasons for coming to study at the *midrasha* instead of going to directly to university. He had come to learn without the pressure of grades, he said. He had come "looking for meaning, but not to find something new; only to consolidate what I already think"; to study Machiavelli, the Talmud and Keynes before having to immerse himself in the kind of degree that will pay the bills.

Like the other students of the *midrasha*, left and right alike, Yoel was a young person in the process of building his theories, founding them on education and testing them on experience. His collected, balanced repose spoke of great self-assurance, but his thoughts and words indicated a hunger for information and counter information, for being proven wrong, on the way to becoming right – a process that we witnessed throughout our stay at the *midrasha*.

However, back in a fully paid up settlement resident's home, amongst older, well established settlers, the open mindedness we had witnessed over the last 24 hours dissipated. Facts here were as well rooted as the foundations of the capacious house that stood immovably on the mountaintop, teeming with kids who ran around the legs of tables laid with cake, and the legs of guests who ate it. With a commanding view through the large windows over the creamy desert mountains and Jordan Valley beyond, there was a lot more at stake here than in the transient caravans of the *midrasha*. The time for philosophising and deliberating on actions was long gone – here the settlement was life, as Nir, the father of the house, with the chiselled high cheek bones distinctive of North African Jews, explained, as he sipped coffee with his friend, Ronen.

"I'm a product of the place. Before I came to the *yeshuv* I didn't have an opinion on the settlements either way. But now I think it's important for us to be here."

Nir's development as a settler was much like the development of a settlement itself, which he describes in similar terms to Daniella Weiss:

"The *yeshuvim* always start small and without permission. The government says go ahead, while it looks the other way, and then once the *yeshuv* grows they give it official permission. That's how they all start."

And just like a fledgling settlement, Nir's personal progress in the West Bank began small, arriving with no clear ideology, before the realities of settlement life eventually affirmed his status as a politically motivated settler. Now his arguments were edged with the same insistent persuasion of countless settlers we had met: that he was doing indisputably good work; that his cause was right and just. This was now about more than the grand scale of living that a factory worker like himself could afford out here. This was about serving the state itself. Indeed, Nir believed that the settlements acted as a beacon of morality for the rest of Israel.

"Israel is a divided country, but here in this *yeshuv* we set an example to the rest of the country – a model of people cooperating together. Where else can you find *datim* and *hilonim* living together like this? We've also got a school for problematic children here, we've got the *midrasha*... we represent the unity and morality that Israel needs. We can start a ripple effect for the rest of the country, in showing them how to behave."

Typically, Nir refused to distinguish between Israel and the West Bank, making Kfar Adumim and Allon an indisputable part of Israel, all of it land that had been won in one war or another. Ronen then went on to reiterate the common argument that the Palestinians are not a nation: "They might say they've been here for generations, but they weren't a people. They've always lived under foreign rule, but as soon as it's Israeli rule, they say they want their own land."

The irony is, of course, that Israel would never have existed, were the same logic to be applied to the Jewish people, but Ronen's denial of Palestinian nationalism served a clear purpose to the settlers' cause, beyond merely denying the right of the Palestinians to a homeland. In lumping Palestinians into one indistinct Arab mass, just as they were perceived during the 1967 war when Israel battled Arab armies on all fronts, Ronen recalled the existential dangers of '67, affirming that the settlements were simply a continuation of old battles and not a new and distinct problem. In doing so, he also denied the settlers' own role in augmenting the Palestinians' national aspirations. To recognise Palestinian nationalism would also be to recognise that the settlers' presence acted as a catalyst in that nationalist movement – an admission that is an anathema to any self respecting settler, as it means admitting to being the cause of their own problems.

"Israel got the land when the Arabs attacked," Nir's wife piped up strongly, "They tried to destroy us. We need the land for Israel's security."

There were no surprises here. Whereas the student voices of the *midrasha* were characterised by discussion and dispute, whether due to their diversity, their status as temporary residents of the West Bank, or simply an academic inclination to entertain the other side of the story, the older, established settlers maintained the establishment settler line, piling their defences one on top of the other, their very lives contingent on the reinforcement of these same assertions. Nevertheless, a younger voice tried its luck. A student from the *midrasha* to my right took issue with Nir's wife's statement, arguing that the Arabs "no longer have the power to destroy us."

"Of course they want to destroy us," she replied bluntly.

"Yes. But they no longer have the ability. That's the point."

But the conversation moved on. This was not the place for dissenting voices, for if you took away the idea that this house was preventing the Arabs from destroying Israel then you shook the very foundations of the house itself. Perhaps the young man realised that, for he didn't push his point. This was not the *midrasha*, and – as the

dozens of children running around the room attested –
there was a lot more at stake.

The academic conflict

Late in the afternoon the students began to make their
way over the dusty mountaintop to Micha's house, where
their teacher gave his weekly Shabbat *drosha* [talk]
before *havdalah* [the service at the end of Shabbat].
Having already tired of the day, the sun had begun to
recede behind the mountainside that climbed to our right,
and, taking the edge off the heat, the shade made our
walk up the steep incline altogether more bearable.
Traipsing up the hillside with me were Oren and Galit,
both guests of *midrasha* students for just a few more
hours until Shabbat was over and they returned to their
respective homes.

Perhaps infused with the spirituality of the day's
events, or perhaps inspired by the widening expanse of
ancient land that stretched to our left as we scaled the
mountain road, Galit returned to her veneration of the
Jewish state and its colonies of Judea and Samaria as
being a performance of God's will. Galit's political religiosity might have been common amongst many settlers
we had met until now, but amongst the students of the
midrasha, citation of the divine decree in political discus-
sions was unusual and Oren was quick to cut her down,
apparently as unimpressed with her way of thinking as
he was eager to expound his own.

"You can't just say we're doing God's will because that
means different things to different people. Everyone can
say they're acting in God's name and then go and do completely different things. There are only practical
justifications and solutions – not divine ones."

Galit scowled and turned her eyes to the ground as she
trudged up the hill in silence, while Oren expanded on
precisely what his practical solutions might be.

"First of all, the Palestinians need their own state. I think we need to give them a big patch of land in the Negev, alongside Gaza, transfer all the Jews from the Negev to Judea and Samaria and transfer all the Palestinians from Judea and Samaria to the Negev, then build a great big wall around it and say 'there you go, there's your state.'

"I'm not saying it will be easy. There'll be a lot of trouble – it will be like a war and a lot of people will die, on both sides, but at least it will be a war with an end – and we'll put an end to this ongoing war that we have at the moment. Right now people are dying, they're suffering and they're afraid. This solution will be difficult; it will take the agreement and cooperation of successive governments and will take at least ten or twelve years to complete, but at least then it will finally be over.

"After that I don't care what happens to the Palestinians. They'll get money from the world, they'll develop their education and improve themselves – I don't care – any problems they have they can take up with Egypt, because they'll be right down on their border. But of course the Egyptians hate them too."

"But that won't stop them attacking Israel," Galit interjected.

Oren agreed, "But at least this way I'll know where they all are. They'll be behind this big wall – and if there's trouble I'll know where to find them. We can just bomb them, without any of this worry about whether we're killing civilians or not – it will simply be a war between two countries. And it will mean less tragedy on both sides – the current situation is traumatic for both, but in the future it will just be a national war between two states and Israel will be able to defend itself whenever it needs to."

Aside from Oren's tough-guy take on matters, the solution he presented was not far removed from the general consensus on a two state solution – two states for two peoples, with a complete end to the occupation – except for one major difference: Israel trades the West Bank for the Negev. Oren's justification for this was simple:

"Giving them the Negev is better than the West Bank because this way Israel won't have to transfer nearly so many Jews."

And as we entered Micha's family home, with its garden crammed with students and children, its flower beds blooming with almond and jasmine, hibiscus and hollyhock, and the buffet tables laden with cakes, sweets and biscuits, it was apparent what forty years of settlement had done to the mindset of many young right wing Israelis like Oren. It had filled the West Bank with Jewish life. How could you simply give that up? In Oren's mind he was just stating the obvious – the fewer Israelis to be moved, the better. So integral has the West Bank become to Israel that it seems easier to give up a part of Israel itself than to give up occupied land.

We loaded our plates with borekas and hummus followed by blintzes, fruit salad and rogelach and continued our conversation on plastic garden chairs. Having established Palestine, Oren got onto the nature of Israel itself.

"We must work towards making Israel a Jewish state," he argued. "Not a democratic Jewish state, but a Jewish democracy, in which the Arabs will have equal civilian rights, but they won't be represented in Parliament. They'll be able to live good lives, but they won't have their own MKs and there'll be no chance of a Muslim Prime Minister. That will be for Jews only. As for the vote – I'm not sure – that can be decided later, but the point is that this is a state for Jews and needs to be kept as such. And the Arabs that don't sign a statement to be loyal and part of this Jewish state can go to Palestine."

Despite sounding alarmingly like far rightist MK Lieberman, with his talk of loyalty and transfer, Oren had already voiced his objection to the Yisrael Beiteinu leader, claiming that he would vote Benyamin Netanyahu.

"Sharon was our guy, but he was corrupt. It's good to have a corrupt guy on your side, but they switch on you – at least Bibi's straight. Lieberman though is a lunatic – we don't want a dictator. He could end up killing all the Arabs or God knows what he could do in four years. Hitler managed quite a lot."

In spite of distancing himself from such hard rightists, Oren's ultra-nationalist rhetoric didn't go unanswered and it was Guy, the dissenting voice from our lunchtime conversation at Nir's house, who delivered the challenge, this time feeling more at ease to see his point through, emphatically rejecting the very notion of enforced loyalty tests for a specific ethnic group.

"You absolutely can't do this. It's essential that Israel is a democracy and it is important that it is open and representative, which means that everyone needs a voice and representation. If not, you'll only drive the extremists underground, where they'll get more extreme, which will come back to upset the whole system. You need everyone in government, even your extremists, in order to stop extremism from boiling over."

While Oren's hard-line approach clearly couldn't accommodate such an outlook, there was no time for him to argue his case, as we were called over to the lawn, where the twenty or so congregants were sat in a circle, quieting down for Micha's talk. A golden-tanned thirty-something with cropped blond hair, a crisp shirt and a warm smile, Micha was a notably trendy mentor and it was clear to see why the students liked him, floating as he did somewhere between the status of professor and colleague. It was also apparent, once Micha began to talk, just what was fuelling the students' passion for debate and discussion, thesis and antithesis. Standing as well as sitting, making eye contact so that he was talking directly to each of the students and drawing on the teachings of Aristotle and Plato, Midrash and Talmud, Ancient Chinese culture and Milton Friedman, Micha's sermon spoke of the perils of a consumerist society and the need to temper our behaviour and lifestyle so as to have a decreased impact on the planet. It was diverse and wide ranging stuff, but as one student beamed afterwards, Micha had "the ability to take two completely unrelated subjects and connect them to create a lesson that you'd never have imagined. It's amazing."

Micha's talk having had a profound impact on the students, the issues were debated for a while afterwards before the darkening sky was slowly pricked with tiny speckles of light and it was time for the Havdalah service. The students stacked their chairs by the house and then reassembled on the lawn, standing in a round, one arm over another's shoulder, as the Shabbat flame burned between them. Even the *midrasha*'s Ultra-Orthodox student was unfazed at being stood arm in arm with his female neighbour, embodying the concept of mutual tolerance that this settlement promoted. Singing and swaying their way through the prayers, the group ended the Sabbath as it had begun, until the flame was finally extinguished and the new week began on a contemplative, spiritual note.

As the students dispersed and began their walk through the crisp, descending night, back to their caravans, it was hard not to be struck by the paradox of it all. Here was an enlightened, intellectual group of students from a variety of backgrounds; a variety of political inclinations, long-haired and pierced and opting to spend their summer before university engaged in intensive study and self-improvement. Nestled in a community that encouraged tolerance and understanding, and inspired by a mentor that cultivated free-thinking and challenging debate, even those at the extreme ends of the political spectrum thought deeply about the issues they discussed and actively sought counter arguments.

Yet here they were on land that the Palestinians' desperately craved to make their own state; and knowingly so. It was not as if they were unaware of the issues, indeed they debated them constantly – and yet none of them, no matter how left wing, had a problem with living in a place where their presence was consensually accepted to be an obstacle to the peace process. Was it because they thought that until there was a resolution their presence was doing no harm, as some had implied? Was it because this was consensus land, so close to Jerusalem that they believed it would never be given back – as others claimed? Or was it quite simply that after forty years of normalisation, the question of living in a settlement like Kfar Adumim was no longer an issue for these young Israelis?

***

With most of the students in another caravan watching a film before the new study week began, we took the opportunity to catch up on our notes and get our things together in advance of setting out the following morning. Just as we were about to go to bed, the caravan door creaked open and a stooping Ya'akov lumbered in through the small entranceway, stopping as he saw us, as though he thought he might have entered the wrong caravan.

"What's up man?"

Ya'akov remained distant, his brow furrowed in a perplexed frown, unsure whether to go to his compartment or to remain standing.

"I was watching a film. *Yossi and Jagger*," he said simply, apparently uncertain whether to go on. Ya'akov's hesitation continued and we wondered if we were doing something wrong, until slowly he continued.

"It reminded me of my army service. I was a medic with a Druze unit which had been operating in Gaza and one of my friends had been wounded in battle. As the medic, it was my call whether to go straight in and rescue him, or to wait for backup. I decided we should wait. But by the time we reached him, the guy was already dead. I'm pretty sure it was my fault."

"How old were you at the time?"

"I was 21."

Ya'akov stood blinking for a while, then turned and sloped off to his room, shutting the door behind him – though the confused look that he had cast lingered long after lights out.

The promised land

Despite the settlements' proximity and accessibility to Israel, the lack of traffic between the mainland and its outposts means that it can take a long time to leave the smaller settlements. Surrounded by bags, on dusty rocks at the dirt road junction between Alon and Kfar Adumim, we waited for a lift to the local city settlement of Ma'aleh Adumim, our stopping point on the way to Jerusalem. Developing the rules organically as the game progressed, we threw small stones at a bigger stone nearby, our boredom so great that you could throw a small stone at it. Seth was undoubtedly winning, when the guard at the ramshackle internal gate to Allon – with surprising vehemence – ordered us to stop throwing stones. When asked for a reason, none was forthcoming, though we stopped all the same.

Perhaps from a feeling of guilt, or more probably from a sense of boredom even greater than our own, the guard then called us over without explanation. Initially we thought we might be in for an earful, but by the time we reached his small, barren compartment, he was offering us cold water and shade while we waited for our lift.

His name was Sammi and he was a Christian Arab from Haifa, who worked as a guard at the entrance to Allon, on a road which could only be accessed from Kfar Adumim after having passed the more rigorous security there. Tired of his work, which saw him spending his week nights in Allon before returning to Haifa at the weekends, Sammi was eager to return to London, a city in which he had lived for four years. His eyes lit up upon talk of the city and he recalled with starry-eyed fondness the places of "Turnham Green, Acton, New Malden, Hanger Lane", as though they were golden realms; lands of mythical fantasy, to which he promised he would one day return.

Refreshed by Sammi's water, it was not long until a car pulled up on its way to Ma'aleh Adumim and we jumped into the air conditioned compartment, leaving Sammi to return to his stifling lookout post. The car scratched over the gravel and onto the path, speeding up as the surface levelled out into a smooth and even road.

Our driver was Eliza, a Moroccan-born Israeli woman who had moved to Ma'aleh Adumim not out of political ideology but for economic reasons, claiming that the flat that she had bought for $160,000 would cost five times as much in Jerusalem, highlighting just how cheap it is to live in the settlements instead of Israel proper. And at just ten minutes' drive from Jerusalem, it was clear to see why the quality of life argument had proved so persuasive for so many Israelis.

Upon hearing of our project, Eliza immediately offered to try and find us people that we could stay with in Ma'aleh Adumim – she would have us herself but her son had just come back to stay in her spare room. We left her our numbers and jumped out at the shopping centre, ready to begin the next leg of our journey, once again struck by how open and hospitable people were that they could offer to let us stay after only five minutes of meeting – so close-knit and trusting were these small communities.

Chapter Four
Efrat: Normalisation

In two minds

With fire in her eyes, our hostess declares "We're *mitna-halim*", as if to set out her stall from the off. Of course, that she and her husband are settlers is a given, by virtue of the fact that their house is located well past the Green Line, but Irit's definition marks her out as an ideological resident, rather than someone who has simply come for the cheap housing. Her initial tone does not last long: she is as motherly and soft-spoken as anyone we've stayed with thus far, and soon settles into her comfort zone as she weaves an intimate family history of how she and Moshe came to settle in Efrat.

Irit's parents were refugees from Europe; Hungarian and Czechoslovakian, they met and got engaged on the ship where they spent over a month waiting to dock in Palestine. In 1939, they finally disembarked the boat – her mother was just eighteen, her father a mere two years older; most of their family would perish in the flames of the Holocaust. The young Orthodox couple spent time in two *kibbutzim*, before moving to the coastal city of Netanya, where they raised their three children. Irit enlisted in the army after the Six Day War, spending one year in preparatory training before completing two years of action service. She met her first husband in 1970 at Ein Tzurim, a kibbutz where she was posted with the army; their first daughter Inbal was born there in 1972, and for a short time all seemed perfect for the young couple.

However, Irit's mother passed away soon after, and in October 1973 Irit's husband was called up for reserve duty to fight in the Yom Kippur War. He was the commander of an IDF post on the Suez Canal, before disappearing during a raid which left numerous soldiers dead, and many more captured by Egyptian troops. "For six months, I had no idea where he was," she recalls. "Finally there was a deal, a prisoner and casualty exchange, and his was one of the bodies handed back in a coffin: we held his funeral immediately afterwards." (Last year, Irit went to Egypt for the first time, along with members of her husband's army unit, in order to see for herself the spot where he fell in battle.)

Irit's father died a few months afterwards, leaving Irit both widowed and orphaned in quick succession, with a baby in tow. It was at this point that Moshe reappeared on the scene: they had known one another from their Bnei Akiva youth movement, and love blossomed between the pair, culminating in marriage and a daughter, Shira. They left Ein Tzurim in 1975: "It was too painful to carry on living on the same kibbutz where I'd lived with my first husband," explains Irit. Despite the financial upheaval of leaving kibbutz life – "we had no possessions or money, since everything was communal on the kibbutz" – they managed to find a small sum with which to purchase a house in the seven-year old settlement of Kiryat Arba, near Hebron. "When I was widowed, the army gave me a car to help me manage; initially I gave it to the kibbutz, but when we left I was given it back – we sold it, and with that money bought our house: that's how cheap property was in Kiryat Arba back then."

Irit was still completing her studies in social work when they moved to Kiryat Arba; Moshe found work as the secretary of the town's council. 450 families were living there when they arrived – "around the same number as today", according to Irit. However, the population of Kiryat Arba is now almost six times greater than it was when Moshe and Irit moved in, increasing from around 1200 in 1975[11] to 7000 today. Established immediately after the West Bank was conquered during the Six Day War, Kiryat Arba's population was largely made up of "extremists", says Irit. "I was middle of the road [by comparison], and it was too much for me: there were demonstrations all the time, illegal settler activity, and so on; after five years I told Moshe we had to leave."

They relocated to Alon Shvut, which was founded in 1970 as a neighbourhood for housing families associated with the then-nascent Har Etzion *hesder yeshiva*[12]. Their move to the town was always temporary: they were simply "waiting there for Efrat to be built". "Anyone who moved from Kiryat Arba to Efrat is no longer an extremist," states Irit, "with the exception of Nadia Matar..." She is referring to Efrat's resident ideologue; Matar is founder and head of the hardline 'Women in Green' movement, who see their mission as ensuring 'the security and Jewish heritage of historic Israel', which translates into fierce opposition to any kind of deal with the Palestinians that cedes territory or control to the other side.

Irit, on the other hand, is far more open to compromise: "If the [government] told me to give up my house for real peace, I would be ready to say goodbye to [Efrat]," casting her gaze out of the window at the verdant lawns of her salubrious neighbourhood. "Right at the beginning, I was ideological," she explains, "but now I'm not so sure if we need to keep the *Shtachim* or return them. If I talk about it, they'll shoot me..." she laughs. She claims that her ideological shift was the result of driving to work each day and observing "the difficult sight... [of] Arabs standing in line every day at the checkpoints,... sitting at the side of the road while the soldiers check them, when the majority are just looking for work."

"Moshe wants to keep the territories, but our kids have run to the left [they have four children]. Our son Elad is embarrassed: he wants to delete from his CV the fact that he once lived in Kiryat Arba. He couldn't take the fact that he had to beat Arab kids when he was serving in the army in Hebron; that was when he switched to the left. He was in the paratroopers' division, and started his service with so much willingness..."

None of their children are religious, "which was hard for us at first, but they've made their choice". Irit reckons that ninety percent of Efrat's residents are religious, to her chagrin. She would prefer a more mixed populace – "like Kfar Adumim" – but recognises that there is little incentive for secular families to move to Efrat, "since our schools are religious, so why would they come?"

She views the Disengagement as a "tragedy", but at the same time she "would not fight if the orders were given to evacuate Efrat". She tried not to think about the security situation – "I don't want to, because that would make it hard for me to commute to work each morning". She is the head of a rehabilitative daycare centre, where she has worked for fifteen years, requiring her to make the daily journey through the checkpoints and tunnels back across the Green Line to Jerusalem. During the first intifada, she drove in all conditions: "through fog, through snow, and past the Deheisha [refugee] camp, where they were shooting at us, throwing rocks... I had my car's windows smashed more than once". During the second intifada, there was "more shooting, less rocks – people were killed. I don't think about it; I don't let it get to me. I don't want to be too frightened to travel to Jerusalem".

At this point, Moshe returns from his Jewish studies lecture, all smiles as he sits down next to his wife at the kitchen table. Irit turns to him and jokes "it's lucky you weren't here to hear what I said about Kiryat Arba..." Moshe is clearly far more committed to the settlement enterprise, and draws heavily from a well of nationalistic pride when it comes to recounting his reasons for moving to Efrat. "Moskowitz used to say 'Gush Etzion fell [in 1948] because there were too few people here to defend it – if we put a city there, they will never conquer it from us'". Moshe was an adherent of the Allon Plan[13] which included the provision that wherever Jews had been in 1948, there would be settlements built in the post-1967 era of occupation. "It was decided that the road from Jerusalem to Hebron would be the Israeli/Arab border, and we looked to see where we could build a city." The founders of Efrat took government land and decided to construct their settlement near Bethlehem. "There was room for thousands of houses; at first, Moskowitz had thought there was room for only a few hundred. At present, there are around six or seven thousand residents here: for security reasons, we won't build any more houses..." – "and because it's Arab land", interrupts Irit mildly, but Moshe doesn't take the bait this time.

The mechanical drone of low-flying army helicopters threatens to drown out our conversation, reminding us just how deep we are into a militarised zone, though Moshe and Irit seem barely to notice the noise. "We began to make plans for the city," he continues, "and we brought in not just Israelis, but outsiders too. Rabbi Shlomo Riskin from Manhattan decided to move to Efrat and to bring some of his community with him – who were very rich – and at the same time a group of South African families settled here as well; they got permission to build houses next to one another here. The demographic was one third Israeli, one third American, one third South African. People spoke English on the street; letters from the city council were at first written just in English, and only later in Ivrit too."

"In 1978, we began to develop the land, and in 1980 we established the Rimon neighbourhood, before bringing in more residents in 1983 [they had hoped to bring them in 1982, but the outbreak of the Lebanon War meant they had to postpone their plans for a year]. It was different here than in Kedumim: people didn't start off in caravans, but rather moved straight into houses. We did it properly," he says proudly. "We registered incoming individuals, built their houses, and then they moved in. We set up schools, a *mikva* [ritual bath], offices, and more. Then we began to build on the hill, setting up public gardens and a synagogue too." Rather than acknowledge Irit's anti-extremist sentiments as reason for their departure from Kiryat Arba, Moshe explains the move by saying he "wanted to move to a place where we could be of assistance". The street where they live was originally designated for South Africans only, but Moshe's influence with the council helped them circumvent the segregationist policy.

"Of course we have to stay here," states Moshe firmly, in relation to Efrat as a settlement entity, rather than to his family's Israeli outpost on their overwhelmingly South African street. He notes that Kiryat Arba has a "stronger sense of ideology", which he puts down to its location deeper in the West Bank – "where they are surrounded by Arabs" – as well as to Kiryat Arba's history, "which is steeped in blood". (According to Irit, "Jews moved to Hebron in 1968 and lived on the Arab's throats"; again, Moshe pays little attention to her reading of events.)

As we come to the end of our initial meeting, the conversation turns to the thorny subject of why Israel garners a seemingly disproportionate amount of media attention round the world. Irit notes that, lately, "the UK is in the Israeli media's focus all the time", thanks to the threat of terrorism on British soil. "Those terrorists are Palestinian," she declares, but Seth refutes that assertion, stating that they are in fact British citizens with links to Al Qaida. "OK, they're Muslims", she retorts simply, and Moshe interjects to opine that Chechneya's problems are "because of Muslims too, as are those of Croatia...", before Irit expands further and says that "*all* terror in the world is because of the Muslims". The ubiquitous 'Islamic threat' rears its head here, as in Mitzpeh Yericho, in fact as in almost every place we've visited thus far, sucking in both hardliners like Moshe and ostensibly more moderate types such as Irit. As the helicopters continue to circle high above the dusty streets of Efrat, it is clear that the thudding beat of their blades is in fact a comfort rather than a nuisance.

Skin deep

Efrat today is the manifestation of Moshe's (if not Irit's) dreams all those years ago. Both the private and public gardens are immaculately kept: in keeping with other major settlements around the West Bank, little attention is paid to the water shortages that so blight the region; instead, water is poured onto the verges and lawns of the city with wanton abandon. The settlers have certainly made the desert bloom in a literal sense, but at what cost to themselves, not to mention their Palestinian neighbours? Beneath the lush surface of Efrat's streets, all is not as calm as would appear from the picture-postcard appearance of the city. Settlers come under regular attack when driving the surrounding roads, from amateur child rock-throwers to militant gunmen; reprisals against the Palestinian populace are swift, meted out by both settlers and soldiers alike. Fear is a hard currency in Efrat; much as many of the residents try to mask their apprehension (as with Irit earlier), the nagging doubts quickly take centre stage when discussing the precarious nature of life in the West Bank. Guns are in abundance, sported by guards at the entrance to the *yeshuv*, by troops manning the checkpoints nearby, and by private individuals who require the extra confidence boost of strapping on their very own sidearm at all times.

Whilst Efrat resembles many other major settlements at first glance – the standard redbrick roofs, the incongruous juxtaposition of wealth and luxury against a wider backdrop of poverty and want – the devil is in the detail. Since Palestinians drive the same roads as are used by Efrat's residents just outside the settlement's perimeter, the settlers take their message of division and conquest to a seemingly juvenile level of vandalism. Wherever a signpost is written in Hebrew, Arabic and English (as is common to most parts of Israeli-administered roads and highways), outraged settlers have sprayed over the Arabic, ramming home their sectarian message to all who pass by. Other posts and poles are plastered in bumper stickers; one atop the other, in an orgy of sloganeering, each perpetrator deciding their mantra is more worthy of prominence than those which came before. Half of a sticker reading 'The People Are With The Golan' sticks out from under another which reads: "UN = Unwanted Nobodies – GO HOME!", mustering all the intellect of an angry five year old.

Beautifully-kept parks and shaded glades of trees are a pleasure to walk through, but it is impossible to escape the feeling that the veneer of calm could be shattered at any point; the tinderbox element of Efrat's existence might be of its own making, but either way it dominates the thoughts of both resident and visitor alike. The cafes are bustling, the pizza parlour welcomes a constant stream of hungry children and adults alike, whilst in the supermarket, tills peal out their contentment as each item is scanned, bagged and stuffed into shopping carts – but the glint of gunmetal can be seen poking out of waistbands and holsters in every shop we pass. If this is the dream of Moshe and his fellow pioneers, then all well and good. Listening to the doubts of his wife, however, and hearing how his own children have left the *yeshuv* far behind them, one wonders why one's man utopia has turned into Paradise Lost for others living the same reality.

Peace sounds nice – but I wouldn't want to live there

"Just like in London, people move out to the suburbs – we came to Efrat because it meant we could have a bigger house."

In the large living room of that bigger house, indeed much like the cushioned comfort of middle class London suburbs, Rachel and Michael discuss their reasons for moving to Efrat. Middle aged *olim* [immigrants] from Wembley and Finchley respectively, the couple describe the settlement as a "dormitory town" for those who commute to Jerusalem.

"Efrat is a fifteen minute drive from Jerusalem, where we both work," says Rachel. "It's an easy journey, which explains why few of the residents work here. Most of them commute."

And just like a suburb, Efrat offered the couple, who met in Jerusalem in 1971, a safe place to raise their children, in contrast to the busy city streets of Jerusalem.

"Look, our twelve year old is outside playing in the street right now and we're not worried because we know he's in the *yeshuv*. You don't have to worry – the only thing you have to fear is cats and dogs."

However, the fact that Michael carries a gun – something that would be unthinkable for this well spoken, bespectacled archaeologist back in London – belies his offhand description of Efrat as a suburb like any other. A number of violent incidents in and around the *yeshuv* also conspire to undermine the conveyed image of a peaceful suburban existence. Rachel plays down the "two or three incidents on the road" during the last Intifada that included the murders of two Efrat women in their car on the way to Jerusalem, while Michael mentions the attempted suicide bombing in their local supermarket – "one of our neighbours shot him before he had a chance to fully detonate the bomb" – but neglects to mention the bombing by a sixteen year old kid in the local medical centre a month later, in which six Israelis were injured. All of these incidents, however, happened over five years ago and a decline in attacks in recent years has left the couple feeling quite safe.

Apparently unsure as to why living in Efrat would even be an issue, Rachel measures her slight, restrained voice, her movements controlled, almost repressed, to portray life in Efrat as nothing out of the ordinary; a quiet town of quiet streets, good schools and friendly neighbours.

"We lead very ordinary lives here. We travel to and from Jerusalem every day; our children are in and out of each other's houses. It's very sociable – real village life."

However, Rachel and Michael admit that others inside the Green Line do not share the couple's impression of their home town.

"When the Intifada was at its worst," says Rachel, "people didn't want to come and visit us, because they thought it was too dangerous. But then again I never went to Gush Katif, out of fear – nor did I go to Hebron or to Kiryat Arba."

"People rationalise their fear," Michael explains. "Everybody had their own place [during the Intifada] where they felt safe. Some wouldn't visit this street or that house, or that room. When we lived in [the settlement of] Giloh during the first Intifada, the Arabs in Bethlehem were firing across the valley at us, but we felt safe in our street even though bullets were flying there. You feel safe with what you know."

Part of the reason people in Israel regard life in Efrat as dangerous is that, according to Michael's belief, the media demonise everyone who lives in the settlements.

"The media is full of derogatory, negative portrayals of settlers. We're seen as extreme right wing cowboys – but most of us are not. It's a function of propaganda – Israel, Israeli Jews are against every settlement over the Green Line and they'll do anything to blacken our name. So we need to show people that we're living a good life, doing good work... that we're not evil or different from them."

Rachel and Michael might not be cowboys, but their presence in Efrat is politically and ideologically motivated, even if their initial reason for moving here was to improve their quality of life. The violence of the second Intifada radicalised them and, as happened to many settlers throughout the West Bank, it strengthened their resolve, making them more right wing. Moreover, Michael now refuses to draw a distinction between Efrat and other West Bank settlements on the one hand and Israel on the other. "This is how Israel started. Israel was one big *yeshuv*. I don't feel like Efrat is a settlement – if Efrat is a settlement, then the whole of Israel is a settlement."

Echoing the logic of the settlement enterprise's system of creating *facts on the ground*, Michael asserts that once a settlement has ceased to be constituted of tents and a water tower, having become an established town of bricks and mortar, it is no longer a settlement. In this outlook, it is practically irrelevant what the international community recognises to be a legitimate state and what it deems to be occupied land; it is simply a case of consolidating *statements on the ground* into *facts*.

Michael believes that another such consolidation is the construction of the security wall, a de facto border between Israel and the Palestinians, which he envisages becoming the permanent border later down the line. Despite this, Michael maintains that the Jewish people have a right to live throughout the Occupied Territories. Invoking a range of justifications, from the archaeological evidence of ancient Jewish civilisation, through the fact that Gush Etzion was Jewish-owned prior to the 1948 war, to the claim that the Palestinians are not even a nation, Michael emphasizes Jewish rights to the land while belittling those of the Palestinians.

When pushed on the subject of reconciliation and a two state solution, Michael and Rachel both claim a willingness to give up their suburban lifestyle for true peace, but their indication of a weak Palestinian leadership and social structure explains their disillusionment with the concept of peace and its pursuit. Or perhaps it is simply an excuse. Leaning back in his arm chair, Michael speaks philosophically about the hypothetical, almost abstract notion of two states, seemingly confident that it is unlikely to be realised.

"If there was a real option of signing a real peace treaty with the Arabs all around us, and that was conditioned by land transfer on both sides, I don't think that's a problem – in return for peace. But we know from our own experience that they've not kept to former agreements. Just look at Gush Katif. They openly say that agreements don't need to be honoured – it's just not part of their culture."

Of course, there was no bilateral agreement that led to the evacuation of Gaza, which was arguably a factor in the rise of the hostile Hamas government there, but by claiming that the differences between Israelis and Palestinians are cultural, somehow innate, as opposed to territorial or historical, Michael emphasises how little he trusts his neighbours.

"All they do is hate us. They don't know why they hate – they just do."

"The Palestinians need to spend time building up their own country," adds Rachel, nodding solemnly. "They need to put in some kind of structure. It's bedlam over there. They're so bent on trying to kill us and push us out, instead of focusing on developing their own country. They're not ready for their own state."

Michael agrees, "The Jordanians are the only ones we can talk to. If they could turn these so-called Palestinians into more reasonable partners then fine, but I don't see how it can be done. They've poisoned the minds of their youngest generation – we'll have to wait another generation now until we can clean it all up."

On cue, the next generation of the family, Na'ama, 22, joins us and Josh asks her whether she will choose to live in a settlement in the future. Unappreciative of the homogeneity of her home town, where she says she felt "strangled" growing up, Na'ama says would choose to raise her own family in the *Shtachim,* but not in a settlement like Efrat.

Michael refers to his oldest son, who now lives in the settlement of Shiloh, when he claims that his children would prefer "a settlement in the making. It's too established here; too well set up. The youth always look for pioneering ventures... They look at their mums and dads as past it; as no longer relevant. That's good. They're not materialistic; they're more interested in the spirit... they want to give to society. There's still a lot of hope in the younger generation. I'm glad to provide for that. I'm happy to be past it."

Michael smiles at his wife and daughter, content with the way his home has turned out. Having arrived in Efrat seeking a better quality of life, only to become radicalised by the Intifada, Michael's journey is quite different to that of Irit whose right wing ideology was undermined through her contact with Palestinians at check points. Where Irit has raised left wing children and wonders whether she will one day leave Efrat in the name of peace, Michael seems to have built himself a world of suburban stability here, safe in the knowledge that his solid home, built as part of what he describes as a "shoelace, growing in Jerusalem's direction", not only strengthens Jewish settlement in the West Bank, but has also given rise to a new generation, prepared to pioneer the Efrats of tomorrow. From a Palestinian perspective, the young minds in Efrat could also be described as "poisoned" – towards building more settlements and taking more Palestinian land, preventing the realisation of a two state solution that could put an end to the ongoing conflict, though of course Michael and Rachel would not see it that way.

Instead, in their tranquil suburb, it would seem that Michael and Rachel have already established their own version of peace – and would be reluctant to exchange it for any other kind.

Talking to a stranger

Walking the streets of Efrat the next day, we pass a building site where a few labourers toil away in the afternoon sun. As we turn the corner, we see another of the workers sitting down in the shade of an olive tree eating his lunch, so we stop and strike up a conversation with him. What we learn from the brief chat serves to reaffirm to us the atrocious state of affairs that exists for Palestinians who are "lucky" enough to find employment with Israeli contractors, who shamelessly exploit them with little regard for anything other than their own profit margins.

Clad in a ragged T-shirt emblazoned with the logo of an Israeli building company, Boel [not his real name] glances furtively around him, then agrees to talk to us for a few minutes, while the coast is clear. And the coast needs to be clear for him to be able to converse with strangers, since Palestinian labourers in Efrat are banned from every activity other than silently doing the job that they were employed to do. Contravention of the rules will result in his permit to work being instantly withdrawn, says Boel, "and I'll end up sitting outside my house all day, with no way to feed my family".

"If I want to go to collect supplies from the gate, the guard must come with me," he told us. "If I want to go to the toilet, the guard must come with me too. If I want to speak to anyone other than my fellow workers, the guard must be present. In fact, I can't even walk more than twenty metres away from the guard, otherwise he'll call the police and have me kicked out of the area." Boel is afforded as much freedom as a rottweiler chained to a gatepost; his invisible shackles are closely monitored by the gun-toting guard, upon whose whims rest Boel's entire livelihood, and who must be treated with suitably fawning respect by Boel.

Boel receives one hundred shekels a day for an eight-hour shift – equivalent to the pittance that the "basket

139

children [Arab child labourers]" earn in the Mahane Yehuda souk in downtown Jerusalem. However, even though the basket children's wages are pitiful, it is somewhat more understandable given that they are underage, unskilled workers. Boel, on the other hand, is in his mid-30s and has a wife and kids to feed – plus he's been working in the building trade for years.

Naturally, given the indifference of his employers – as well as the government, which refuses to enforce the labour laws – there is no insurance policy in place to assist Boel and his friends in the result of accident or injury. Boel laughs bitterly at the idea that anyone would care enough to provide such cover. "If I get hurt, then I don't work and I don't earn," he says. "Plus I have to deduct any medical expenses from the hundred shekels I earned that day."

Despite all of this, Boel actually feels fortunate to be working on the Efrat project. There is no work whatsoever for him in his home village, and the alternative to this job would be to seek employment illegally in Tel Aviv or Haifa. There, he says, the exploitation is even more severe, where those hiring know that they have the workers over a barrel, since Palestinian ID-holders aren't allowed in those areas at all.

"Over there, the work isn't even fit for dogs or donkeys," Boel says. "And any Arab who tries to sleep on the site overnight will get attacked by the soldiers on patrol. I have a friend from my village who was heavily beaten with a stick by a soldier – he ended up in hospital, and he can't even see any more, let alone work."

The abuse isn't always physical, Boel tells us. "Here in Efrat, the guards empty out my food containers every day searching for weapons, even though they've known me for twenty years. Everything that the Israelis do to the Arabs is no good," he states flatly, instantly conflating his parochial experiences with a far wider assessment of how the two sides interact. "In the Qur'an, it says that the Israelis will do this to us for years," he says, finding solace for his predicament through his religious learning. "But it also says that our time will come. This won't go on forever."

The ongoing conflict means that both sides can cite reasons for their own abhorrent behaviour toward one another. Efrat residents we meet tell us "it's a shame we have to treat the Arab workers like that, but they've attacked us from within before", referring to several murders that were perpetrated by Palestinian workers over the last few years.

And, on the other side, when the likes of Boel see and experience the rampant racism and oppression that he's on the receiving end of every day, it's easy to see why the more militant amongst his community find excuses to rise up against the state they perceive as oppressors, however unpalatable and unacceptable the violent methods they employ.

There appears no way out of the impasse while these perceptions persist. If Palestinian workers feel like they are chained up like dogs while they work, it is near impossible for Israelis to win their hearts and minds. If they, in turn, resort to indiscriminate violence against Israelis to exact revenge for their mistreatment, they'll find their pleas for a better life falling on deaf ears among those who once might have heeded their calls.

In the meantime, however, a wage increase and insurance cover for workers such as Boel would go some way to alleviating his valid concerns that his Israeli employers couldn't really care less about his welfare. However, he – along with anyone else familiar with the situation here – isn't holding his breath for change any time soon.

Hollywood

Verdant, well-watered lawns surround the paths tracking neatly through the grounds of Kfar Etzion, a well-kept religious kibbutz, primly overrun with florid banks of colour and patches of welcome shade. Quiet and serene, the landscaped grounds are interspersed with clusters of modest housing, and the occasional passing *kippah* or long skirt is the only marker of difference between this kibbutz and any other in Israel.

The bedrock of the eponymous Etzion bloc, Kfar Etzion was first settled by Yemenite Jews before the creation of the State of Israel, in 1927, and was deserted and resettled several times prior to its eventual abandonment in May 1948, when it was captured by Arab forces. In a bloody day of a vengeful war, Arab irregulars massacred the last 127 men and women of the fallen kibbutz, one day before Israel declared its independence.

When Israel conquered the land in the 1967 war, a few residents of the original kibbutz requested that they be allowed to rebuild the settlement. Prime Minister Levi Eshkol's eventual consent meant that the settlement was the first to be established inside the West Bank after the Six Day War. Whilst many, including Eshkol, felt that this was a return to an area of emotional significance to the Jewish people, due to its recent history as a Jewish settlement, the Prime Minister was nevertheless aware that Israeli civilian settlement in the West Bank was illegal according to international law; a contravention of the Fourth Geneva Convention that states that an "Occupying Power shall not deport or transfer parts of its own civilian population into the territory it occupies". For this reason Eshkol ensured that the settlement was established under the guise of a military base.[14]

The pre-state history of the Gush Etzion means that the settlements here are afforded special emotional status amongst many Israelis who know the land's history. Many West Bank residents hold up the existence of pre-48 settlement at Kfar Etzion as a justification for the return of the 1948 Jewish refugees and the re-establishment of a Jewish neighbourhood, though of course they don't apply the same logic to the Palestinian towns that were abandoned within what is now Israel. Kfar Etzion then, as part of Gush Etzion, is regarded as being rightfully Jewish by those who live there, and a small, permanent museum within the kibbutz proudly champions the Jewish history of the area, Biblical and recent, in an attempt at justifying the legitimacy of the West Bank settlement to its undecided visitors. The cornerstone of the museum is a short film that plays to small groups of tourists eager to learn more about why Israel is right to be in the West Bank. The film's narrative recounts the pre-state Jewish settlement of the land, its fall at the hands of the Arab forces, and its subsequent re-establishment following the 1967 war. Principle amongst this narrative though, is the telling of the massacre.

Ostensibly a documentation of the tragic murder of civilians by over-zealous soldiers, the film is couched in wild, propagandist terms and sloganeering, while the graphic action plays out to an orchestral score worthy of Hollywood. An American man's voice comically sensationalises the narration, as superhero music accompanies the brave Jewish pioneers at work, while an evil horror movie soundtrack characterises the surrounding "hostile Arab villages". With continued reference to war, the Holocaust and death, the tragedy of the loss of the Etzion area is trumped only by the triumph of the Jewish people's return in 1967. Their "memories", combined with reference to the Biblical resonances of the ancient land for the Jewish people, help to create the impression that Jewish settlement of Gush Etzion is ancient and uninterrupted, but for the nineteen years when it was under Jordanian rule, obscuring the reality that the settlement had only existed for twenty-one years prior to its fall in 1948, and even then not continuously.

Aside from the tragedy of the massacre, the video describes the tragedy of the loss of the settlement itself, claiming that "in one sudden burst, the War of Independence ended the dreams of the people of Kfar Etzion." Tellingly, the video speaks of the War of

Independence – the war that effected the establishment of the Jewish state of Israel – as simply a war that ended the settlement of this small patch of land. In celebrating the return of the settlers then, it is hard not to be struck by the sense that this kind of propaganda is happy to undermine the value of the state of Israel itself in favour of emphasising the import of this small West Bank settlement. As the guide states afterwards, "in my father's generation Kfar Etzion was more important than Tel Aviv, but now the rest of Israel's not interested." It seems missed on the guide that Kfar Etzion and other land lost when the 1949 armistice lines were drawn were the price the Jewish people paid for finally gaining a state of their own. Only when the IDF rolled back into the Gush, in 1967, were people like the guide allowed to have it both ways.

The film feels like little more than a propagandist piece designed to evoke sympathy and support for the suffering residents of Kfar Etzion in the face of ongoing Arab hostility. One would be forgiven for leaving the auditorium with the belief that the persecuted residents of the Gush are holding on by a thread to a tiny patch of land that the marauding Arabs are continually pulling from beneath their feet. Once outside the darkened auditorium and in the dazzling light of day, the truth is plainer to see; trilingual road signs in Area B are reduced to bilingual, the Arabic having been petulantly sprayed over; barbed perimeter fences and manned, reinforced gates segregate the Area C settlements from the regions to which the Palestinians are granted access. Meanwhile, the film's implication that the poor settlers are steadily having their land robbed by aggressive Palestinians goes beyond hypocrisy.

With the film's vivid action playing over in my mind as we walk along the sweaty tarmac, one can't shake the feeling that the film does a great a disservice to the original pre-state settlers of Kfar Etzion, who were intent not on preventing the realisation of another nation's independence, but on building a state of their own. Instead of commemorating the victims of the massacre, however, the film politicises them, using their blood to justify a political agenda; creating martyrs for the settlers' cause. The fields are steeped with Jewish blood, the viewers seem to be told. The current residents have earned this land through blood, sweat and tears.

Banging the drum

We had been warned by Irit that Nadia Matar was something of a firebrand and, as we walk towards her front door, it appears that the assessment had been an accurate one.

Matar's battered Chevrolet van is swathed in scores of political bumper stickers, professing hate for both the Palestinian leadership and Israeli government alike, and a huge orange flag, in support for the anti-Disengagement movement, flies on the well-kept front lawn. Sitting at a table to the side of the house is Nadia herself, barking into the mobile phone clamped to her ear, and scowling with frustration at the person on the other end of the line.

When she sees us, she mellows somewhat, breaking out into a well-polished smile and motioning for us to sit down opposite her. A couple of her kids peer at us curiously from the front door, then Nadia hangs up the phone and we get down to business. The next hour is spent with her firing off soundbites like a Gatling gun, as we struggle desperately to keep up with the transcription. She packs as much rhetoric and opinion into the interview as she possibly can, adamant that she'll make the most of this opportunity to spread her message, given that she doesn't enjoy the best of relations with the Israeli press.

"They're very left wing," she tells us, "especially the state media. Anything that Peace Now say gets straight into the papers here, whereas whenever I put out a release, it just gets ignored by and large." She is the head of Women In Green (WIG), an activist group that she founded along with her mother-in-law in order to "protect the Jewish people's right to this earth, so that our great-great-grandchildren can still live in the land of Israel".

The group is made up of both religious and secular Jews – Nadia calls herself Orthodox, yet is wearing trousers when we meet her – and this dichotomy is reflected in WIG's policies. "Our ideas are based on both the religious and historical connection between Jews and the Land of Israel," she states, "however, we're not just doing it for the Jewish people's benefit..."

"It's in the world's interests that we stand up and be strong against the Arabs," she assures us, getting more and more animated as she warms to her theme. "The Arabs won't stop if they get the *Shtachim*, they won't even stop if they get all of Israel. No, that would just be the first course in their quest to take over the world."

According to Nadia, as well as to many others we've met lately, this is the opening salvo in "the war of Islam versus Judaism and Christianity. The Arabs have a saying – 'first the Saturday people, then the Sunday people.' If we cave in, then the next step will be turning Europe into Eurabia." Explaining her family's presence in Efrat, she tells us proudly that "we're the bulletproof vest for the rest of Israel and, by extension, the world."

This idea of selfless sacrifice permeates the rest of the interview, with Belgian-born Nadia declaring that she knows far better than the native Israeli Jews what's best for this troubled country and how things could be righted, if only she had some kind of power. However, since she is staunchly "extra-parliamentary" (due to her disgust at the "corruption of the Knesset, which is in the hands of the leftist elite") it is hard to see how she ever hopes to wrest control of the political reins and bring her plans to fruition.

She appears, to all intents and purposes, to be yet another frustrated extremist, sidelined even further by a self-imposed ostracism from the mainstream. However – and this is where she and her followers differ from the kind of people who just sit around bemoaning their fate – the most alarming part of WIG's hysteria is how pro-active they are in seeking to take on the powers that be.

Nadia herself has been slung into jail for her protesting "many, many times" and, at the end of July, the group planned to flood onto a contested hilltop called Givat Ha-Eitam to "build a settlement there in order to counter the government's policy of retreat and capitulation to the enemy." She speaks defiantly of the inevitable confronta-tion with the army: "it's up to them if it descends into violence, but we'll turn out in force regardless."

And this is only the start, according to Nadia's grand designs for the future of the conflict. Citing the world's opinion of Israel as being based on anti-Semitism, she maintains: "we can only counter their views by being proud Jews." She declares that, "no one respects a person who crawls; the only time the world looked up to us was after the Six Day War, when we crushed the Arabs deci-sively. It's a psychological thing. People respect those who respect themselves."

If she had her way, "during the next war, we must get rid of all the Palestinian leaders, just as Europe destroyed the Nazi Reich. We must kill all of Hamas, all of the PA, all of the PLO, and smash their infrastructure, just as the allies did in Dresden. It's either that, or being wiped out ourselves." She apparently used to believe in coexistence, but "now I've become radicalised thanks to the new generation of Arabs who can't fathom the idea of a Jewish state where Jewish sovereignty rules the people."

She explains away the entire left wing camp in Israel as being "mentally unwell." "They have a sickness," she says with a sad shake of her head, "and it's called 'beaten wife syndrome.' Whenever the Arabs attack us, the left think it's their own fault, and try to do everything they can to appease them – such as handing over land and

147

power to them." And nowhere is safe when this mentality takes hold, according to Nadia. "Peres and the other architects of Oslo are responsible for 9/11," she states flatly. "They gave legitimacy to Arab terror, and made the Arabs believe that they could forever get what they want through slaughter."

She delivers these words without the slightest trace of irony in her voice. The same woman who, moments earlier, had been advocating the mass extermination of the Palestinian command is now declaring that the Arabs shouldn't be allowed to get their own way through the language of war.

Quality of life

"Nadia is *the* fanatic of Efrat," Avigail exclaims. "She's crazy! Have you any idea how many times she's been to prison?!"

A meeting with Avigail, a 31 year old mother of two and her graphic designer husband, Chen, puts our meeting with Nadia Matar into perspective. According to Avigail, an Efrat resident since the age of sixteen when she returned from an eight year stint in the US, "99% of Efrat's residents would disagree with Nadia, [who is] in her own place entirely" – a place of which Avigail is highly critical, taking particular issue with her influence over the youth: "she finds young people, gives them a slice of pizza and then gets them to do all her dirty work."

We're sitting in the living room of Avigail and Chen's modern two-bedroom flat, in Efrat's only apartment block, on the edge of the settlement – an area currently being developed for more housing. Bright plastic toys have been tidied to the edges of the linoleum floor and three-year old Maya waddles from her mummy to the visitors, slapping my hand as she says hello. With five-year old Hila running in and out of the room to demand attention from her distracted mum as Chen busies himself in the kitchen, Avigail admits that Efrat attracted her for what it had to offer her children, not for what it represented ideologically.

"There are amazing schools in the area – award winning – and although they're religious we balance that at home so that our kids won't become too *dati*. Just as long as they don't turn out Ultra-Orthodox I'll be happy."

A progressive religious Jew herself, Avigail also speaks highly of the comfort and sense of community in Efrat, believing that it is these quality of life factors that entice the majority of residents, who she claims have none of the violent vitriol of the settlement's unofficial spokesman, Matar.

"Most people come here not because it's a settlement but because it's a good place to live. It's not as if we don't think we should be here, but most people don't come specifically for that reason. It's basically thought of as part of Jerusalem – at about a twenty to forty minute commute into town – and for us it's good because it doesn't have acceptance criteria, so you don't have to be religious to live here. That makes it less oppressive – we've got lots of *hiloni* friends and they can drive into the *yeshuv* to visit on Shabbat."

"And within the settlement we all know each other – there are committees for everything, so say a woman gives birth in the town, a committee will organise to send meals to her home for a week. Or if people are low on funds for their wedding, there will be a fund available for them to turn to."

Despite this village-like sense of community, Avigail admits that Efrat has its share of social problems, particularly amongst young people. A former youth worker herself, Avigail has a progressive outlook on the handling of such concerns.

"There are tons of drugs problems and theft. For a few years Efrat buried its head in the sand and did nothing about it and all the kids were out on the street, bored, vandalising the place. They had no place to be, no structure; they were in a bad state. So it was up to our generation to take charge. We set up a youth club, along with a school for difficult kids and now people come here from all over Israel. We woke up and tackled the problems head on and it's a lot better now."

With her progressive attitude towards religion and society, her brightly decorated apartment and her eagerness to chat with us in her excellent English, Avigail's young, trendy image defies the stereotypical image of Israeli settler – religious, armed, aggressive and patriotically communicating in Hebrew only, unlike most urban Israelis. Keen to embrace the wider world, Avigail and Chen have raised their children to speak both Hebrew and English and lament the fact that they were not raised speaking more languages. With their own families hailing from Iraq, Turkey and Morocco, Avigail and Chen could have had a further four languages between them: Arabic, French, Kurdish and Turkish, but, as was the way with new immigrants to Israel at the time, their parents insisted that their children spoke Hebrew only, an idealistic tradition which Avigail describes as being "messed up" and which now seems to be most prevalent in the settlements.

That an outgoing, open-minded and modern young couple like Avigail and Chen can be found in the settlement of Efrat is testament to its perceived status as a consensus settlement amongst Israelis, within the separation wall, and close to Jerusalem.

"The government has said over and over that Efrat, along with Ma'aleh Adumim, will never be given back," Avigail affirms, smiling at her daughter as she clambers onto her lap. "They'll be made into parts of Jerusalem, to provide a continuous area... It's growing too – there's room for it to expand. There are going to be another 700 houses in [the Efrat neighbourhood of] Dagan, between 500 and 700 in Tamar and another 400 here. There's a huge amount of building going on all the time – and the prices are high. Efrat is probably the most expensive settlement, with a three bed apartment costing around $170,000."

Nevertheless, despite the normalisation of Efrat, Avigail does not deceive herself over the settlement's controversial status, nor does she attempt to deceive others with the politically loaded vocabulary of those like Nadia who speak of the "liberated territories" and the danger of giving land "away" rather than "back" to the Palestinians. Avigail and Chen are reminded of just how contested their home is by certain friends of theirs who refuse to visit them in the settlement.

"It took our best friend a year and a half to come and visit us here. We don't normally talk politics together but we said to her put your politics aside for one day and come and visit us, and she did – and that was the first and only time she's ever crossed the Green Line. We haven't spoken about politics since."

This element of controversy makes Avigail alert to the fact that Efrat's future is not altogether secure, despite the settlement's ongoing expansion. Chen's family lived in the Israeli settlement of Gush Katif prior to the withdrawal from Gaza and, reappearing from the kitchen momentarily, Chen is quick to criticise the government that he feels betrayed his family.

"My brother was kicked out of Gush Katif. He had lived there for fifteen years with his family in a beautiful house – we fell in love with the place when we went to visit – and he didn't believe they would actually have to leave. They stayed till the very end, until they were taken out on the buses, and now he's living in a tiny caravan with his wife and six children, instead of his enormous house. It's changed him politically. He used to vote [the left wing party] Meretz, but after this he switched to Likud"

"That's why we wouldn't trust the government to take care of us," Avigail chips in. "The majority of Israelis think whatever happens to the Jews in the territories, they've got it coming. I wouldn't be surprised if Efrat was given back at some point, although I think it would

151

be the last to be given back, but if we had to leave we'd be the first to go. We wouldn't put our trust in the government to look after us. And if there was trouble here, I wouldn't trust the government to look after us either. There's no pressure on the government to look after the settlers."

Nevertheless, Avigail does not oppose the idea of leaving Efrat on principle "providing it was for the right reasons."

"If I could find the same quality of life elsewhere I would be happy to leave; I don't mind if it's inside or outside the Green Line. You never know if a settlement's going to be given back. Personally I believe the Jews have the right to be here, but if we believed there was to be real peace, we'd give up our house for its sake."

That said, Avigail is unwilling to make the first move, putting the quality of life for her family above all other considerations. She believes that the same is true of other Efrat residents, even the oxymoronic left wing settlers amongst them.

"People live here and vote Meretz, and they will leave their houses when they're asked, but they're not going to lead by example."

Avigail herself votes for Likud, even though she doesn't like their leader Benyamin Netanyahu, supporting the centre-right party "by default", as the only non-extreme, non-religious party that does not actively promote the evacuation of the settlements. And just as Avigail's ideal of a peace agreement between Israel and the Palestinians is undermined by her preference of a right wing party, so is her vision of co-existence marred by disillusionment, as she blights her own image of the perfect Middle East with doubt:

"Ideally I'd like to think that Jews and Arabs could live together peacefully, but I'm pessimistic about the chances of that happening."

For the time being, though, Avigail feels relatively secure in Efrat, believing that the settlement is, for now, safe from both the threat of evacuation and the danger of violence or terror.

"In 2002 the security was bad here, but since then I feel more secure on the streets of Efrat than I do in Tel Aviv. It's a suburb, a nice little town that feels very safe. I feel safe on the road to Jerusalem too. Maybe these are delusions, but that's how it feels."

Perhaps there is an element of Michael's "rationalised fear" to Avigail's sense of security, but there is a tangible reality to this security too and after our encounter with Boel, it is clear to see the price at which the Efrat residents' sense of sanctuary comes. Avigail listens with a furrowed brow as we relay Boel's story, and the discomfort on her face is evident as she hears about the flipside of the settlement's quiet streets and homogeneous neighbourhoods.

"It's embarrassing that the guards have to stand over the Arabs while they work," admits Avigail. "But the bottom line is that the people who brought in the bombs were labourers themselves, known by all the residents of the *yeshuv*. They weren't strangers. We didn't used to have guards with the workers, but we've had to learn from experience."

"But I don't like it," Avigail concedes, after a pause.

The thought appears to have revived a memory, buried beneath the polished stone and clean streets of Efrat, of another period of interaction between Jews and Palestinians, before the walls and the violence tore the two peoples apart. Hardly a golden era of friendship and understanding, but Avigail recalls her relations with the surrounding Palestinians with genuine fondness.

"There used to be a lot of interaction with the Arabs around here. We used to go into Bethlehem and Hebron all the time to go shopping, or to have an ice cream. It was a completely different way of life – I used to holiday in Sinai as a kid, but not any more. The first Intifada changed all that. It will never go back to how it was."

Avigail points to the economic benefits of the previously more benign occupation, like others before her who have highlighted the economic success of Palestinian market towns like Bidya and Mescha that enjoyed high levels of Israeli custom before the outbreak of the second Intifada. However, in doing so Avigail seems unwilling to recognise that, like any nationalist movement, Palestinian nationalism will not be sated by financial provisions alone.

"It was good for them and good for us. People used to drive into Beit Jalla to have their cars fixed or to do their shopping, but now it's all gone. They've got no money and no economy."

If the first Intifada turned Israelis away from visiting Palestinian towns, the violence of the second cemented the walls between the peoples and cloaked any sense of hope for those like Avigail behind an impenetrable veil of mistrust.

"Efrat used to be such an example for Jewish Arab relations. The former head of the town was very good friends with the Arabs in the surrounding towns and made a point of improving relations between us. We had an incredible medical centre here which was opened and the whole point was that it provided free medical services for all the Arabs in the region, and the ambulances used to travel all over. But then a suicide bomber walked into the centre and blew it up."

"My cousin's husband was one of the injured and he had skin grafts all over his body because of the scars. So now there's no relation. Efrat was such an example at the time and now it's all fallen apart."

Irit and Moshe claim that a survey, conducted to investigate people's reasons for living in Efrat, found the top four reasons to be education, society, value for money and ideology, in that order. Certainly Avigail and Chen seem to fit neatly into those statistics, seeking a certain quality of life rather than making any specific ideological statement. On the other hand, it would seem that this is only half the picture. Because for all of Avigail and Chen's youth and liberal outlook on social issues, despite their trendy flat with its modern Ikea furniture, their secular, progressive ideologies and their refreshing lack of ethno-religious dogma, a house in Efrat is a statement in itself and, as intelligent, politically engaged people, they must be aware that if they are not making that statement loudly, they are nevertheless giving it credence. And like most residents of the *Shtachim*, ideological or otherwise, they are left jaded by years of conflict. For all that Avigail and the Meretz supporters around her might claim to be prepared to move out for the sake of peace, peace remains far from the horizon, a horizon to which their backs are turned in any case. And in the meantime the quality of life in Efrat – a quality enforced by armed guards, at a considerable expense – ensures that they are going nowhere in a hurry.

A bigger picture

At just a twenty minute drive from Efrat, our table in the small, ramshackle garden of the Aroma coffee shop set back from Jerusalem's fragrant suburban streets, is a world away from the settlement's recurring red-roofs and silent tarmac roads. Our notebooks don't turn the heads of the coffee-and-cake queuing customers, nor do we feel out of place amongst the diverse and dissociated tables of drinkers, smokers and chatters. It is fitting then that when our interviewee – Irit and Moshe's 29-year old son, Elad – wanders in, his shaved head, broad, dozy smile and large hoop earring sets him peoples apart from the average Efrat settler.

Elad has had just two hours sleep since his night shift at a residential care home for disabled adults, and when he greets us it is with the languid air of the under-rested but content. Naturally at ease, Elad orders a coffee and, in flawless British English, begins to tell us how he went from being a religious settler kid in the notoriously extreme Hebron settlement, Kiryat Arba, to a Jerusalem-residing left winger, with dreams of a binational Israel for Jews and Palestinians.

With his father Moshe the *mazkir* [secretary] of the *yeshuv*, Elad spent the first three years of his life in Kiryat Arba, a period he describes as "a black hole in my past", before moving with his family to Efrat. A resident of the settlement until he joined the army, Elad was aware that his status as a young Israeli settler set him apart from others.

"I was a part of Efrat growing up, but I always had an attraction to not being separate from the Israeli mainstream. When we walked around with *kippot* on our heads we felt different from most people. You felt strange, like a bit of a weirdo, but I didn't want to be different; I was very attached to the mainstream Israel culture. I wanted to go to concerts. I liked secular people. But at the same time I had this religious background that made me different."

Nevertheless, like all Israeli teenagers, Elad turned eighteen and prepared to enter the army, the great leveller of Israeli society, where his feelings of difference would doubtless be smoothed away in the country's biggest melting pot. But his dreams of achieving oneness with his country didn't turn out as he expected.

"When I was young I hoped I'd be a hero. I wanted to give my soul to my country, so I became a paratrooper, believing in the need to defend our country. But when I got there I found myself doing things that I didn't think I would have to do. Doing things that I don't identify with, and I found myself changing my mind."

"I started to understand the Peace Now slogan 'the occupation corrupts'. I grew up in Efrat so I was used to going through the checkpoints every day, seeing all the Arabs standing in the queues to get through – it was something I was blind to. But it was only once I was in the army that I realised that in order for me to live in Efrat the army needs to go to homes in the middle of the night, and that I'd have to do lots of things that felt really wrong... For example, on one occasion we were inside a village in the middle of the night, going into a house and waking the entire family up so that we could take a sixteen year old boy, by force, to a Shabak [Israeli internal security] investigation – we didn't know why, but we had to accept what we had been told. No one knew what the boy had done, but some of my friends felt the sense of justice so strongly that they started to beat him up."

Elad shakes his head slowly, and for a moment he appears distant, tired; lost in the past, but he comes to with an assertion of his current principles, demonstrating the extent to which his present outlook has been shaped by the lessons and mistakes of growing up amongst war.

"The most important thing for me is that we shouldn't harm innocent people. We need to have a system that allows us not to harm innocents – that demands us not to. That's the principle that I feel most strongly about – hurting innocent people harms our chances for peace. This goes together with my Jewish sense; with all the principles I grew up on... Probably most of my friends won't agree with me and will say we have no choice; that we're not doing it on purpose; that we're in a situation of survival and if we're not strong we won't survive. But I believe we're stronger than we see ourselves... The army changed my views when I saw the price we have to pay to continue this situation. I realised how the army works. How much force we use. I'm not saying we shouldn't use force to secure ourselves but there's no doubt we're using way too much."

A spell in Hebron, beside his birthplace of Kiryat Arba, opened his eyes further still.

"In Hebron I saw how the army acts out of frustration based on things that don't relate to the situation there. Lots of things the army does are based on boredom, with no particular thought behind them. As a soldier you're on an eight hour shift, then you have eight hours off and then you're on again. It drove me crazy. You get so bored that sometimes people do things just to have action. They try to create a situation where they can use their weapon, to pass the time – which is wrong. When you have a weapon in your hand it's not a game."

When he finished his army service, Elad was a changed man. Far from having become the hero he had dreamed of being as a child, he felt a different emotion altogether.

"I had to run away; to leave Israel. I was so un-proud of what I had done in the army that I wanted more than anything to feel proud again, so I started to do things to *make myself* feel proud again. I came to Ireland and England and I got involved in youth work – which changed the way I thought about the world. England is a place where the concept of tolerance is much more wide-spread. It's very different from Israel – and I learned from that. And my contact with the Jewish community in England expanded my Jewish perspective, because until then I had been very influenced by the Jewish Israeli per-spective.

"Then when I came back to Israel I started working with disabled people and I realised I didn't want to go back to the army [for *miluim* [reserve duty]]. I didn't want to use a weapon again. I realised that when I was in uniform I wasn't so much a messenger of the state of Israel as a messenger of other things. When you're wear-ing your uniform you're supposed to be serving your country but I wasn't serving it in the way I wanted to – I thought maybe I'd be sent to do things that I'm not happy with.

"I thought about refusing – but it's very hard to refuse in this country; to make the statement that I'm not will-ing to take part. Then you have the fact that my parents still live in the territories and the government says we need to secure them with force – and I didn't know any other way. So instead I do my *miluim* and I spend my time trying to raise awareness amongst my friends in order to make us act more humanely. And in fact the last *miluim* in Gaza was the first time that I felt that what we were doing was legitimate. It was the scariest *miluim* of my life – we were based on the border going into Gaza on daily operations, getting into real fights – but it was the first time that I felt my role was justified. We were guarding a legitimate border and the operations were to find tunnels going under the border to blow up IDF bases. I felt that at last, after five years of doing *miluim*, we were doing the right thing."

Nevertheless, Elad hates his reserve duties, the gravity of his slow, considered sentences reflecting the thought he has given to the reality of what it means to serve as a combat soldier in the Israeli army. With Irit's first husband having died in the Yom Kippur War, Elad grew up in a family where "the presence of this dead person was always around" and that has added to his sense of the fragility of the soldier's situation.

"I fear something similar will happen to me. When I go to the army I'm afraid of dying. I've reached a state where I know that just by leaving to go into the army – even just to go into training – the army is a place where you have to kill or be killed and you have to be *willing* to kill or be killed. I have strong feelings that maybe I shouldn't be doing this. I want to live, but it's very hard to live when you know you have to do that.

"I've talked to my mum about this and although she understands me she feels, unlike me, that even though we're using force we have justice on our side and that we're right to use force. The things that drive me crazy don't drive her crazy... And when I ask her to write a letter to say 'I lost one husband, I'm not willing to lose another boy', she refuses. She won't take responsibility for releasing me from the army."

Elad's gradual shift from right to left means that he no longer wants to live in the Occupied Territories, nor is he comfortable in his home town any longer. Drawing stares from the residents with his earring and without a *kippah*, Elad says there is now "nothing for him in Efrat" other than the occasional family dinner. Nevertheless, his views on whether Israel should pull out from his parents' settlement are not black and white. Describing himself as "kind of left wing", Elad supported the Disengagement from Gaza in 2005, believing it was "the right thing to do". And unlike many Israelis who hold up the cross-border conflicts that have continued since then as proof that the Palestinians are not ready for their own state, Elad expected that there would be trouble between Israel and Gaza in the short term and supported the *hitnatkut* regardless.

The lesson that Elad has taken from Gaza is that it is not good for Israel to act unilaterally, without agreement from the other side. And despite waiting to see what the situation with Gaza will be "in the long term", the rocket barrages from Gaza have qualified his support of further withdrawals from the West Bank.

"On the one hand I think that if this [Disengagement] is what we need to do for peace, then we should do it, but on the other hand, how can we be sure that it will bring peace? We need to strengthen the moderate Palestinian leaders. In principle I believe that peace can come – I really believe that if we want it, we can achieve it, but it is hard to believe in it."

And what about Efrat? Would he be able to move his own family out for the sake of peace?

"No. If I had to take my parents, my family, my friends, out of Efrat, I wouldn't be able to do it. I would say this is my home, my house – no, I don't want to think about it. On the one hand I believe we have a moral and historical right to live in the Territories... And Efrat and the Gush Etzion are different to other settlements because they were Jewish areas pre 1948. The lands were bought by Jewish people; there's a large population of Jews there now and not a big population of Palestinians. I believe we have a right to be in Gush Etzion. In principle... But on the other hand we need to separate from the Territories. Maybe one day we can live together with Arabs but now the price is too high. People are dying.

"I want to get to an agreement that gives the Arabs their rights. There's no doubt we're using too much force in order to secure the settlements. There are some small settlements, like Har Hebron that demand lots of force to sustain them, but then there are the big settlement blocs like Ma'aleh Adumim, Ariel and Efrat – these are different. I don't believe it's simply about 1967 borders. We need a new situation on the map."

However, the complexity of the situation leads Elad to come to some rather unorthodox conclusions for an Israeli Jew, let alone someone from the settlements. It is hard to tell whether the slight glaze in his eyes is due to tiredness or to the contemplation of his ideal, or both, but Elad has a clear vision for the Middle East he would like to live in one day.

"My aim is to live together on the same land. The first stage is to establish a Palestinian state, but after a few decades we could dismantle it and have one shared state. The Jewish state is a necessity now, especially after the Holocaust, but in fifty years from now maybe the state could be binational – you'd have a state for Jews, but it wouldn't be a Jewish state. Some say that if the land is mine then only I should be here, but I see Judaism in a different way – I believe that if it's mine I can share it with others. We don't need to discriminate... When I really, really try to think about it I think it can't go any other way. There's no other solution; we're so caught up together and we both want to live in the same place. I'll be sad if I can't take my children to the landscapes I grew up in; the landscapes that I'm attached to. Judea is as historic as Jerusalem – we read about it in the Torah – so why shouldn't we be able to walk there? Because we're not wanted there. But I want us to be wanted there. If we can live in peace together, why can't we live in the same state? But the question is how do we learn to live together?"

These words might not seem radical to some, but they mean the end of the state of Israel in its current form and for many Israelis, not to mention Elad's former neighbours in Efrat, that idea is anathematical. So how do Elad's friends and family feel about his transformation from one extreme of the Israeli political spectrum to the other, and his transition from religious to secular? And how does Elad feel about his family and former neighbours who hold very different views from his own?

"The people I love, I love because of who they are, even if I disagree with them – and I do strongly disagree with some of my friends. But I'll never hate [them]. I want to separate the friendship and the ideology. Just as I think I can live in peace with Arabs, I can live in peace with those people who are different from me; those who have different opinions from my own. As long as we both have respect for one another; and my friends do respect me. And whoever doesn't respect me – well, I'm not going to fight for that.

"I feel I'm continuing in the way I was raised, even though I'm different from how they tried to make me. I'm going along with my Jewish principles. I was raised to be human and I've had all sorts of conflict and I've found my own way to live through it... I can think what I think and it's not like my parents don't talk to me, or my friends don't respect me. I've created my own identity; my own way of thinking. And I think people respect me for that."

Again, that tired, languorous gaze is laced with contentment, as though Elad is at last satisfied with who he is now, and as we finish the interview and Elad heads off to his work for a party at the care home, his parting words lend weight to that look in his eyes. He smiles.

"I love my work," he says. "It's work that makes me proud of what I do."

Chapter Five
Karnei Shomron:
Jews versus Israelis

Taking the wheel

"There's a war going on here – between the Israeli dream and the Jewish dream."

The calm tone and quiet voice with which Moshe Feiglin utters this sentence give the far right Likud party subversive an air of measured rationality, but an intense fire burns within the pinprick pupils of his tiny eyes, augmenting his words. Feiglin, who in 1997 served six months of an eighteen-month jail sentence for sedition, has been fighting the Israeli mainstream for years; a personal enemy of Benyamin Netanyahu, the wiry resident of the West Bank settlement of Karnei Shomron was then engaged in a fierce battle with the Prime Minister for control of the right wing mainstream party, with the decision to be taken by party members at the primaries, six weeks later. Having begun his political career as an outsider pissing into the mainstream political tent, creating the Zo Artzeinu [This is Our Land] movement to protest the Israeli government's cooperation with Yasser Arafat, Feiglin's time in jail persuaded him that the only way he could change the Likud party was by entering the tent himself – and proceeding to piss all over it.

"I joined Likud in 2000, saying from day one that I am joining to run to become the head of Likud and the Prime Minister. I don't want to be part of a new direction – I want to take the wheel and lead it. I have my own political agenda, the Jewish Leadership movement [his new organisation], and I want to use Likud as the tool to implement it... The politicians of Likud understood that there was a big force here and each one tried to bring me near to them – but then they understood that I'm independent and they began to fight against me."

With one leg stretched onto a plastic garden chair on the patio of his large home, stately mountains rising behind his lawn at the edge of the settlement, Feiglin seems like a man who is utterly sure of himself and the path he has chosen. A resident of Karnei Shomron for fourteen years, he describes life in the *Shtachim* simply as "great" and was unfazed by two Intifadas, not once having considered leaving the settlement. His mission now is to effect a complete overhaul of Israeli politics and society, beginning with the takeover of the Likud party, with the mobilisation of the supporters of his Jewish Leadership movement. Once in charge of the mainstream political party, Feiglin intends to rectify what he perceives as the declining Jewish identity of the state of Israel. Representing the many disaffected voices we have heard throughout the territories that bemoan the Israeli mainstream's lack of Jewish values, Feiglin gives political voice to Esther of Mitzpeh Yeriho's perceived dichotomy between those who are Israeli and those who are Jewish. For Feiglin, the problem lies with the Israeli establishment whom he deems to be anti-Jewish and a corrupting influence on the traditional values of the state.

"There has been a war of dreams since the first day of Israel – whether to have a country of all its citizens, or a Jewish state. Most people in Israel want a Jewish state, but a small minority wants to erase any sense of Jewish identity and create a Singapore of the Middle East. And this minority is running the country."

For Feiglin, the peace process is just another step on the road towards the eradication of Jewish identity in Israel.

"I understood that Oslo was not a peace process but rather it was a process wherein so-called Palestinians are brought here to help the Israelis to force their opinions on the Jews. 70-80% of Israelis, if asked whether they see themselves as Israeli or Jewish first, will say 'I'm Jewish,' but the country is run by people who see themselves as Israeli, not Jewish. The state is run by those who want a liberal, Western state, built around whatever the latest popular values are, that has nothing to do with Jewish values."

Echoing the persecution complex that afflicts many of the settlers we have spoken to, Feiglin speaks matter-of-factly about how the Oslo accords, all the way through to the Disengagement from Gaza, were not about peace, but rather about crushing the settlers and eradicating any sense of Jewishness from the state of Israel.

"Oslo used the ideas of peace, territory and war to force new Israeli values on the majority, but you can't *create* an Israeli identity. When you live in a Jewish state in the land of Israel, with the patriarchs buried in Hebron; Rachel's tomb; the Temple Mount in Jerusalem and all the territories mentioned in the Bible, Jewish identity is calling from under your feet, from beneath every stone. So the whole process of getting rid of the territories is about getting rid of the Jewish connection to the land so that they can erase the Jewish identity of the state.

"And the settlers are the biggest threat to those who don't want a Jewish state. We connect Judaism to history through the land. We're the people who are paving the road for a modern Jewish state to be developed on holy land... [so] for me it was obvious that when we had 10,000 refugees [of the Israeli settlement in Gaza] in our own land, it was a move designed to destroy the settlers. [The government] had to show them."

Feiglin's foray into mainstream politics, then, is to tackle this perceived problem of Israel's de-judaisation head on and "replace the leaders with an Israeli dream with leaders with a Jewish dream." But what exactly is this Jewish dream? And what are Feiglin's proposals for achieving it?

165

At the more moderate end of his manifesto are rather benign policies that would not seem out of place in the old One Nation Tory handbook, including increasing the levels of religious education at school and bolstering the family unit in the face of its perceived erosion. However, by the time Feiglin gets onto the subjects of immigration and territorial conflict, it becomes clear why even the right wingers of Likud have come to fear the damage he could do to their party's mainstream image.

"Who is a Jew? It is as the Torah says – anyone with a Jewish mother. So our immigration laws must be made to fit this – either the mother must be Jewish or you must convert in the traditional way. We have half a million people from Russia who are not Jewish. They go into the army and they take an oath on the New Testament. The Jewish Russians complain about them – there are tens of churches in Ashdod and Ashkelon. Why are they so important for Israel? They don't want it to be a Jewish state.... I think Jewish citizenship in the Jewish state should go to Jews, based on nationality and, in very specific cases, to non Jews who prove that they accept the Jewish sovereignty on their land... As for the Russian Jews who are already citizens, I don't know how to deal with them. I would hope that many of them would convert and accept Judaism and that the others will understand that this is not their place and will find their future elsewhere. We will have to endure a few generations of payment for the stupidity of bringing them here in the first place."

"As for the Arabs – and I make no distinction between Arabs within the Green Line or without – they have proved that they don't accept Jewish sovereignty over the land of Israel... They build wherever they want without permits. They don't pay taxes. They're like a growing state within Israel... We need to admit we have a problem, but Israeli politicians don't like to talk about it. We should explain to them who this country belongs to – I don't want to get into details about how to do this, but the problem is not the Arabs, it's the Jews. When the Jews finally begin to understand for themselves that the land belongs to them and they gather around Jewish identity and are proud of who they are, the Arab problem will disappear slowly... Even according to existing laws we can solve most of the problems. Tens of thousands of buildings can be destroyed according to Israeli law. When Israel is ruled by proud Jewish leaders and the Arabs understand that these buildings will be destroyed, they'll begin to obey."

In Feiglin's view, a truly Jewish Israel would favour Jews of the world over non-Jewish residents of Israel, and that hierarchy would be enshrined in the country's political system.

"I would like to see two houses in the Knesset. The upper house would represent the entire Jewish nation and would be constituted of 70% Israeli Jews and 30% from world Jewry. It would be for Jews only, voted for by Jews only and the lower house would also include non Jews, would be voted for by all citizens of Israel and would deal with regional things like sewage etc. This is a Jewish state, so every Jew would have a vote – and that includes from outside Israel. I would also change the law that says an Arab can be the Prime Minister."

Feiglin's uncompromising model of a Jewish state is intended to leave so little room for any non Jews, specifically Palestinians, as to squeeze them out. But in case they don't get the message, Feiglin advocates catalysing their departure.

"With the money that Israel put into the Oslo process – $200m since 1995 – we could have given $0.25m to each so called Palestinian family to start a new life elsewhere in the world. Today most of the Arabs want to leave the territories because their fight means that the standard of living has fallen by 90%. They want to leave, so instead of working on bringing non Jews to the country we should focus on... convincing and helping Arabs to leave the country by offering them the kind of money that they'll have to take. We have to transfer our efforts from a false Israel dream into a Jewish dream and we can solve the problem. The question is do you want a Jewish state? I have human solutions to the problem."

Incredibly, Feiglin is adamant that the international community will respect such ethnic cleansing and give its consent to mass population transfer.

"The world will react well. They won't call Israel racist. Surprisingly, when Jews behave in a proud way, upright, without bending over, the world respects them. It's when they give up their national pride and try to be nice to the world that they get more pressure from the outside world. When you try to gain the world's respect by giving up your national honour and identity, you get the opposite reaction from the world."

In the tranquil setting of his private garden, it is easy for Feiglin to exude such confidence. But as a right wing settler Feiglin is geographically, politically and religiously remote from the centre of power and the Israeli mainstream and one gets a sense that his war between Jews and Israelis is being fought more virulently in his own head than in the consciousness of most Israeli citizens, whose voting behaviour at least does not condone a radical shake-up of the Israeli political system. Voices similar in kind to Feiglin's that we have heard so far have been sounded from the remotest reaches of isolated, extreme settlements and it is hard to imagine that Feiglin will find enough support to bring his extremist policies to fruition. In his own words it "looks like we need a miracle" for Feiglin to win the Likud primaries, with Bibi Netanyahu leading his closest contender by 75% to 14%.

However, the fact that Feiglin's democratic revolution has made him a prominent force in one of the most significant mainstream Israeli political parties reflects the growing volume of these isolated, disaffected settler voices and suggests that they have started to galvanise themselves into a coherent political bloc; a self-confessed

Jewish army in the war against the Israeli state. In the absence of a miracle[15], it is difficult to say whether Feiglin will pale into insignificance or whether his success is portentous of things to come. In either case though, the voices that Feiglin represents are unlikely to disappear and, whether they are represented independently or co-opted into the mainstream, they look set to have an increasing influence on the Israeli political system for as long as they remain on the landscape.

A friendly face

When we first arrived in Karnei Shomron, and before we'd spent time with the *yeshuv*'s hardline politician-in-residence, our host collected us from the bus stop to drive us to his home. "Just behind you is where the *pigua* [attack] happened," he stated flatly as we clambered into the car; the five-year old incident still worthy of mention, but not of elaboration – at least, not so early on in our acquaintance. Later on, we are told that the bombing killed three local teenagers and injured thirty other diners at the settlement's pizzeria. The memory is seared on every resident, haunting their nightmares and dominating the way in which they view the political situation, thanks to the highly personal and highly savage way the conflict was brought to their doorstep all those years ago.

Our host, Ritchie [not his real name] carries a pistol on him at all times: "It's really not easy to get, or keep, a licence," he complains bitterly, hoisting up his trousers to keep the gun secure in his waistband. We have stopped by the roadside on a quick tour of the settlement, and as we get back in the car Ritchie points up the street, telling us that just outside the perimeter of the *yeshuv*, atop the tallest hill in the area, stands Moshe Zar's fortress-style mansion, once reputed to be the largest private residence in the West Bank.

Now an elderly man, the wealthy Zar is one of the most notorious settler figures in the occupation's forty-year history, having bought and allegedly stolen vast amounts of Palestinian land throughout the region. Loathed by his Arab neighbours, Zar is a legend in his home-town of Karnei Shomron.

Ritchie's wife, Rebecca [not her real name] welcomes us into their home with the same effusiveness common to most families we've encountered thus far. Shabbat will be upon us in a few hours, and the house is a hive of activity as she prepares food and sets the table for the evening meal; we are shooed upstairs to get settled into our room before coming back down to introduce ourselves properly to our hosts.

Rebecca explains that some parts of the *yeshuv* are more religious than others: "the Russians here are mostly secular – they refuse to make an 'Israeli home', but their kids will. We've got the kids, but the adults aren't ours," she notes. When the couple married and moved to Israel from the States, they first set up home in Gush Katif, living there between 1981 and 1983, before moving back across the Green Line to Ra'anana, whilst they waited for their house to be built in Karnei Shomron. "Living in Ranaana, or Netanya, or somewhere similar [inside Israel proper] would have fulfilled my Zionist dream," says Ritchie, "but living in the *Shtachim* does as well, plus slightly more on top..."

We set off for Friday night services at the *shul*, which is a standard settlement structure, teeming with modern Orthodox men (and a few women behind the dividing screens). On the way home, Ritchie has to make a detour to drop off an M16 semi-automatic rifle at a friend's house; the carrying of weapons being permitted on the Sabbath, since they are necessary for *pikuach nefesh* [preserving life], and thus exempt from the stringent rulings governing Shabbat activity.

Dinner is a noisy affair; friends of Ritchie and Rebecca have been invited, along with their four children, and high-spirited conversation flows from the off. One of the daughters sets out her stall early on: when we mention our recent visit to Kfar Adumim's *wadi*, she agrees that it is a sight well worth visiting, on one condition – "the *wadi is* fun", she remarks, "but only when it's not full of Arabs". There is no trace of hostility in her voice, nor even of guilt or shame at making such an explicitly racist remark. Life in the *Shtachim* has conditioned her to believe that either such talk is not a social gaffe, or that – in fact – it is an admirable quality to display; that showing one's antipathy towards the Palestinians is a way of reminding those within earshot that the speaker is fully 'on message' when it comes to the settler take on the conflict.

Politics by no means dominates the discourse, with a raucous debate breaking out on the subject of the national lottery. Everyone round the table has strong opinions on whether or not it is worth buying a ticket; one of the guests' sons smugly declares that he wouldn't enter the 50m shekel draw "because then I'd have to share the winnings with someone else"; he'd rather enter the 20m shekel version, which he believes attracts fewer punters, thus reducing the chances of the top prize having to be divided up. Soon, however, conversation turns to recollections of the 2002 bombing of the *yeshuv* pizzeria. Some suggest that the bomber must have had inside help, since he had apparently been able to access the most crowded part of the mall area before setting off his explosives – speculation abounds, but of course no one at the table knows for sure. Two of the older children at the table had worked regularly with Arab labourers in local businesses up until the outbreak of the second Intifada – "but once it began, they were all fired".

Having quizzed me on my army service, Miriam – daughter of the guests – suddenly realises that my unit must have been involved in the Disengagement of 2005, and more specifically that we had been part of the operation to clear out the West Bank settlement of Homesh.

My participation is seemingly tolerated by Miriam and her siblings, who likely put it down to me being a straight-off-the-boat immigrant soldier only following orders, rather than perceiving me as a die-hard anti-settlement activist. Earlier in the meal, two of her brothers had boasted of having lived in Homesh at the time of the withdrawal, having seen it as their duty to bolster the numbers of those protesting the evacuation – they still go to anti-government rallies, they tell us, including the recent 'Return to Homesh' march which we attended as well. Moshe, the older of the two (and a student at Bar Ilan University), says that he is part of Panim Mul Panim – a settler group who "go door to door to explain to secular city dwellers what settlers are like as people". Such canvassing is seen as vital to win the hearts and minds of the Israeli mainstream; Moshe and his fellow activists set much stall by breaking down prejudices and stereotypes via personal contact – consequently, they seem happy to talk to us as part of our research, in order to utilise any opportunity to state the case for the settler enterprise.

Mention is made of a local legend in which a resident of a nearby Arab village wandered into a grocery store with his sister's head in a bag; honour killing is cited as another reason why the culture clash between Islam and the West is too severe for the sides to ever live side by side in harmony. Rather than see the 'head in a bag' story as an extreme manifestation of a malaise that afflicts adherents of patriarchal religions the world over, it is politically more expedient to isolate Muslims as the sole practitioners of such crimes.

A discussion starts over whether to take precautions when living in the *Shtachim*; Miriam declares her outright refusal to wear a bulletproof vest when driving: "It's our country – why should I have to?", as though ownership of the land will keep her safe from enemy fire. Seth asks her why she takes such a view, given that she would wear a seatbelt in order to protect herself in the event of a collision; her mother interrupts with a strange comparison: "It's like the annoying security tags you get when you're trying on clothes – why should I be punished because of thieves?" Her analogy is confusing; her sentiments in relation to the Palestinians less so: "An Arab could walk into any *yeshuv* or Israeli city and feel safe, but no Jew could walk into an Arab village [and remain secure]".

Such proclamations seem incongruous in the wake of what we heard in Kedumim, when Aryeh described nonchalantly buying ice creams for his family in nearby Arab towns; likewise Israeli activists pay daily visits to Arab villages to participate in joint protests with their Palestinian counterparts without encountering any danger at the hands of their hosts. At the same time, Boel – the worker we met in Efrat – maintained that many Palestinians felt unsafe setting foot in Israeli towns, despite the assertions of Rebecca that settlers wouldn't harm a hair on a visiting Palestinian's head. Her son Moshe goes a step further: "I doubt they'd even make it out of there alive". Rebecca picks up the baton, recalling the time she "got a puncture when driving through an Arab village – I kept on going just on the rims, just to get away..." No one walks outside the *yeshuv* any more, we are told; the sense of fear and doubt has them all in a vice-like grip, akin to Londoners considering parts of the inner-city no-go areas thanks to perceptions of street crime and violence.

Miriam, ever keen to voice her opinions – no matter how crude – tells of soldiers who relieve boredom at checkpoints by "going up to an Arab, hugging them, and saying 'hi – you're the *mashtap* [collaborator], aren't you?'" within earshot of other Palestinians. "Then he's dead for sure..."

Her mother is an English teacher in Ra'anana, and recalls the time she asked her pupils to write an essay on 'the perfect murder'. One asked whether anyone could be the victim – she said yes, so they asked if Prime Minister Rabin could be the target. "You'll get an 'A' in that case," she replied. "And then that weekend Rabin was killed. I was terrified I'd be arrested," she says smiling.

The younger generation complain that their university professors are all "biased against settlers", as well as the Israeli police – "who beat settlers at marches" – and even security guards in city malls ("one wouldn't let us in because we were wearing orange shirts"). The sense of being sidelined and maligned by the mainstream is obvious; they wear the 'outlaw' tag with a hint of rebellious pride, it appears. Ritchie and Rebecca speak proudly of their son, Elitsur, writing an essay in which he called for Gush Katif settlers to be compensated "for their loss of community" in the wake of the Disengagement. "His professor was very impressed, and said he hadn't thought of that aspect before," remembers Rebecca. In her eyes, it is of major importance that *yeshuvim* have a sense of being "a community, rather than simply a neighbourhood". She says there is no racism amongst the children in Karnei Shomron – "they all get along, and don't distinguish between Russian, Ethiopian, Yemenite, and so on". However, when it comes to Arab youth, she still thinks "they shouldn't integrate with Israeli kids" – demonstrating a two-tier approach common to the Israeli right: racism between different sectors of Jewish society is strictly forbidden; integration and coexistence with Arabs is different, and (more often than not) an unacceptable proposition to swallow.

Ritchie tells us that there will never be peace in the region: "The only solution is a military one. We have to annihilate the enemy; the Talmud says that he who is merciful to the enemy ends up becoming an enemy of the merciful". Hindus, on the other hand, "are OK – because they're always ready to kill a Muslim", he laughs. We ask whether he considers Palestinians to be Amalek[16], given his talk of annihilating enemies and showing no mercy; he stops short, considering his response. "I don't think Palestinians are necessarily Amalek," he replies. "They're more like Moabites – the Moabites felt aggrieved at their land being taken, whereas the Midianites attacked the Israelites for no reason whatsoever. Therefore the Israelites slaughtered the Midianites, but because the Moabites had a slight justification, a deal was made with them instead of killing them – they became slaves, or something..."

Rebecca then returns to the sense of ostracism that she, and her family and friends, so keenly feel. "Settlers are seen as expendable by the rest of the country – whenever a settler is killed, the first thing people say is 'but why did they choose to live there? [in the *Shtachim*]'. That's why we feel like sub-standard citizens in our own country. The government doesn't care about us – they used to let the bombs fall on Gush Katif all the time; the bombs were seen as 'inevitable'. But we have the right to *fight back*," she declares animatedly. "They wouldn't let us fire on people throwing rocks – why? I say there will have to be collateral damage [when dealing with the Palestinian militants]... If we have to destroy a family's home because snipers have taken it over, then so be it." Ritchie agrees, when asked how to deal with opponents of Israel. "Placating them isn't the right way," he says. "We need to decisively take control of the situation, and show them that we're strong," he concludes, before inviting the guests to open their prayer books to say grace after the meal.

Never again

After the family have returned from *shul* on Saturday, the lunchtime conversation casts some light on the origins of the family's hard line attitude.

It is hardly the most original thought to argue that the Holocaust has shaped the way that Israel conducts itself, and it can be overly simplistic to try to use the Jewish nation's past either to condone or condemn the country's attitudes towards the Palestinians. As Amos Oz writes, "in real life some victims of oppression... become more... sensitive to the sufferings of others... whereas other victims... become more vindictive"[17]. The claim that the Jews' history of suffering means they should know better is easily countered with the argument that their near annihilation means they must now be strong at all costs – and neither argument really allows for the complexity of the situation. Nevertheless, as we sit at the Shabbat lunch table, over-laden with meats and salads, and listen to Rebecca's family history, it is hard not to make the connection between the butchering of her parents' Jewish identity and her own political outlook, which prioritises the prosperity of Jewish identity above all else.

Rebecca's narration is matter of fact, her momsy smile now pulled tight, set with regret, as she clips her sprawling Brooklyn diphthongs from their usual sing-song, driving the narrative forward with a grim determination; this feels like an oft-told tale, though still not believed. She begins with the story of her mother, who escaped from Poland to New York at the start of the war, where she tried to earn money to pay for her brothers and sisters to come and join her but was unable to reunite her family, losing all but one of her ten siblings in the Holocaust. When that one surviving brother eventually went back to Poland to try and discover what had happened to their family, he "he was shot dead in the street by Poles."

Rebecca's father also came from Poland and managed to avoid being taken to the camps by going into hiding: "My father was a bit of a playboy and he went to a Polish girlfriend he had, who hid him."

The girl took him to her house in the country and concealed him and his brother inside a wall, where there was just enough space for the two of them to stand. Every day, the girl fed the hideaways, and at 3am each night she would fetch them from the wall and let them run around outside for a few minutes, so that they could stretch their legs, before returning to their hiding place. As for going to

176

the toilet, Rebecca says they "would do their business standing up". They remained in that hiding place for 29 months.

Once the war was over, Rebecca's father got on a boat for South America, but jumped ship at New Orleans and ended up in Brooklyn, where he met Rebecca's mother, who had begun work in a sweat shop to make ends meet. The couple married, but Rebecca's father died within seven years of respiratory illness, probably caused by his time living in the wall. As an illegal immigrant in America, not once did Rebecca's father vote in an American election.

Her parents' short marriage meant that Rebecca was an only child and when her own children were grown up, Rebecca recalls how her mother tried to dissuade her son from travelling back to Poland for the March of Living, an annual trip that brings Jewish teens from all over the world to Poland, to march from Auschwitz to Birkenau, in commemoration of the dead and celebration of the living. According to Rebecca's mother, such a trip ought to be rejected as it gives money to Poland, but Rebecca's argument was different, claiming that it was "the best kind of revenge – to come from a Jewish country and walk tall, with a *kippah* on your head, alive and healthy and proud to be Jewish." This, she claimed, was the ultimate response to the Poles "who shot and betrayed Jews, but never paid the price."

For Rebecca, this sense of Jewish pride against the odds shapes her attitude towards the Jewish people's collective conduct. It is as though the Jews have been given another chance in Israel, and Rebecca is eager for the Jewish people to live as a proud and prosperous nation; to continue to walk with their heads held high, their *kippot* placed prominently atop their crowns. Rebecca laments what she sees as a gradual erosion of the nation's Jewish identity.

"We feel so at home here. Everyone knows what Shabbat is, what Yom Tov[18] is. We can hold our heads high and there's no fuss... But Israel itself is becoming Hollywoodised; westernised. It's lost track of its character and no longer knows who it is... Israel wants to be a global village, to put democracy over its Jewishness and we're losing our Jewish identity. The Arabs know who they are, but the Jews in Israel are less Jewish than Jews in the rest of the world – it's like we're trying to give ourselves away."

Whilst Rebecca perceives a loss of Jewish identity throughout Israel, she believes that settlements like Karnei Shomron go against the grain, with the "global village" being replaced by a village of Jews from around the globe, but where she believes the sense of Jewish identity is stronger than elsewhere in Israel.

However, Rebecca's conception of Jewish identity, along with that of her husband Ritchie recalls that of their neighbour Moshe Feiglin: narrow and unwavering, and based entirely on their orthodox interpretation of religion. Settled in his place at the head of the family table, Ritchie seems well used to regaling his guests with tales as they eat the bounty of food before them, peppering his stories with metaphors and parables from the wealth of ancient Jewish literature that fills the bookcase to his rear. Whilst Ritchie's allusions to kings and prophets are more illustrative than dogmatic, they nevertheless conspire to indicate the kind of Jewish identity that he considers to be definitive. Israel, he argues, exists to be a Jewish state and although many believe that this refers to Jewish culture and not religion, Ritchie claims that these people's references – like those that populate his own sentences – are all religious in kind. For Ritchie and Rebecca, then, Jewish culture is nothing without the religion; the Jewish religion is what ought to define Israel's Jewish identity and it is Jewish religious education that Israel lacks.

This desire to fix Israel's Jewish identity in their own image influences the way that Rebecca and Ritchie regard their Palestinian neighbours. In having been given another chance in Israel, Rebecca cannot bear to see the Jewish people "give themselves away".

"The answers to Israel's problems aren't in trying to be like the West, but in admitting that Israel is a Jewish state... We must return to this, with more Jewish education, and then the Arabs can respect our sovereignty and have full civil rights [in Israel], but not political rights... This is Jewish land and Arabs must accept our sovereignty."

Sounding remarkably like Feiglin in their desire to establish full, permanent rule over the politically disenfranchised Palestinians of the West Bank, Ritchie and Rebecca do not share the politician's distrust of new immigrants who can be used to swell the ranks of the Jewish population of Greater Israel. In contrast to Feiglin, Ritchie is pleased of the fact that Israel "found one million Russians, who were almost all Jewish" and speaks optimistically of the chance of another million Jews coming to Israel from America. "Demography is a bugaboo," he says dismissively.

And as the Jewish people in Israel augments its sense of national religious pride, it must, according to Ritchie, assert its control over the land it holds, refusing to go soft on the enemy.

"The media demonise Israel and we give in too easily," Ritchie claims. Instead, he argues, Israel should "stand strong and destroy the enemy. We can't keep giving. We tried to give Arabs decent housing but they refused – they constantly preserve their underdog status in order to undermine Israel and make it a pariah."

However, as Ritchie and Rebecca project an image of an increasingly proud Jewish nation, with swollen numbers of new immigrants, standing strong in the face of an Arab enemy, Rebecca realises that such a confrontational model is liable to breed trouble of its own.

"Violence breeds violence and dialogue is important – we have to see that we are all human and have similar concerns – but what can you do? Islam is not a bad religion but fundamentalists have taken over who want to kill Jews. How can you stop people who only want to destroy Israel – who hate the foreign influence that attacked the heart of the Islamic region?"

Ritchie, too, admits that Islam itself is not the enemy, stating that "Islam has a good place for Jews. It can tolerate them – it won't kill them like Germany did, just because they're different."

Nevertheless, when it comes to finding a way to prevent the opposition between Jews and Palestinians through dialogue and contact, Rebecca's desire for the preservation and purity of Jewish identity trumps all.

"Dialogue is good but integration, bringing Arabs and Jews together, is not the key. We need to preserve our Jewish identity. Israel is too keen to lose it."

As if to illustrate the uniqueness of Israel's position, Rebecca holds up the example of the Israeli football team to make her point: "the Arabs in the team don't sing *HaTikva* [the national anthem]. Where else in the world could this happen? It's crazy!?"

The mention of the football team recalls the allusion of a young officer we had spoken to in the settlement of Elkana a few weeks earlier. Strikingly though, where he had used the image as a model to aspire to, Rebecca uses it to demonstrate the shortcomings of integration. The origins of Rebecca's eagerness for a strong, proud Jewish nation are obvious, and just as she wanted her son to flaunt that pride in the face of the Poles two generations after the Holocaust, she wants Israel to unite around its Jewish identity and ignore the call of the Western world to embrace democracy and Westernise in its image. By her own admission, however, Rebecca recognises that pitting a strong Jewish nation against a common Arab enemy will likely breed more animosity, but still she is unwilling to encourage models of integration or cooperation that might overcome such enmity. Instead, by fixing Israel's Jewish identity as religious, unmoving and without room for progression

180

or diversity, Rebecca and Ritchie's model of Jewish Israel begins to become repressive and restrictive, and, what's more, isolationist; at odds with both the West and its Arab neighbours. Rebecca's 'trust no one' attitude is perhaps understandable given her direct experience of recent Jewish history, but whether the channelling of such rejectionist nationalist politics, through the likes of Moshe Feiglin, is in fact likely to lead the Jewish people down the safest path to self-preservation is doubtful. Little wonder then that the mainstream voters of Israel, despite their jaded attitude towards the peace process, tend to reject such extremist politics for those that, in theory, allow for negotiation with the Palestinians, as well as the maintenance of a Western democratic political system.

Despite holding sway over the machinations of Israeli politics, inasmuch as they maintain control over the West Bank, people like Rebecca and Ritchie are marginalised when it comes to effecting the kind of Judaisation of the Israeli mainstream that they would like to see. As such, their isolationist politics have the effect of polarising them from the mainstream, while their rejection of mainstream Israeli Jewish identity as inauthentic risks pushing away the very people they want to influence. By promoting a single, contemporaneous model of Judaism and Jewish identity, and attempting to impose it on an unwilling society, they restrict the progressive, timeless nature of that identity that has allowed it to survive for millennia, suffocating its vitality and adaptability, thus strangling the very thing they seek to preserve. As a result, despite the efforts of the Panim Mul Panim project, the politics of settlers like Rebecca and Ritchie are likely to continue to scare off and alienate those who they wish to change, and further entrench the divisions between the right wing settlers and the mainstream Israeli centre.

The mask of authenticity

The sense of Jewish communal prosperity that Rebecca had championed is evident later in the afternoon when we visit some younger family friends of our hosts, who have instinctively invited us over for *seudah shlishit*, the third ritual meal of Shabbat. Several young couples sit around the large, open plan living room, dressed in crisp white shirts and summer dresses, children pouring over the sofa backs and under the table, and, as soon as we have stepped through the door, over our arms and shoulders too.

In the midst of their weekly social event, the parents of these young families are old friends, mostly having moved to the settlement as children from Canada and the US, and the quiet tree lined streets and bright green lawns outside are where they grew up. Despite a few incidents with stoned cars in years past, these families are comfortable and happy with their lives here, and as they talk of day care and jobs and the lengths of their commutes, they are reminiscent of young suburban families the world over.

However, beneath the chirpy surface of conventional conservativism lie some startlingly radical values that remind us just where we are. As we speak to Tuvia, the young father of the most sociable children in the room, he tells us that he has been arrested in the past for his right wing activism and he insists that the views of Moshe Feiglin are widely supported amongst him and his friends.

These might seem like your average Western middle-class family friends, but they are trying hard to be otherwise, with Tuvia insisting that values like "acceptance, diplomacy and democracy" are all Western concepts which have no place in the Israel-Palestine conflict. "We're dealing with Arabs. This is a Jewish state. It isn't a Western system," he maintains. "We play by different rules."

As far as Tuvia is concerned, the Muslims have one thing written in the Quran, whilst the Jews have another enshrined in the Torah and the two are irreconcilable. They are Ishmael and we are Isaac, he says, clarifying the inaccurate analogy of Jacob and Esau that we heard in Kedumim. With diplomacy not an option, there are no political solutions to these two conflicting views and so, concludes Tuvia, the only answer is that everyone "lives under Jewish rule".

When asked why not all the Jews in Israel – and in the government particularly – do not agree with this analysis, Tuvia's friends raise the argument of the mixed multitude, essentially a Jewish conspiracy theory; the pro-Semitic equivalent of legends of a New World Order run by Jews and Freemasons. According to the theory, the Jewish people has been infiltrated by impostors; non Jews who escaped with the Israelites from slavery in Egypt, assimilated, and are now corrupting the nation from within. Some of the guests even claim that these impostors include government minsters, which they believe explains why the Israeli government is against the settlers: because they are not true Jews. The theory is made more incredible by the fact that it is expounded by seemingly intelligent, everyday conservative families – a far cry from the hill-billy backwaters of the American South, where one might expect to hear such stories.

It is hard to take this seriously. Far more startling, though, is the readiness with which Tuvia dismisses the modern humanist values which the Jewish people have historically played a significant role in shaping. It seems that in building up this settlement from nothing, people like Tuvia are intent on establishing a new value system to go with it, one which they claim is traditional, but which is in fact an absolute rejection of the continuum of development of modern socio-political thought, and is therefore a thoroughly radical upheaval, whose consequences cannot be anticipated.

Beyond this, though, such conversations also reveal just how far politics is intertwined with these people's lives. In most similar situations in the world, one would expect a discussion of politics in this house, it if happened at all, to be about little more than the current level of taxation and the nature of the education system. However, politics here is everything and it even extends to whether or not the families of the neighbourhood will be able to spend another year in the homes in which they grew up. On top of that, their houses are themselves an embodiment of their political ideologies: these people's lifestyles and their politics are in fact one and the same. Little wonder then that in such extreme circumstances extreme viewpoints abound.

A long way back

Ritchie drops us at the gate and we wait with a handful of people for the bus ride back over the Green Line, a lone *Haredi* boy mixing up the otherwise modern orthodox crowd. On the bench behind me, an elderly German woman talks to herself in a mixture of Yiddish and heavily accented English, before launching, confusedly and unprompted, into a random list of Arab leaders, old and new. Before long the bus swerves towards the pavement and even the old woman jostles with the rest of us to be first through the door. And as the door closes, the nasal shrill of the local Muezzin resounds throughout the settlement – then the bus pulls through the thick metal gate and into the crying night.

As the gaggle of girls behind us switches effortlessly from Hebrew to English, we take stock of the events of the last weekend. Recalling how approving our recent company has been of the prospect of our book and its inevitability to counter the image of the crazy settler, it is hard not to be struck by the paradoxes and contradictions of those we had met in Karnei Shomron. On the one hand, here was a group of remarkably warm and outgoing people; funny in their conversations and generous in their hospitality. Ritchie, with the strained, questioning inflections at his sentences' ends that suggested that he might be wrong, even though he quietly supposed he was right, had an avuncular charm that complemented Rebecca's attentive manner perfectly, whilst the younger generation that flowed in and out of their friends' homes discussing house prices and their children's latest habits could have belonged anywhere in the world.

And yet beneath this surface lay another side to the settlement – one of Feiglin's isolationist, expansionist policies; of subjugation and population transfer and the triumph of Judaism over democracy. Whilst our visit did indeed permeate the veneer of the crazy settler, what lay beneath could be disturbing, or simply confusing, and, as talk of the mixed multitude, the deconstruction of democracy, and policies of ethnic population transfer abounded, it became incredibly hard to reconcile such normal people with such extreme views. And as the bus passes through Palestinian villages, Hebrew and Arabic signs recalling a bygone era of interaction; as it glides through heavily manned checkpoints, through segregated zones, on the way back to the Green Line; as minarets on the receding landscape appear like smudged green specks through the bulletproof glass, one wonders just what kind of a country the residents of Karnei Shomron would like Israel to be.

Ginette[19]

To the north east of Tel Aviv, almost entirely engorged by the encroaching roads of the beachside city, lies the nondescript satellite town of Hod Hasharon, its main street a clogged dual carriageway heading dead straight from Petah Tikva to Kfar Saba. Every so often, amongst the rows of unmemorable high street shops and orange lottery booths, a patch of grass scrubs up a particular corner, pitifully ineffective beside the tarmac and traffic and hissing passing buses. This is a long way from the West Bank.

The corners themselves lead off into calmer side streets, where palm trees and bushes soften the rigidity of the newly developed housing. As the streets progress from the spinal thoroughfare they relax from their blocked formations, winding into smaller, quieter roads, and it is a smart apartment building on such a street that makes the ideal anonymous retreat for Ginette Thaler, whose experiences in her previous home in the settlement of Ginot Shomron made her move where nobody knew her name.

We take a seat at the breakfast table of a gleaming open plan kitchen-living room in Ginette's modern tenth floor flat and drink glasses of coke, as Ginette, a London-born Israeli, decants crisps and seeds into bowls in the centre of the table. The snacks make for the perfect distraction from the gravity of the forthcoming conversation and both Ginette's son Leor, who joins us at the table, and we help ourselves mechanically for the duration of the sitting.

We have come to talk about how, on the 27th of February 2002, Rachel Thaler – Ginette's daughter, Leor's sister – died of wounds sustained in a suicide bomb attack on a Karnei Shomron shopping mall twelve days previously. The same attack that had been briefly discussed at the dinner table with Ritchie and Rebecca. The same attack that had made rather jaded headlines during a spate of bombings at the height of the Second Intifada. And now here we are with the victims themselves.

How does one begin such a conversation?

We find ourselves skirting around the issue, mentally trying to reconcile the subject with such banal details as the cola bubbling in our mouths and the curious dog Gypsie scratching around our feet. We are unsure of the words to begin, but once Ginette and Leor get started it seems that the words themselves are almost immaterial;

strangely the telling almost seems to hold what happened at bay. As Ginette pushes into her narrative, her voice remains constant, the words following swiftly on from one another, as though if she gains a sufficient head of steam the momentum will see her safely through to the other side.

Ginette's daughter Rachel was 16 when she died, the victim of a suicide bomber who had been on his way to Tel Aviv when he was turned back at an army checkpoint and opted for the mall in Karnei Shomron instead. Leor, who was 14 at the time, was also present at the blast, in which, along with his sister, he lost his best friend Nehemia too. The burst ear drum he sustained prevents him from hearing properly to this day.

Ginette says she had a feeling that something terrible was going to happen, ever since a string of shootings and attacks in the Karnei Shomron area in 2001 brought the violence of the Second Intifada into her immediate surroundings. However, Ginette's daily journey along the dangerous West Bank roads meant that she worried about how her children would cope if she was the victim of an attack. Not once did she imagine that it would be her children in the firing line. And in fact, as Ginette recalls, it was only by chance that her children were at the mall at all.

"I didn't know that Leor was there. He had gone over to his friend Nehemia's house after Shabbat and I had taken Rachel to the shopping centre. She was on her way to Jerusalem for the night and she was meeting her friends at the pizza place first. I kept saying 'I don't want you to go to Jerusalem tonight, it's too dangerous'. I was convinced that something would happen there and not on our own doorstep.

"I left them there and went back home. It was a beautiful evening and I had the window open as I worked at my computer, when about an hour later I heard a loud noise. I wasn't sure what it was and I emailed my friend in [the nearby neighbourhood of] Neve Aliza because I thought it might have been something that had come over from the [Palestinian town of] Azun – a Qassam maybe. But two minutes later I got an email back saying no – there had been a bomb in the shopping centre.

"I knew something had happened. I knew that Rachel was there and I remember that on the way to my car my neighbour tried to tell me something about Leor being at the pizza place too, but I ignored him. I couldn't hear him. When I arrived at the shopping centre I found it all cordoned off and surrounded by people. I wanted to find Rachel, but no one was being let through. I kept asking if anyone had seen Rachel. Then [Ginette's youngest son] Zvi saw Rachel's friend in an ambulance which confirmed that Rachel had been there. People were making a list of all the names they thought might have been in the shopping centre and I gave them Rachel's name – then Zvi saw Nehemia's name on the list and I realised that Leor was there too."

As Ginette ploughs on with her narrative, Leor's hard stare is fixed on the far edge of the table and he continues to pick seeds from the bowl in front of him, crushing the husk with a frown, before grinding his jaw intensely on the flesh. Equally steadfast, Ginette's voice remains flat, almost matter of fact, refusing to allow herself to be pulled down by her memory.

"It was a long time before I learned anything about either of them. Eventually I was told to go to the Bellinson Hospital where Rachel had been taken, but as someone drove me there I got a phone call from a hospital in Kfar Saba asking me to describe Leor's clothes. I had no idea he would be so unrecognisable. Leor and Nehemia had dyed their hair green or red and I must have told them that because they kept asking me to describe what he was wearing – down to what kind of underwear he had on.

"I thought about going to Leor's hospital but the driver persuaded me to go to Rachel's so I had a friend go and meet Leor in Kfar Saba. I couldn't find anyone to speak to, so I walked through to the operation room and found a nurse who told me that Rachel was having surgery on a broken jaw. I sat in the waiting room with another family who had two injured girls. One of them had a nail in her heart and they had to open her heart to take the nail out. There were doctors talking to the families and I kept waiting for someone to tell me about my kid. Then I got a call telling me that Leor had had a nail removed from his throat. He had nails and shrapnel all over. His gall bladder had been removed, his ear had almost been ripped off and he had two nails in his neck, one that they had pulled out and one that they had to remove in surgery. Then I found out that Nehemia was dead. He was like part of the family, but they kept it from me until someone had called to tell me about Leor. But there was still no news from Rachel.

"Finally at 2am the doctor came and explained to me about Rachel's facial injuries and a couple of hours later a neurosurgeon told me the details about the shrapnel that was in her head. I realised it must be serious. An orthopaedic doctor operated on her broken shoulder blade and eventually at 5am she came out of surgery. Meanwhile, the other girls that had come out of surgery were transferred to the children's hospital, but when Rachel came out of surgery she wasn't transferred. I thought this was strange and it became obvious that they didn't expect her to survive. I went up to her room to see her – and she was lying there in bandages, wired up to machines. Rachel was born prematurely and she was on an incubator. When I walked in and saw her lying there like that I thought to myself, she's going to go out of the world exactly as she came into it: taped up to wires."

For just a moment a lump catches in Ginette's throat, but she refuses to let it rise.

"They transferred Rachel to the ICU at Schneider Hospital but I knew she'd never make it. She was brain damaged, in an induced coma and she never regained consciousness. They took her off the drugs ten or eleven days later to see if there was any function, but there was no activity, no blood to the brain, and they decided to take her off the respirator. And that's what happened to Rachel."

Behind her thick framed glasses, Ginette's eyes contort in an empty smile, and it is clear that she will not allow herself to be dragged down. She pushes on, barely even pausing for breath as she recounts how she coped with two wounded children in separate hospitals.

"I didn't see Leor until he'd woken up. He was in the ICU and he was in terrible shape, I couldn't even recognise him."

Travelling back and forth between hospitals whilst Rachel was still in intensive care, Ginette eventually managed to have Leor transferred to Schneider, so that her two children would be in the same hospital. When Leor woke up, he couldn't speak so he wrote his sister's name, wanting to know how she was. He learnt that Rachel was then still alive, but Leor still didn't know that his best friend had died.

"He kept asking about Nehemia, but I avoided answering. I thought it wouldn't be good for him to know until he was stronger, but the doctor said that that he ought to know. I couldn't do it, but I didn't want to lie so I said that he was somewhere else. At first I thought about getting the psychologists to tell him, but then when he asked again I thought how can I have strangers tell him? So I told him myself. He was like a brother to Leor. It was the hardest thing I've ever had to tell him."

As Ginette looks at her son, Leor remains stone faced, keeping his eyes at the same point on the table. After a while Ginette goes on, remembering how amazed the doctors and nurses were by the numbers of children that came in and out of each hospital, visiting the injured.

"If people in the city lose someone, they don't know how to deal with it. No one talks to the families... But in the settlements it's another story. One kid is everyone's kid."

On the day of Rachel's funeral, large crowds turned out

190

to show their love for Rachel, but Ginette recalls the service being marred by an angry Daniella Weiss who used the occasion to begin a shouting match with an attendant MK [Member of Knesset, the Israeli Parliament] in the middle of the service. "She was screaming her head off. I totally lost respect for her after that." As for Leor, he came from hospital in a car with social services, "holding a tube that led to a bag, draining his wound". An ambulance followed closely behind, in case of emergency.

"On the day before the bomb, I was driving with Rachel past a cemetery in Kfar Saba and there were a lot of people there for a service. I remember Rachel turning to me and joking 'if it was your funeral there wouldn't be so many people, but if it was mine there'd be even more.'

"After the bombing we had a ceremony for the victims by the mall where it happened and there were so many people there. Then when we went to the cemetery I looked at the crowds – so many friends – and I said, 'Rachel, you were right. Just look how many people have come for you.'"

Ginette raises her eyebrows, so that they hide beneath the red tips of her dark hair, and sighs. A brief silence is filled by the crack of seeds, the husks adding to a steadily growing pile in front of Leor, who sits in inscrutable silence. Ginette seems eager for the emptiness to be filled and she encourages her son to talk. Leant forward on his elbows, his broad shoulders spread beneath a shaven head and earring, Leor half shrugs, turning his palms up as begins to recount his version of the evening, as if there is nothing to be gained from the telling, but tell he will, if asked. In clear American tones Leor moves efficiently from one necessary detail to the next, with nothing in between. It is a dry statement of events; like his mother, Leor does his best to keep the pain at bay.

"I went over to Nehemia's house. Then after about 15 minutes I got a call from this girl – the one who had the nail in her heart – to say that she was going home. So Nehemia's brother drove us up to the mall so that we could say goodbye. We were only going to be there for five minutes and then leave and we were sitting down having pizza when Nehemia called me and I got up and looked to the left – and then I remember waking up by a post.

"I remember hearing people laughing in my head – I thought maybe someone had thrown something, like at Purim. A firework or something. I saw the TV on the ground and so I thought maybe the TV had exploded. I got up and walked towards the pharmacy and it was all dark. I wanted to go to security to tell them something had happened, then I looked down and saw that my pants were down and my clothes were all burnt and ripped. I carried on to security, walking down some stairs, when I started scratching my arm and I pulled out a nail. Then I realised that something must have happened, but I didn't realise that I was bleeding.

"I remember trying to run to tell my friend's mother that she was ok, then running back to the mall when I see Nehemia's brother Moshe running towards the pizzeria and I call out to him and Moshe sees me with a nail in my neck and he puts me on the floor. I try to get back up but I am too weak, so I stay there. And then I black out.

"More people were put down next to me and I was talking to my friend – the one with the nail in her heart – and talking and losing hearing and I kept saying 'I can't hear you. I can't hear you'. Then I lost consciousness. I remember a pharmacist going round with rescue drops to calm us down. And three women taking care of us, taking our clothes off and checking our injuries. Then I lost consciousness again and then I was pulled into an ambulance and asked questions. Then I lost consciousness again. I woke up two or three times on the way to the hospital and when I arrived there were journalists taking pictures... I was rushed into surgery where a doctor asked me my name and put a mask on my face and that's the last thing I remember until I woke up the following afternoon."

When Leor awoke he had difficulties breathing due to "gunge inside my chest that kept coming up" and wanted

Ginette to hold him while he was coughing, but she says she was "scared to do it because of the surgery. He was getting angry with me. I was a terrible nurse."

Shortly after the blast, Leor couldn't feel any pain, other than his face burning, but the next day his injuries began to become painfully clear. All his hair, which had been brightly died a few days before, and his eye lashes, had been burnt off, which explains why the doctors had asked Ginette to identify what clothes her son had been wearing.

Leor expands on his injuries:

"I had two nails in my throat. My ear was ripped off and my ear drum had burst and wouldn't grow back. I had surgery for a new ear drum, but I'm still practically deaf in one ear and have problems with the other one. I had my gall bladder removed because of a leak, and had an infected bile duct. I had first and second degree burns and I still have a nail and shrapnel inside my stomach."

Leor's father, Michael, lives in America and couldn't get the news until a while afterwards. He bought a ticket to fly to Israel and was reading his children's names in the newspaper before he'd even had a chance to talk to them. As for the bomber, a 16 year old dispatched from Qalqiliya, no one is really sure how he got there. Leor doesn't remember seeing him arrive, while according to Ginette a couple of girls who sat at the table with Rachel and survived the blast recall seeing him stood next to them and calling "Allahu Akbar" [God is great] before everything went dead.

"I like to think how Rachel would have answered him," states Ginette, wryly. "She was a fighter. A real tough cookie."

Ginette goes into her bedroom and reappears with a large box of photos, which she begins exploring, pulling out picture after picture of her young children. There are photos of Leor in his hospital bed, his face covered in cuts and bruises, attempting to smile for the camera. And there are many of Rachel as a young girl.

"You have so many photos from when they're little but as they're growing up you don't take as many. Then when it was too late I realised that I didn't have any photos of Rachel and I was craving them. I went to all the photo shops in Karnei Shomron to see if there were any films that she hadn't picked up and developed, but I couldn't find any."

Other memories, though, offered comfort to Ginette after her daughter's death and the landmarks of Karnei and Ginot Shomron, as well as her burial site reminded her of her daughter, while the chance to see Rachel's friends and classmates on the local streets allowed Ginette to feel close to her daughter. But where at first these people brought comfort, they soon began to have the opposite effect.

"For a while after Rachel died I could look at her friends every day and imagine what Rachel would be doing now. But as they grew older and left school it felt like Rachel was being left behind. I could no longer imagine what she would be doing, or what she'd be thinking. Would she be married? What job would she be doing? When her friends were in school it was ok, but when you can no longer make the comparison, it gets difficult. The years go by and you need to get away from it all.

"What you need at the beginning – a framework of support – soon turns against you... For a while we used to be involved in organisations that raised funds for injured bomb victims and their families... I'd go and talk at these things and people would feel so good about themselves for giving money and I would just walk away feeling shit."

No matter how well intended, Ginette grew tired of people's pity, which came in a number of forms, some worse than others. With a laugh Ginette remembers a trip laid on by some wealthy American Jews, which brought Ginette's family and other Israeli bomb victims to the States for a holiday and culminated in an absurdly misguided visit to a traumatised horse sanctuary, so that the bomb victims could gain inspiration from the way in

194

which the horses had learnt to live with their grief.

As Leor grew sick of his therapy groups, experiences like this eventually made Ginette realise that she couldn't be a part of the victim brigade any longer. They moved to Hod HaSharon, where the busy streets and endless housing provided Ginette, Leor and the youngest son Zvi anonymity that they had not known since coming to Israel. Nevertheless, the family remain close enough to their old home to visit Rachel's grave, and Ginette's attitude on the return of the West Bank is unrelenting. Having moved to Ginot Shomron because they liked the place, rather than out of any specific ideology, both Ginette and Leor now believe that to exchange the West Bank for peace would be a security disaster for Israel. Indeed, their hopes for peace itself are non existent.

"There will never be peace," says Leor, bluntly. "Both sides have been injured, wounded and killed, which just makes more and more enemies. Between Jews and Arabs there won't be peace any more. That's how I see it."

A growing pile of photos now spills across the table and still Ginette is busy in the box, smiling and shaking her head as she talks, passing around photo after photo of how her family once was. Eventually she gets to one of Rachel and her friend Keren – the third fatality of the bombing – and shows it to us. Rachel is blindfolded and being led by Keren, who holds her hand, to her surprise birthday party, two weeks before the attack. Looking at this photo, Ginette explains the meaning she sees in the image.

"Keren was the first to die and just as she's leading my Rachel to her party in the photo, so she ended up leading her on to..." She trails off.

"It's a way of looking at it," she adds, apologetically.

Ginette manages a smile then returns to her box, unsatisfied that this is not meaning enough. She talks instead about how Keren, Rachel and Nehemia were the three victims, and the first letters of each of their names spell Keren in Hebrew, as well as being the root of the name of the settlement itself, Karnei Shomron. Again though, this meaning is insufficient and Ginette is drawn back to the box, lingering over photo after photo, long after they have ceased to be passed around the table.

At last the words appear to have dried up and the emotion is no longer held at bay. It is time for us to leave.

On our way to the door we pass a large framed portrait of Rachel, her hair cropped short, her eyes determined and powerful and with the ghost of a smile on her lips, revealing traces of both the humour and the "tough cookie" that her mother had described. Although she has left Karnei Shomron, Ginette has made sure that she remains surrounded by memories of Rachel. And so we leave her to return to her box of photos and the search for meaning that is unlikely ever to bring Ginette the answers she needs.

Chapter Six
Ariel: City state

Lessons from the motherland[20]

At precisely 8pm, as the lengthening shadows of Sderot Hen are fading into the Tel Aviv twilight, I am joined at my table by Yossi Gurlevich, who highlights his punctual arrival with a smart grey shirt, pressed black trousers and polished shoes, the very picture of precision. Yossi has agreed to join me at the end of his day's work conducting algorithmic research, developing finance cryptography and other such arcane activity, to talk about growing up in the city settlement of Ariel. Fortunately Yossi speaks more than one language and he eschews tech-talk in favour of a notably replete English to discuss his home town, a non-religious, economic settlement, famed for its large Russian-speaking population. Yossi himself is one of those Russians, having been born in Soviet-era Moscow before moving to Israel with his family in 1988. With measured sentences funnelled through a tight, nasal accent, Yossi discusses the transition from living under the Communist regime to life in the Promised Land.

He tells me that before he was born his father was an employee of the Soviet space programme, putting his maths and physics Masters degree to good use. However, when he got married to Yossi's mother, he decided to put his long-standing Zionist ideals into practice and filed a request to move to Israel: he was fired immediately, and spent the rest of his years in Moscow working as a street cleaner, clearing snow from the roads, because, as Yossi wryly observes, "there's no such thing as unemployment in Communist Russia".

It was the politics more than the religion that caused problems for Yossi's family and although they could not easily practise Judaism in Moscow, they managed to maintain their cultural Jewish heritage and Yossi remembers being able to go to the *shul* to collect boxes of *matza* for Pesach. He also recollects Sunday school lessons where he studied Hebrew, Jewish history and Zionism, but it was the latter that attracted the attention of the authorities. Yossi's parents' political ideology was a problem for the repressive regime and Yossi recalls the KGB being permanently stationed in a car outside his front door "taking notes of all who came and left the house... They were not spying because we were Jewish but because my parents were active in the Zionist movement."

Having lost his job, Yossi's father had little left to lose and submitted another request to leave the country when his first son was born, but was again denied. On his third request, however, Yossi's father was successful and in 1987 Yossi, his parents, his brother and the cat were granted a permit to leave the USSR for Israel. When they arrived, Yossi was struck by the economic difference between the two countries – "there were stores everywhere and new cars. And you could buy food without having to stand in line". Nevertheless, Yossi's early years as a new immigrant were spent in relative poverty, passing the first year in a Jerusalem absorption centre, a complex of buildings "that would flood during the winter", along with other impoverished new immigrants from Syria, Morocco and Ethiopia, amongst others. After a year in the centre, Yossi's family took advantage of extremely low house prices and government incentives to move to the Occupied Territories and bought an apartment in the young settlement of Ariel.

With the economic freedom of his new life came liberty of conscience, and the contrast with his experiences of living under a dictatorial regime still shape his attitude towards life in Israel. He casts his eyes around the busy streets that enclose Rabin Square, rear headlights and reflections glancing off one another, streaming into the balmy night.

"I can appreciate what I have here, but lots of people take it for granted. They know nothing else – because they're born into it they think it will always be like that. They can't understand what it means to be without democracy, without civil rights, because they have been accustomed to it from birth. And they think everyone else lives like that – they think that democracy and civil rights exist for everyone in the world, but it's not true."

However, Yossi was surprised to discover that such ideological freedom resulted in attitudes that he could not recognise. Not all of the promises of the Promised Land were to his taste.

"I wasn't used to democracy or to freedom of thought. I thought that everyone in Israel was a Zionist because I'd been taught about Ben Gurion and Moshe Dayan and the brave Zionists who had fought the War of Independence and the 1967 war – and then I came to Israel and for many years I found it very hard to understand how there could be left wing people here; how they could just give away parts of their land when in Russia there would have been a great big war over a tiny patch of land that no one even lived in. [In Russia] we were taught to believe that your country is your country and you need to be patriotic. Then I came here and people were giving away their land; their future lives; their country – it was very hard to understand... And it's still really hard for me to see that most people don't care– they just want peace, quick, and don't care about struggling for their ideals."

However, whilst it was a combination of right wing Zionist ideology and economic incentives that brought Yossi's family to Ariel – and could entice him back in the future – the same is not necessarily the case for a large section of its population, which swelled rapidly in the early '90s, on the crest of a large wave of Russian immigration to Israel, following the collapse of the Soviet Union. Once a community *yeshuv* like Kedumim or Mitzpeh Yeriho, Ariel is now a city of almost 20,000 residents and a further 10,000 students – an inflation that

Yossi accredits to one man: Ron Nachman, the City Mayor.

"When the Russian *aliyah* [immigration to Israel – lit. 'going up'] arrived, the mayor went personally to the airport to meet the new *olim* and told them to come and live in his city – and he doubled the population. The change happened over a few years... and now, because of the college, lots of students come to Ariel from the centre [of Israel]. In the last few years a very big population of students has grown, with dormitories and apartments which are very cheap compared to Tel Aviv."

This economic incentive to live in the settlement, added to the mayor's reportedly tireless drive to recruit more residents, means that Ariel is not perceived to be ideological like the community *yeshuvim*, but rather it is economic; a cheap town of convenience. Nor, with its large population of secular Russians, is it perceived as being religious, a fact which, according to Yossi, means that it will be harder to gain Israeli public consensus for withdrawal from the Ariel bloc than from the more religious community settlements of Gush Katif or Homesh. Indeed, according to the BBC, in his election campaign of 2006, Olmert said of the West Bank's second largest settlement that "the Ariel bloc will be an inseparable part of Israel under any situation. Ariel is Israel."[21] This despite the fact that the settlement's size and its obtrusion 22km into Palestinian Territory that is only 52km at its widest point, make it the most obstructive settlement to a contiguous Palestinian state.

The reason for mainstream support of the retention of Ariel, argues Yossi, is that there is "a lot of antagonism towards the religious in the media, in the papers, on the TV; [they are] against the religious settlers. But people know that the people in Ariel are not religious – they are seen as normal. They don't go around with a *kippah* and sandals and an Uzi... The media are much more familiar with Ariel residents. There's less 'us and them'... so it would be much harder [to evacuate them]."

As for the settlers evacuated during the Disengagement from Gaza, Yossi is "100% sure that they were being targeted. It's easier to marginalise some individuals. To focus on them; on their difference; on the weird people. They say they do it for the greater good; for the big peace, but they target these people because they are easier. It would not be so easy with Ariel."

Ironically then, cheap housing and Nachman's courting of new Russian immigrants has had the effect of creating a population of residents that have no strong ideological attachment to the West Bank, whilst paradoxically consolidating the settlement as one of the hardest to evacuate, precisely because the Israeli public doesn't regard its residents as real settlers.

Furthermore, not only do many of Ariel's residents have no ideological attachment to the West Bank, beyond calling the city home, there are those like Moshe Feiglin who argue that the Russian population of Israel has no attachment to the Jewish state at all, worrying that many of them are "not Jewish". However, according to Yossi, the reality of the relationship between Israel's Russian speaking population and the state of Israel is rather more complex than that.

"Lots of Russians came to Israel for a better life, not for Zionist reasons. I know lots of Jewish Russians who are trying to escape from the army, who feel nothing for their country – lots of them have already left – back to Russia, or to the US or to Canada. But I know a Russian Christian who loves this country and was an officer in the army, so it depends on the person. There is always animosity towards every immigrant group from certain people in Israel. They're used to making generalisations – they say all Russians are prostitutes, or that they're all Christians and we all eat pork... it was a big issue at the beginning of the 90s but people have grown up... Until 1999/2000 there were still issues about immigrants but now there are more important issues, such as the Intifada or last year's [Lebanon] war... Lots of Russians started going into combat units and serving as security guards, and then suddenly you saw lots of Russian names in the obituaries and people saw that they were no different; that they're dying for the land just like us – and so they started to accept them."

As someone who arrived in Israel over three years before the large Russian *aliyah* of the early 90s, Yossi sees himself as more integrated than the wider Russian community – "most of my friends are Israeli... [whereas] the new *aliyah* don't try to make friends with Israelis". His family's reasons for coming to Israel were Zionist, rather than economic, and he is observant of Jewish culture. And although those like Ritchie and Rebecca in Karnei Shomron might dispute his notion of Judaism, Yossi is comfortable with his interpretation of his Jewish heritage as cultural rather than religious, stating that the Bible is "a document of a civilisation, not a holy book that I should live by." Accordingly, Yossi rejects the idea that the West Bank must remain in Jewish hands for religious reasons, stating that he doesn't have "a messianic view that if we keep the *Shtachim* the *moshiach* [Messiah] will come. I wish it was true, but you can't plan your life by it."

Nevertheless, Yossi's notion of Zionism, imbibed in Russia where he was "taught that your country is your country", doesn't allow for territorial concessions. In his view, it is in Israel's strategic interest to maintain full control of the West Bank.

"Without the *Shtachim* Israel is 16km in width. That's half a marathon – no land at all... If Israel withdraws to the 1967 borders, even if all Arabs were peaceful Buddhists, there's not enough land or water for the next generation."

Beyond this, Yossi believes that Israeli control of the West Bank is militarily important, pointing to the rise of Hamas in Gaza as evidence.

"Judea and Shomron are full of militants. [If Israel withdraws] they will fight against themselves, and against Israel. They'll fire rockets on us. At the moment they fire rockets from Gaza on Sderot, but from Judea and Shomron they'll fire on Jerusalem, Kfar Saba and Netanya too. It will be an even bigger disaster, from a security point of view, than the last *hitnatkut*. Also, we're not talking about relocating thousands of Jews, but hundreds of thousands. We couldn't do it with Gaza, so how can we do it from Judea and Shomron?"

Despite sharing the same territorial end goal as the most fundamentalist religious settler, Yossi's desire for a Greater Israel is more Lieberman than Feiglin. Having voted at the previous election for Avigdor Lieberman, the Moldovan leader of the far rightist party Yisrael Beiteinu (whom even the relatively extreme Oren had, in Kfar Adumim, described as a "lunatic... who could end up killing all the Arabs"), Yossi advocates a strong Israeli nation over a strong Jewish one; a subtle but significant difference. And whilst right wing ideological settlers like Esther in Mitzpeh Yeriho have spoken of transferring Palestinians to surrounding Arab countries, Yossi believes that Palestinians and Arab Israelis can make loyal Israeli citizens, provided their political leadership and nationalist aspirations have been smashed. Unlike Feiglin, Yossi does not propose such racist policies as political representation for Jews only, or funding the transfer of the West Bank's Palestinian population. Instead Yossi's model bears similarities to the expansionist policies of his native Soviet Union, albeit with an elected government, wherein the Israeli state is all, separatist dissent is crushed by a powerful government and the individual is nurtured to be a loyal, patriotic citizen of the state, regardless of his ethnicity or religion.

"All the Hamas and Fatah members and those imported by Rabin to serve as the Palestinian police must leave. The inciters must be expelled or go to jail, while the people who just want to live – the farmers, the family people – would be allowed to stay in Israel. As for the vote, just as in Iraq the US changed the dictatorship to a

203

democracy overnight and no good came of it, you can't do that here. The first stage would see the Palestinians have the same rights as us, and their children educated in our schools. Then the children, who have been educated out of Islamic violence, should be allowed to vote – but they shouldn't have the right immediately... Nothing can be done until the Fatah and Hamas ideology and the religious inciters and the people in the Friday prayers calling for jihad and killing Jews... are stopped. Only after they leave can we start something."

"As for Israeli Arabs – they're in a difficult situation. Israeli people [sic] are very suspicious of them. They're mistrusted and mistreated in their jobs. But they have to survive – they've survived the Ottomans, the British – they have to survive the Jewish state, so if Israel is weak the Israeli Arabs will choose to side with the stronger side. They have a lot to lose and they need to survive. But if Israel is strong they will be loyal. Israeli Arabs can be loyal citizens. I believe that every citizen is an asset to its country – and Israeli Arabs can be an asset to Israel too."

Yossi no longer lives in Ariel and prefers the big city life of Tel Aviv. Whilst he doesn't like the steep prices, he enjoys the convenience of the place – "that you can buy milk on Shabbat when you want a cup of coffee" – as well as the theatres and festivals, the clubs, beaches and cinemas. The freedoms and indulgences that were missing in his native USSR weave vibrant colour into the fabric of his social life. And yet it is hard not to be struck by a cold authoritarianism in Yossi's political outlook and whilst he appears still to value the freedoms and liberties that his life away from the Soviet Union have granted him, one is struck by the sense that his politics have never quite surpassed those of the old country. Having resented the strong arm of the state in the USSR that restricted his parents' national aspirations, he advocates a similar state of Israel to subdue the nationalism of Israel's Palestinian neighbours.

Nevertheless, Yossi's political outlook is neither myopic nor simmering with righteous anger. Referencing a number of Palestinian, Lebanese and Egyptian blogs that he reads regularly, not once does my interlocutor raise his voice. Each of his sentences is uttered with the patient, logical rationale that one would expect of the son of a Russian scientist and, well versed in the politics of the other side, Yossi's claim that "he can understand the left wing position and could argue it for the sake of debate" feels entirely credible. And yet facts on the ground have shaped Yossi's politics and for political, military and strategic reasons, as opposed to religious or ideological, he advocates the annexation of the Occupied Territories to Israel. It seems that as the facts on the ground increase, so too does their immutability.

Yossi heads off, in time to keep another appointment, and I settle up, then head down Frishman, my back to the foreboding expanse of concrete that is Rabin Square. Here, in 1995, the eponymous Prime Minister was assassinated and now the square stands a sorry landmark; a broken wasteland, dark and desolate under the night sky. Blood has watered this ground, too, and the concrete and paving stones seal its place as yet another fact on the ground. Only this one, apart from the odd demonstration, remains empty of people. And whilst stats and statements fertilise the furious growth of settlements like Ariel, the dull grey square lies fallow, as pitiful and incomplete as the great man's legacy.

The outsider

The eye of the storm is often cited as the safest place to be – but it can also prove the loneliest. As the headline-grabbing conflict between the Israelis and Palestinians rages, those in the region with unconnected, yet equally pressing, predicaments find themselves unattended and their causes left unchampioned. So we find in Ariel, where we meet a man whose unique status as a non-Jewish Israeli has proved to be an almost insurmountable obstacle in his quest for acceptance.

For Dima, a Ukranian-born engineering student living in the city-settlement, issues of identity and feelings of rejection by his adoptive countrymen have left him in a quandary with regards to his loyalty to the Jewish State. Calling himself "a Zionist – at least, everything except the religious part," Dima is philosophical about not having his feelings of love and loyalty for the state reciprocated by the governing authorities.

Although he served at officer level in the IDF, Dima's non-kosher blood means that he would not be buried in a military cemetery were he to fall in battle. The irony of the situation is not lost on Dima, and neither is the hypocrisy of those writing the rules. His strawberry-blond ponytail swaying as he talks, Dima declares frankly: "Israel is a racist society, and that works as much against the Russian community as it does against the Arabs."

Dima's family emigrated to Israel from Dnieperpetrovsk as soon as the Iron Curtain lifted, seeking a better life for their offspring and falling back on their part-Jewish lineage to enable them to qualify for Israeli citizenship. From the off, Dima tried his damnedest to fit into Israeli society, sacrificing the ease of encasing himself in the Russian-speaking community in favour of a strict Hebrew-only environment.

"Many of the Russian immigrants speak only Russian, watch only Russian TV and so on, but that keeps them separate from their Israeli neighbours," he says. "I didn't want that, so now I speak perfect Hebrew – which means that now many Russians also treat me as an outsider." As for the Israelis he encounters: "I sometimes get racist comments on the bus – but having big arms helps negate the problem." He smiles, flexing his thick biceps to emphasise the point.

As an avowed atheist, Dima isn't overly concerned whether people view him as Jewish or not for purely academic reasons, but it is the importance that the state places on religious status that sticks in his throat. "I'm angry that I can't be buried in a Jewish cemetery. I'm angry that I can't marry a Jewish girl in Israel," he says hotly. "Christians and Muslims determine their religion according to the father's bloodline. The idea that Jews inherit their mother's status is a relatively new concept," he explains. "I consider myself technically Jewish – but that means nothing in the eyes of the government."

Perhaps it is his outsider status however that gives Dima a degree of sympathy with his Palestinian neighbours, particularly those who seek work in Israeli cities and settlements. With stories reminscent of those we heard from Boel in Efrat, Dima describes how Palestinian workers are at the mercy of their Israeli bosses.

"Israeli people use them. The Palestinians have to work here, to make money, so the bosses can easily take advantage of them and not pay, or only give them a fraction of what they told them. Many Palestinians are abused in this way and they can't do anything about it."

Having worked with some Palestinians from Nablus who attained work permits from Ariel security, only to be duped in such a way, Dima advised them to take their bosses to court, but they told him they were too scared to try. Dima offered what advice he could, but realised there was little he or they could do to change the situation.

Despite the country's faults and his own bitterness, Dima is a staunch defender of Israel's right to exist, and politics appear to be at the forefront of his mind. His family ended up in the West Bank after being met by Ariel's mayor Ron Nachman when they stepped off the plane from Ukraine, who persuaded them to make their home in the newly-established town.

As a result, Dima has grown up on the front line, both in the army and at home. He sees himself as "middle of the road, politically – I realise that the Palestinians need a state, but at the same time I'm not sure where I stand on giving up West Bank settlements... But there's no other solution. The best idea is for most of Judea and Samaria to be a Palestinian state. Maybe Ariel and the other blocs would remain Israeli, but if the government said to us we had to leave, many of us would go – ideologies here are weak. We're not like [the religious settlements of] Elkana and Itamar."

After witnessing the aftermath of the last Disengagement, Dima claims that "the left wing offers no solution. We gave the Palestinians what they wanted and still nothing happened. But then the right wing are problematic too because we can't simply kill or expel the Palestinians."

For now, he is opposed to any further concessions, at least until the Palestinians prove their commitment by "sticking to a quiet period" in terms of attacks on Israel.

He says that the uniqueness of Israeli politics is that "most people choose a party according to their stance on the Palestinian question," meaning that issues that could make or break governments in other countries are largely ignored by the Israeli electorate. "Even I wouldn't be swayed much by a party dedicated to helping the Russian community, such as Yisrael Beytenu," says Dima, "since my priority is which party will deliver peace to the region."

The more Dima talks about Israel as though referring to a beloved, sickly family member, the sadder it becomes to watch him, given the second-class status bestowed upon him by the state. This is a boy who wants "my children to grow up Israeli, first and foremost", who is prepared to lay down his life defending its borders, yet whose body is not holy enough to be interred amongst those of thoroughbred Jews were he to make the ultimate sacrifice.

Although there are a multitude of explanations given by the religious authorities that set rules for who qualifies as a Jew, Dima is doomed to remain an interloper – no matter how long he resides in the country and how much he contributes to the state.

His plight won't make headline news around the world, since his cause isn't as obvious as those of the similarly-mistreated Palestinians who live under the yoke of Israeli rule. Instead, the likes of Dima will continue to soldier on, in every sense of the word, physically on the inside of Israel's borders, but in every other way an outsider.

The blame game

Our guide around Ariel for the afternoon is Sivan, a twenty-four year old microbiology student and resident of the town since the age of three. She walks us through her neighbourhood streets, which, despite the settlement's city status, feel very similar to those of other *yeshuvim* we have visited, albeit on a larger scale. The same box-like apartment blocks stand stacked along uniform roads, giving way to familiar red roofs of newer, wealthier housing; the same scrubby patches of dirt and bush bare themselves between undeveloped plots of land; the hilltop horizons of Palestinian villages are the same too, or they might as well be from here, given the lack of contact.

The place is, of course, bigger than your average settlement, having grown a great deal since Sivan first arrived, and with a gym, tennis courts, 24 hour shopping, pubs and restaurants there is far less reason to make the hour drive into Tel Aviv. However, the absence of things like locked doors, traffic lights, or even traffic, marks this out as a distinctly suburban kind of city, and, although she likes the place now, Sivan admits that Ariel was a boring place to grow up.

Having been born in Argentina to her Argentine father and an Israeli mother, Sivan's parents were courted at the airport upon their return to Israel by the industrious mayor Nachman, who encouraged them to come and live in the caravans and *ashkubiot* of the fledgling settlement, eventually complying a couple of years later. Sivan remembers how from the age of nine, Ariel began to change as waves of new Russian immigrants were pumped into the city. At first there were separate groups of Russians and Israelis but now, she says, "most of my friends are Russian. They had a stigma at high school – that they were criminals, or always smoking or taking drugs, but it's not true. The Russians I know are polite and friendly and well cultured."

We sit at a small plastic table outside a spruced up old café, which does slow but steady business despite the time of day, and order something to drink. Sitting quietly across the table, Sivan seems slightly bemused by our interest in her life in Ariel, hanging her head shyly and smiling almost apologctically as she tries to think of things to tell us. She doesn't like speaking about politics, she explains, and as for the settlement itself her deflective shrugs suggests that this is just normal suburban life – what else is there to say? She likes the place and feels safe here. She's not sure whether the separation barrier contains Ariel but is not concerned either way. She's not a *mitnhahelet,* she explains. She's not a settler.

An old woman comes over and asks us something in Russian. None of us is able to respond and the woman wanders over to the next shop, where an elderly man is able to answer her question in her own tongue. "It's common for Israelis and Russians to mix together," explains Sivan, as if answering Dima's earlier assertion that a degree of segregation still prevails. She tells us that her own boyfriend is Russian and that although the settlement is much bigger now than when she was younger, most of the residents still know one another. She likes the variety that the expansion has brought; the only people that she doesn't interact with, she claims, are the religious communities within the *yeshuv*, who "keep themselves to themselves".

Sivan supports Yossi Gurlevich's description of Mayor Nachman's role in expanding the settlement and recalls playing her own part in his drive for Ariel's growth.

"I was in a singing troupe when I was in high school and we went on a tour of the US with the mayor, singing at various concerts to raise money for the *yeshuv*. He's a very pushy man and he managed to collect a lot of money, especially from the Christians. They gave us loads of money – they loved us far more than the Jews."

Sivan's friend Avital expands on what Nachman has done for the settlement.

"Mayor Ron Nachman was here from the start and he made Ariel a big, powerful city. He was in the Knesset with Likud and always pushed to give more strength to Ariel as a city – for banks, medical centres, social services. We have a branch of each government office here, as well as a law court. These things wouldn't be here if it wasn't for him. He also pushed for loads more people to come here which, in general, was a good thing, but... he persuaded people to come because it's cheap and you can have a big house with a garden for the price of a small flat in Tel Aviv, so people with little money came here to improve their quality of life. But they brought their problems with them."

Sivan has brought us to meet Avital, a 26 year old graduate from law school and the daughter of Russian immigrants who were amongst the initial thirty families to come to Ariel, camping in tents before the first permanent housing was erected. As a descendent of the original kernel of Ariel settlers, Avital is part of the settlement's establishment and, after leading us past the rows of Russian language novels that line the shelves of her staircase, and onto her roof terrace, she gestures expansively across the broad vista of surrounding hills, with the hauteur of old money that has looked down to find the nouveau riche a little too close for comfort.

"The old Ariel was different. Now it's pretty big and full of people that I don't know if I want to live with. There used to be a stronger sense of community and the people were better. Now you have more troubled people, bringing violence and drugs and alcohol – people from a lower economic level that bring their socio-economic problems with them and lower the quality of life here."

We are admiring Avital's commanding panoramic views so that she can point out her other neighbours – the Palestinians (a word she insists was unheard of until after the Oslo Accords) – in their villages that mottle the hills both near and far. She claims that for a couple of years before the first Intifada Ariel had "good relations" with its Palestinian neighbours, and residents "used to visit Palestinians in their homes and vice versa."

"When I was a baby I used to sit in cafés with my parents in [the Palestinian town of] Safit. But then the first Intifada happened and some Palestinian workers that had worked in Ariel for years came and stabbed a Jew in the back and killed him. My father lost all faith in the Palestinians after that. He stopped buying from them. He had nothing more to do with them."

Avital then recollects the "good times" after the Oslo Accords when again the "relationship flourished... My ex-boyfriend's neighbour and his Palestinian contractor remained good friends and visited each other's families, but when the second Intifada started one of the main events happened in Bidya [a local Palestinian town]and they were stoning and shooting every car that passed for a few days. For three days it was like a war zone and we were unable to leave Ariel because it was too dangerous. The Palestinian contractor told my friend "don't leave Ariel, it's too dangerous". They had a really good relationship. But then extremists on both sides ruined it."

It is interesting to hear Avital apportion some of the blame with her fellow settlers as well as with her Palestinian neighbours across the fence, and by way of explanation she breaks down settlers into various types; a kind of hierarchy of ideology. Her father, she says, came to Ariel not out of "extreme ideology – that we need to settle every inch of the land, but just because he was searching for a better quality of life. But of course there's ideology too. We have to create and build a new place, so that's part of it. I do believe that we have every right to live here as in any other place."

"However," she continues, "in Hebron they do *davka* [things just for the sake of it]... There are very extremist Jews in Hebron and I don't accept their behaviour at all. Being a Jew you have to respect yourself and those you live with, but they terrorise the people around them in such an undignified way. I have no respect for them... Radicals and lawbreakers act against Jewish law. No matter how Palestinians are behaving, or what violence they are using, it doesn't justify the way these settlers are behaving... [The nearby settlement of] Yitzhar is pretty much the same. Kedumim has a history of getting along with its neighbours – they talk and negotiate with the Arabs around them; with the *mufti* [leader] of the village and don't create clashes, but they're still sort of extreme though."

"Then you have the rich Jew who buys land like Moshe Zar who lives in Karnei Shomron. His son, who was the security officer for all the *yeshuvim*, was murdered by Palestinian terrorists who surrounded his car and ambushed him. It was a targeted killing – they knew who he was. He wasn't very polite with the Palestinians. For them he symbolised all the settlers who try to take their land."

However, despite railing against the more extreme type of settlers, Avital holds up the Palestinians as the reason that there is "no sense of hope now".

"Extremists are now in control of the Palestinian government... The leaders make the common people think that Israel is the problem with everything. They're educating hatred. There's still a stigma that Israelis drink Palestinian blood... I don't see any group who could rise up within Palestinian society and say 'enough of violence, we want peace'."

One relationship that she does think is improving, however, is that between Ariel settlers and Israelis within the Green Line, though not for the same reasons as Yossi.

"When I tell people in Tel Aviv that I'm from Ariel they're surprised – I'm not religious or an extremist. I don't carry an Uzi. They say 'what the hell are you living there for?' Ariel has a stigma in the centre [of Israel]. When you tell people you're from the *Shtachim* they look at you in a funny way. You're different. You're not like them. I anticipate a reaction when I say that I'm from Ariel. But now I think there's less of a divide between Israel and Ariel. I feel I've been getting more normal reactions over the past few years when I tell people where I'm from. I think the *hitnatkut* changed the way that people look at settlers. They see that we're not extremists. We're just everyday people living normal lives."

Since the shooting on the roads into Israel during the second Intifada, a new road has opened to Ariel, providing safe passage away from the Palestinian towns. At the point at which the road crosses the Green Line, someone has daubed a streak of green paint on the mountainside to emphasise the start of occupied territory, but the fading mark is largely ignored. As Ariel becomes sanitised and normalised, and Israelis view Arielis as normal compared to the extremists of Hebron and Yitzhar, Ariel is augmenting its position as a consensus settlement, "an inseparable part of Israel" as Olmert asserted. It is all a matter of perception. Appearing to be normal, Ariel has made itself acceptable. In making itself acceptable, it has become inseparable. Everyone retains their own idea of what's extreme and what's not, but as long as there are extremists who can shoulder the blame, the less extreme can become moderates and then when someone even more extreme comes along, the extremists won't seem quite so extreme themselves. And of course, despite what Avital says about her father's motivations, the original thirty families in Ariel would themselves have seemed extreme to the rest of Israel, once upon a time.

Back with Sivan on Ariel's quiet residential streets, we continue our tour and she uses the opportunity to qualify

214

what Avital had said about the new Russian arrivals to Ariel.

"Not all the Russians are bad, like Avital said. Many good people come to live here too. But it's the non-Jewish Russians that are the problem. They've got no connection to Israel and they don't want any. They just prefer Israel to Russia, that's all. It's people like Dima, who feels Jewish, who are the good guys."

Whether it's regarding Russians, Palestinians or settlers, everyone, it seems, has their own definition of who's extreme and who's not; who's ok and who's beyond the pale. It's all relative. And as long as everyone has their own scapegoat; as long as there's someone left at the end of the line to point to, there's really no need to try and tackle the problems closer to home. Indeed, there's no need to tackle problems at all.

Funds for foundations

Ariel is fortunate to be on the receiving ends of large amounts of private donations, on top of the state assistance given to the city. Buildings all over the settlement bear the proud names of their sponsors in large, bold letters – including the Milken Family Cultural Center, paid for by the philanthropic trust set up by disgraced-financier Michael Milken. As with many other settlements – indeed, as with many other Israeli towns and cities on both sides of the Green Line – the omnipotence of the state lottery, Payas, can be felt thanks to the gymnasia and school buildings it has commissioned for Ariel's population. Spotting the Payas logo here, as elsewhere in the *Shtachim*, reminds the observer just how normalised the settlements have become. Every link forged between public or private initiative back in the motherland to the peninsula of settlements in the Territories helps increase the settlers' sense that they are – to all intents and purposes – as much a part of the state

215

as anyone else, regardless of the contentious and controversial location of their homes.

Wealthy Jews are not the only ones funding the settlements and a great deal of money pours in from American evangelical Christian groups, too. Sivan takes us to the 'Randolph A Hearst Sheltered Workshop', which was established by Victoria Hearst, in memory of her late father, via the Friends of Ariel – an American group of donors from the Baptist Church. The sister of Patti Hearst and granddaughter of media magnate and, ironically, reputed anti-Semite William Randolph Hearst, Victoria's Baptist beliefs led her to believe that if all the Jews returned to Israel, the Messiah would return to Earth – hence she saw supporting projects in Judea and Samaria as an important way to help hasten His coming. In less ethereal terms, the benefaction of the Hearst family has translated into a place where both elderly and handicapped residents of Ariel can find gainful employment, their skills put to use in a variety of ways to help them supplement the meagre welfare they receive from the state.

Sophia, who runs the workshop, fills us in on the history of the mini-factory. Founded fifteen years ago, the intention was to provide disabled residents of the city with "something to do, rather than have them just sit around lonely at home, or spend all day in the cafés drinking coffee". At first, there were just six workers, "but it grew and grew, and now we have seventy-five people employed here". There are around thirty disabled employees; the rest comprise Ariel's pensioners. Each worker receives around 600 shekels per month for their toil, and at the same time "gain a great deal in terms of friendship with one another, and those Russians amongst them soon learn to speak Hebrew as well". The workshop packages plastic cutlery for airlines, prepares vacuum-packed dressings for the army, produces both ceramic objets d'art and electrical cables. "It's great for their families to see them work, and to know that they have

216

something with which to fill their days," Sophia tells us as we wander round the factory floor. "And because they have something to do, they don't call on the social services and doctors so much," she notes. "We try to make it like a second home for our staff – we celebrate their birthdays, Jewish holidays, and even Russian national holidays, such as the anniversary of the victory over Germany." What began as a 24 square metre room is now a thriving 400 square metre workspace, testament to the success of an inspired idea coupled with a healthy injection of overseas funding from a seemingly unlikely source, and is yet another example of the way in which the settlements are being stitched into the fabric of Israeli society.

When we bid goodbye to Sophia and her team, we head to a neighbourhood which houses a ragged collection of internal refugees, who have apparently received precious little help from either the public purse or private donors. Dwelling in cramped caravans huddled together in a field are a group of families from Gush Katif, who were removed from their former homes during the Disengagement of 2005. That they still haven't been rehoused in permanent structures two years after the evacuation is a sign of how poorly-handled the withdrawal was, as we have heard time and again from disgruntled settlers we've met.

When leading us to the caravan site, Sivan says that she imagines all the Gush Katif crowd are black-hatted *haredim* – "we don't see them that much", she says, but her ignorance also highlights the starkness of the divide between the settlements' *hiloni* and *dati* communities. The residents are not clad in black coats and fur hats; rather, they are attired in more modern clothes, the uniform of the national religious settlers everywhere. Religious nonetheless, the Gush Katif evacuees have constructed their own synagogue in the midst of their ramshackle homes.

Abandoned in caravan sites and cut off from their new neighbours – if not physically, then certainly culturally –

217

the plight of the Gush Katif evacuees is plain for all to see. At the same time, that they are still living beyond the Green Line at all gives the lie to the lofty ideals attached to the Disengagement by its chief architects in the government. Moving Israelis from one settlement to another might have appeased critics in the immediate term, but – given that the *yeshuvim* of the West Bank are just as contentious an issue as were those in Gaza – it is cold comfort to the Palestinians to know that by weakening the Israeli hold in one part of the Occupied Territories, the state simply bolstered their numbers and strength in another.

Chapter Seven
Disengagement:
Give and take

Leaving paradise

If, as Moshe Feiglin claims, the Sharon government's
Disengagement plan was meant to crush the settlers'
spirit then it would appear to have had some effect, if our
encounter with Sarah, a former resident of Gaza's
Nisanit settlement, is anything to go by.

As we approach the rickety house on the edge of the
blossoming seaside *moshav* [cooperative village] of
Bustan Hagalil in Northern Israel, we are greeted with
fluttering bursts of colour from a parakeet cage on the
patio's edge. The heat of the sun and the blooming
flowerbeds around the springy *moshav* lawns combine
with the salty sea air to give the sense of being in some
kind of holiday resort, but as we cross the threshold into
Sarah's front room, we find our host cooped up in the
oppressive clutter of a sweltering room that is stifled in
shadow, belying the apparent harmony of the environment. In fact, for Sarah, the only thing holiday-like about
this place is that she is a long way from home.

Following the Disengagement from Gaza in the
summer of 2005, residents of the evacuated Israeli settlements were compensated and re-housed in various
communities around Israel, as well as resettled in the
West Bank. However, two years on, much of the permanent housing has yet to be built and many former Gaza
settlers, like Sarah, complain that the compensation
wasn't enough to replace the kind of lives they had
grown used to in Gaza.

Indeed, this is part of the problem. In his exceptional
overview of Israeli settlements, *Occupied Territories*,

Gorenberg describes that having begun to establish military outposts in Gaza in 1972 in order to suppress Palestinian militancy, General Ariel Sharon had sought to establish permanent Israeli settlements in the region:

"In Sharon's autobiography, he recounts standing on a dune with cabinet ministers, explaining that... he wanted 'fingers' of settlement separating [Gaza's] cities, chopping the region into four... By Sharon's account, it is worth noting, the Gaza campaign was virtually over, the militants defeated... But breaking up the occupied territory and dividing the population fit Sharon's long term strategic view... The purpose was to shatter the territorial contiguity of the Arab population, in the conviction that doing so would ease permanent Israeli control."[22]

So it was that poor immigrant families like Sarah's (Sarah originates from India, and her husband from Turkey) were encouraged by the cheap housing to come and live in seaside communities like Nissanit and play their part in the Israeli government's latest plan. Rather than moving out of religious ideology, they were reassured that the land belonged to Israel and that the move would be a strategic one, expanding and bolstering the borders of the Jewish state in the face of a surrounding Arab enemy. A patriotic act, but more importantly a chance to live in luxury that was unimaginable for such families inside the Green Line, nestled comfortably amongst the same picturesque dunes on which Sharon had stood and composed his grand scheme.

However, Sharon – Prime Minister Sharon by then – changed his mind. At last the free, or rather subsidised, lunch had to come to an end, and although there was majority support for the Disengagement throughout Israel, it is unsurprising that the settlers who had been coaxed to the land when it suited the government were unwilling to be the rulers' Risk pieces once again, now that the government had decided to try their luck at diplomacy. A challenge was made in Israel's Supreme Court on the settlers' behalf, contesting the legality of the

Gaza Disengagement, but as Gorenberg describes the Israeli government's argument was "fraught with irony. The state argued that while it had ruled the West Bank and Gaza Strip for thirty-eight years, the character of its rule was inherently temporary... Settling Israelis on occupied land was permissible – so the government said... – because the settlements... [were] always capable of being erased.

"Yet the purpose of settlement, since the day in July 1967 when the first Israeli settler climbed out of a Jeep in the Syrian heights, had been to create facts that would determine the final status of the land."

No wonder then that as Sarah sits in her stuffy home, with her former neighbours whom she describes as "one big family" now scattered across Israel, she describes herself as "no longer idealistic."

"I won't vote any more," she states. "The government will continue to do what they want anyway."

Just hundreds of yards away lies the patch of land earmarked for the housing complex that is intended to house Sarah, her husband and her five children along with several other families from her Gaza community. However, two years on and not a clod of earth has been shifted, not a brick laid. Sarah claims that every few weeks a letter arrives informing her that work will soon begin, but still there is no progress, and every day that Sarah is made to sit and wait merely compounds her misery, augmenting what she woefully describes as her "awful life." According to Sarah, her husband "doesn't show that he is sad" and is currently trying to open a shop, having left his previous business behind him in Gaza. In the meantime, they fritter their compensation money on the rent for their flimsy prefab home while they wait for the place they've been promised. Their possessions lie festering in a storage container somewhere, waiting for collection, but time and weather have long since damaged them beyond repair.

Time has eroded Sarah's spirits too and unlike her husband Sarah is unable to put a brave face on things.

Claiming she has "no reason to get up in the morning", Sarah has found herself unable to integrate into the new community, marking the contrast with the familiarity and warmth of her previous social circle.

"I am friends with the people here but it's not like [in Nisanit]. I don't have any faith in the people here. One day they smile at you and the next day they turn their back."

There are political differences too, highlighted by Rakefet, Sarah's daughter, who now sits beside her mother, comforting her as her memories track a wet path down her cheeks. Despite having adapted more easily than her mother, Rakefet recalls arriving at her new school shortly after having been removed from her old home – her family was amongst the last to leave, vainly hoping that some kind of miracle would prevent the evacuation from going ahead – where she learnt that the majority of her new classmates had supported the Disengagement. Reluctant to speak about Rakefet's experiences, her classmates had avoided the subject, but when it eventually came up in conversation Rakefet learned that her classmates "wanted to give the land back to the Arabs. They're from another world." Indeed, from the segregation of occupied Gaza to the mixed communities of the North of Israel; from the far right of the political spectrum to the centre left, the relatively short distance of Rakefet's journey belies the huge transition that she has had to make.

For Sarah, that transition has been too much and with her home she has shed not only her possessions and her friends, but also her religion. Where she was once an observant Jew, stringently adhering to all the commandments, she no longer believes in God.

It is easy to argue that the Jewish settlers of Gaza brought it on themselves; that, as the Israeli government contended, they were always aware of the impermanence of their status. Equally, one can say that they should not have even been there in the first place. However, to do so is to miss the point, for it is not only the continued Qassam rocket fire from Gaza that has turned the Israeli public off the idea of further evacuations, it is also the consideration of trying to relocate 280,000 West Bank settlers. Had the government done a fine job of the first wave, perhaps the public would have some hope for the feasibility of continuing on a grander scale. But Sarah's story is not unique. In fact, two years after the Disengagement, work has begun at just two of the 26 sites intended to re-house the evacuated communities. Many former residents, such as those we met in Ariel are still living in caravans and prefab housing, which were intended as a stop gap measure, waiting for their new homes to materialise. The Gush Katif Settlements Committee now predicts that this temporary housing could be in use for up to five years after the date of Disengagement. And such a grand failure to adequately orchestrate the relocation of just 9000 settlers does not bode well for the practicalities of a potential Disengagement from the West Bank. Whilst one might argue that the logistics are irrelevant – it is simply something that must be done – Israel, within the Green Line, remains a democracy and if people don't believe that the Disengagement is practical, they simply won't vote for it, which could mean many more years of flip flopping on the realisation of a Palestinian state.

Meanwhile, former settlers like Sarah are left ruminating on the kind of government that cajoled them to move into hostile territory and build their lives there in the name of national security, only to pluck them out again when the time was right.

As she pushes open the flimsy front door and leads us back out into the blinding sunshine, Sarah stops to show us an incongruous garden ornament, arranged amongst pots of flowers on what has become her front lawn. It is a Qassam shell, a souvenir from her Gaza home, where the rocket landed in her back garden. A curious memento of what is supposed to have been an idyllic life, the Qassam has been replaced with a new kind of missile since Sarah arrived in Bustan Hagalil. During The Second Lebanon War, the north of Israel was under daily attack from Katushya rockets fired by Hezbollah guerrillas from across the nearby Lebanese border. But whereas in Gaza Sarah would have taken refuge from such an attack, as the rockets rained down on the *moshav* during those summer weeks, Sarah sat in her garden and drank tea, the sirens wailing around her. Faith in God is not the only thing to have left Sarah since leaving Nisanit: sadly, she seems to have lost faith in life itself.

Digging in

Whilst Sarah's glass is half-empty and still leaking, others in the settler camp have begun to organise large scale demonstrations in order to make their political points heard. With a sense that they are being persecuted by the Israeli mainstream, but nevertheless boasting a great deal of political representation, settler groups have set their sights set on recapturing both the land they left in 2005 along with the esprit de corps of the early settler pioneers. Two years after the Disengagement, many believe that the time has come to return to, and resettle, the land they were forced to quit – and one of the focal points of their activism is the abandoned West Bank settlement of Homesh.

Standing precariously close to the edge of the mountain, two boys gazed down at the town below them as they waved their outsized flags with pride.

But they weren't a couple of valiant explorers who had successfully scaled a previously unconquered peak, and they weren't inviting the villagers below to share their sense of jubilation. Instead, they were two religious settler youths who'd come back to Homesh and were taunting the townspeople below with the Star of David.

Why? In their words, "to show them that we're back – and that we're not going anywhere."

"Nothing can stop us," said Aron, the louder of the two, when asked what message he wanted the Palestinians below to get from their display. "I want them to see that after 2,000 years, the Jewish people have returned – and yeah, I hope waving the flags did wind them up, so they know how it feels."

The pair of flag wavers was not alone. Fifty buses had been chartered to take settlement supporters to Homesh, in the heart of the West Bank, which had been emptied during the Disengagement and which the settlers are desperate to reoccupy. Marching under a six-foot high banner proclaiming: "We will not forgive, we will not forget," the thousands of protesters swarmed around the ruins of the former settlement, planting trees and preparing the ground for their "inevitable" return. The event was organised with the approval of the IDF, which prompted the more extreme branches of the settlement movement to boycott the march, in protest at the collaboration of the settlers with the same army who evicted them two years ago.

In spite of the split in the movement, settlers were out in force on the site where Homesh once stood. Bands played soft rock numbers to the mainly young crowd, people sang and danced in the overgrown fields, politicians gave speeches – and all under the watchful gaze of the army. One soldier we spoke to told us "I understand how the protestors feel – this was their home after all," as he nonchalantly described what his unit would do if the crowd refused to leave the hilltop at the allotted time. "We'll try to eject anyone who attempts to camp out here," he said, "but if they won't leave, we'll have to stay up here and guard them until they do."

According to this soldier, the army had no problem taking a half-hearted, laissez-faire approach to protestors challenging the soldiers' authority, and it was "understandable" that people ejected from their homes should want to come back to the site and lament their loss. Such an attitude contrasted sharply with the army's approach to the same kind of protest on the Palestinian side of the divide.

The Homesh demonstrators weren't looking for a benign location to vent their frustration and despair. Instead, this was a march of return and a statement of intent; to remind the Palestinians who's boss, as the two flag-waving provocateurs on the hilltop perfectly proved. "We have three options for dealing with them," said Yitz, pointing at the village below with his flagpole, "make them live in peace with us, let them carry on with their terrorism, or kick them all out. All the people down there want us dead – giving places like Homesh back to them isn't enough, in their eyes."

Sarah, who lived on a nearby settlement and had come to Homesh to make a similar point, gestured expansively to the hills on the horizon and declared "in the long term we'll be on that hilltop, and that one, and that one and Gaza too. It'll be a slow process, but it will happen." She lamented the fact that "round the world people have an image of us as the bad guys, but they [the Palestinians] can build their houses anywhere and not get killed, whereas whenever we settle somewhere we need the army to come and defend us. It's ironic."

In a report written the same week as the Homesh demonstration, the EU's Alvaro de Soto suggested that "If Israel ... was seen to be moving earnestly to end the occupation, I believe it would aid rather than handicap its legitimate fight against terrorism."

It is frequently argued that with evacuations like those from Homesh and Gaza, Israel made precisely such "earnest" moves. And yet not only has the settler population risen since the 2005 disengament, but the assistance of Israeli forces to those who attempt to retake evacuated land sends out a highly ambiguous message. Settlers are taken from Gaza and re-placed in Ariel; outposts are illegal according to Israeli law but are supplied with water and electricity; the world is told that settlements are a temporary security measure and yet the facts on the ground are undeniably permanent. Such ambiguity defines the settlers' relationship with the government: the state takes with one hand and quietly gives back with the other. With such duplicitous actions, it is hard to see Israel as "moving earnestly to end the occupation" and even as the settlers at Homesh protest to the government about all they have lost, the very fact that they can do so with the state's assistance suggests they ought also to thank the government, for all they have gained.

Another demonstration in Jerusalem brought home this ambiguity, as right wing settlers walked the walls of the Old City at once to bemoan their losses and flaunt their gains. The march was conducted by Nadia Matar, and having been in battle mode even in the quiet garden of her home, the Women In Green leader was perfectly suited to such a role, as she pulled the strings of a few thousand puppets in the heart of Jerusalem.

An annual event, the march coincides with Tisha Ba'av, the saddest day in the Jewish calendar. By fasting, and reading the Book of Lamentations, Jews around the world commemorate the series of tragedies connected with this date that have engulfed the Jewish people over the centuries (including the destruction of the First and Second Temples, the expulsion from Spain and the Holocaust).

However, subdued mourning and introspection seem not to appeal to Nadia Matar and her merry men and they hijack the occasion to send a stern message to the Arab residents of East Jerusalem with their inflammatory march.

It is, to all intents and purposes, the Mediterranean equivalent of the Orange Order parade in Drumcree. Even the colours are the same, thanks to the presence of the anti-Disengagement crowd whose orange T-shirts and flags bear their latest, shamelessly sectarian slogan, "The Land of Israel for the People of Israel". Two thousand people gathered in Kikar Safra, West Jerusalem, where Nadia worked herself and the crowd into a frenzy, stalking around the square in her trademark green baseball cap while preaching her message of division and war through a microphone.

We asked a passing demonstrator if he was worried that the Arabs might react badly to such an incendiary march, but was reassured that "they know better than to mess with a crowd this big". The man strode off into the distance, heading towards Damascus Gate, where the parade was due to begin.

The roads were cordoned off and manned by a huge police presence, meaning that the protesters were free to act as provocatively as they liked. One burly man, dressed in sackcloth in honour of the occasion, spotted a group of Arab youths on the other side of the road, and purposefully stormed over to wave his flag in their faces as he smirked triumphantly. When asked why he chose to make his point in such a fashion, Eliyahu explained in his booming American accent that "I don't hate them, I just want them to understand that they can only live here under Jewish rule." As we struggled to keep up with his frantic pacing, we asked him whether he thought this method of getting his message across was likely to do more harm than good in terms of Judaeo-Arab relations.

"Look," he screamed, "I don't care whether they like it or not. They need to understand that they lost the war; we won, they lost. Why it's taken them 40 years to get the picture I don't know, but we're not going to stop until they understand who's in control."

Warming to his theme, he went on to deride "the chutz-pah that the Arabs have – they demand that we can't even live in their midst and want us to withdraw. You're from England, so answer me this – what if all the Pakistanis in England said we don't want any whites living in our area, they've all got to go? What would you say to that?"

For all his incendiary posing, Eliyahu was no major player at this event. That accolade belonged to the rightwing Knesset member, Arieh Eldad of the National Union, whose firebrand speech was as chilling as it was surreal. With the walls of the Old City lit up behind him in a fluorescent glow, he bellowed out his message: "We must take back the Temple Mount, if we are to avoid another *churban* [destruction] befalling the Jewish People. We are doomed unless we bring in a strong Jewish leader to rule a land which is meant for Jews, a land which is not meant for Arabs." He left the stage to thunderous applause, the crowd lapping up his battle cry.

Having heard from residents throughout the national religious settlements in the West Bank that they are marginalised and ostracised from mainstream Israeli society, speeches and demonstrations such as these indicated that they remain a significant political force. The drivers of the settlement entertprise – the nationalistic religious activists who support Israeli Jewish sovereignty over the entire West Bank – might be wounded following the evacuation from Gaza, but these demonstrations prove that they are as organised and determined as ever. The night belonged to the rightists and nationalists, and they came together as one to demonstrate their unswerving solidarity with one another, and their equally determined separatism in relation to their Palestinian neighbours.

The Israeli government meanwhile remained at once a friend and enemy – an institution to be mistrusted, but the one which facilitates settlement growth and even demonstrations such as these. Well used to creating facts on the ground and vehemently promoting them, the nationalistic settler vanguard knows precisely how to deal with such a government, having begun as a rebel organisation that fought with the government even as the state assisted them. With talk of destruction and loss, Eldad reminded his audience of the need for expansion and gain: one step backwards two step forwards. Eldad,

Matar and others like them might see themselves on the back foot for now – but for them, it is perhaps the best way to move forwards.

2009

Two years later

Two years on from our tour of Israel's West Bank settlements, a great deal has changed at the political level.

In December 2008, a long running stand off between extremist settlers and Israeli authorities over a group of settlers' right to occupy a Hebron home led to the largest confrontation between settler organisations and the Israeli state since the Disengagement of 2005. Promising to "go to war" with the government and the Israeli forces conducting the evacuation, right wing extremists opposed their removal by attacking Israeli soldiers and rampaging through Palestinian neighbourhoods, provoking disgust and contempt throughout Israeli society. It seemed the right wing settlers were becoming increasingly marginalised and that the war between them and the rest of Israel was heating up.

However, just over three weeks later Israel launched Operation Cast Lead and the Gaza War erupted, as Israel engaged Hamas in a hugely controversial military campaign. Despite widespread international condemnation, the war precipitated a massive lurch to the right within Israeli society and Benyamin Netanyahu was able to point to his opposition to the Disengagement from Gaza in 2005 as proof of the fact that he had been right all along. If only the country had listened to him in the first place, Israel would still be in Gaza, Hamas wouldn't have gained power and Israel wouldn't be sending its troops to war. Despite coming second to Tzipi Livni's Kadima, the right wing parties triumphed overall and Netanyahu was able to stage his long awaited political comeback, arm in arm with far rightist Avigdor Lieberman, promising a new era of old policies: no mention of a Palestinian state; no movement on evacuation of settlements; no divided Jerusalem. The settlers could rest easy.

Over in America, however, politics moved in an entirely different direction and the prioritisation of a solution to the Israel Palestine conflict as a key international policy target distinguished new President Barack Obama from his predecessor, suggesting there were arguments to come between the two old friends, America and Israel.

When we return to the settlements in spring 2009 to discover the mood on the ground following such upheaval at the top, the first clash is already warming up as Israel's demolition of Palestinian homes in East Jerusalem provokes the consternation of US Secretary of State Hilary Clinton who appears determined to make America's new approach known amongst Israel's political echelons.

It seems appropriate, then, that we begin our journey in the holy, disputed city, where we speak to Israelis and Palestinians about what both the right and the left agree is a policy of Judaisation of the Israeli-annexed Palestinian residential areas of East Jerusalem.

We then travel to Hebron to discover the mood there, before heading to the South Hebron hills, a focal point for settler attacks on Palestinians, talking to local settlers and Palestinians alike. Next we take a look at two sides of one particularly contentious stretch of the Separation Barrier, and talk to Palestinian, Israeli and international activists about the various means of resisting appropriation of Palestinian land.

Finally we speak with a former elite soldier and unique Israeli settler now going to war with the Israeli government as he tries to persuade them to enable settlers to leave the West Bank and move back into Israel. Many settlers, he tells us, have had enough.

A great deal may have happened in Israel and the Middle East in two years – but how much has really changed in the settlements of the West Bank?

Chapter Eight
East Jerusalem:
The lie of the land

From the left

In a small patch of wasteland, a short walk from the imperial splendour of East Jerusalem's American Colony Hotel, a shabby tent stands pitched amongst a few old cars, a large sign tacked to its side in English and Arabic: "Stop Ethnic Cleansing". Chairs line the edges of the low ceilinged structure, holding a mix of stern-faced Palestinians and international activists; quiet, like the bereaved in a mourning tent. From the surrounding roads a trickle of pedestrians spills onto the dusty land to congregate outside the booth and soon those inside file out to face an assembling camera crew. The content: the Sheikh Jarrah Neighbourhood Committee's protest against what they describe as the Israeli authorities' "ultimate goal... to evict the Palestinians from Jerusalem and annex their land."

Specifically this is a protest against the imminent eviction of two families of the twenty-seven facing evacuation from their homes in the East Jerusalem district of Sheikh Jarrah, to make way for a housing development of 200 units to house Jewish settlers at the heart of this Palestinian residential area. More generally, however, the sign on the tent refers to a perceived wider problem of the Judaisation of East Jerusalem, whereby Palestinian homes are demolished to clear the way for Jewish developments. In this way, according to a confidential EU report of 2008 cited by the *Guardian* newspaper, Israel is "actively pursuing the illegal annexation of East Jerusalem."[23]

According to the Israeli Committee Against House Demolitions (ICAHD), demolition of Palestinian homes in

East Jerusalem has accelerated rapidly over the last few years, with a total of 512 buildings demolished in the six year period between 2001 and 2006 compared to 137 in the previous six years. Demolition orders are even reported to have spread to Convent homes in the Christian quarter of the Old City, as the Jerusalem municipality ostensibly cracks down on illegal construction. However, Israel's claims that the demolitions are a purely municipal matter are countered by the UN, the EU, the PA and the US, as well as various local and international NGOs, all of which claim that the demolitions are a political move in contravention of Israel's road map commitments and a major obstacle to peace.

According to a report by the UN Office for the Coordination of Humanitarian Affairs (OCHA) in April 2009, the phenomenon of Palestinian construction in East Jerusalem without permission is a result of "the failure of the Israeli authorities to provide adequate planning for Palestinian neighbourhoods", with just 13% of Israeli-annexed East Jerusalem zoned for Palestinian construction, compared to 35% designated for Israeli settlement. The report claims that "the gap between housing needs based on population growth and the legally permitted construction is estimated to be at least 1,100 housing units per year"[24]. Indeed, according to *Haaretz*, even the deputy mayor for East Jerusalem affairs, Yakir Segev, believes that the municipality's policy of withholding permits for Palestinian construction is what drives residents to build illegally, stating that "to get a construction permit in East Jerusalem you have to be more than a saint."[25]

Driven to illegal construction, around 60,000 East Jerusalem Palestinians are now estimated by OCHA to be at risk of having their homes demolished, with up to 1500 buildings already believed to be facing demolition orders. ICAHD maintains that the practice of withholding permits and evicting Palestinian families is part of a "vicious", nationalistically motivated policy to drive

Palestinians from East Jerusalem, "thereby furthering the Judaisation of the city."[26]

However, it is not just illegal construction that threatens Palestinian families with eviction and their homes with demolition. In the case of the two Sheikh Jarrah families, the grounds for eviction stem instead from an ownership dispute. According to Nahalat Shimon, the construction company that intends to demolish the entire Palestinian neighbourhood and build 200 housing units to form a new Jewish settlement, Shimon HaTzadik (named after the neighbouring grave believed to be of the Jewish High Priest of the Second Temple), the land was purchased from a Jewish organisation, the Sephardic Community Committee (SCC). The latter claims to have first acquired the land in the 19th Century and, following Israel's annexation of East Jerusalem in 1967, it reclaimed ownership of the land, demanding that the resident Palestinians pay them rent. However, the Sheikh Jarrah Neighbourhood Committee claims that the SCC's ownership claims are forged, whilst the Israeli Supreme Court has recognised that the SCC's ownership registration is incomplete, but has said it is not its domain to adjudicate on the matter. For their part, the Israel Lands Registry has refused to overturn the SCC's ownership claim, saying this is a matter for the courts. Stuck in the middle of a complex, bureaucratic legal system, the Palestinian families who have been living in the homes since 1956 claim that they were supposed to have received ownership of the land as part of an agreement between UNWRA and the Jordanian rulers at the time, although the ownership was never fully transferred to the families.[27]

It would appear that the difficulties faced by these Sheikh Jarrah families in dealing with the Israeli courts are symptomatic of a bias within an Israeli system that favours Israelis over Palestinians. According to a report by Ir Amim, a not for profit organisation that promotes coexistence in Jerusalem,

"A broad look at recent events in Sheikh Jarrah reveals the differential use of the legal system to (a) carry out eviction orders against Palestinian residents but not against settlers, and (b) to support pre-1948 Jewish land claims in East Jerusalem while opposing pre-1948 Palestinian land claims in West Jerusalem. This systemic distortion results in the cynical use of the legal system in the service of advancing an inequitable and inflammatory political agenda."[28]

According to the report, the Shimon HaTzadik plans can be viewed as part of a wider concerted effort to create a string of Jewish settlements throughout Palestinian districts, much like the shoelaces of settlements that spread across the hilltops of the West Bank, laying claim to the land in between.

"In Sheikh Jarrah to the north, the Mount of Olives to the east and Silwan to the south, development plans aim to ring the Old City with Jewish settlements and public projects, cutting off Palestinian territorial contiguity with the Old City. These developments unilaterally create an integral population link between the Old City and West Jerusalem [and] strengthen Israeli control of this sensitive area."[29]

Indeed, as *Haaretz* has reported, this is the stated aim of both former Mayor of Jerusalem Uri Lupolianski who in 2004 sought permission to build the Jewish neighbourhood in Sheikh Jarrah, "in order to strengthen the connection between the Jewish neighbourhoods" in East Jerusalem, and of National Union MK Benny Elon, who, according to the paper, "supports building the new neighbourhood [saying] it is designed to create a Jewish continuum surrounding the Old City, where there currently is a massive Palestinian majority... by declaring open areas to be national parks and placing state property back-to-back with lands under Jewish ownership."[30]

Moreover, the drive for increased Israeli settlement in East Jerusalem is not just a top down approach, initiated by the municipality, but is supplemented by grass roots settler organisations and individuals who move into Palestinian houses illegally and become permanent squatters there, as well as by wealthy individuals like the American billionaire Irving Moskowitz, who buy up land and homes in Palestinian areas intended for Jewish developments. Such a combined effort has enabled Israeli settlement of East Jerusalem to continue at what the EU has described as a "rapid pace"[31], sparking a major international controversy.

Unilaterally annexed by Israeli in 1967, East Jerusalem is internationally regarded as occupied territory, but amongst Israelis the notion of re-dividing Jerusalem is highly controversial, explaining why politicians from across the political spectrum persistently reaffirm the Basic Law that Jerusalem is the "eternal, undivided capital" of Israel. Some 190,000 Jewish Israelis now live in East Jerusalem and the *Guardian* cites the EU report stating that a further "5,500 new settlement housing units have been submitted for public review, with 3,000 so far approved" since late 2007.[32] In the face of this gradual takeover of East Jerusalem by Israeli residents, the Palestinians remain unswerving in their demand for East Jerusalem to be the capital of a future Palestinian state.

Against this backdrop then the Israeli municipality's suffocation of Palestinian growth and the encouragement of Jewish expansion both in predominantly Jewish suburbs of East Jerusalem as well as densely populated Palestinian residential districts like Silwan, right beside the Old City walls, can be understood as a deliberate policy to create facts on the ground and impact on a future peace agreement with the Palestinians by preventing the re-division of the city which would allow the Palestinians to claim East Jerusalem as their capital. This contentious affront to the Palestinians' national aspirations and the prospect of a negotiated pace settlement, according to Ir Amim, "threaten[s] to spark a dangerous escalation of the conflict in the city and to preclude an agreed-upon political resolution in Jerusalem."[33]

On the other hand however, can it be that Israel is so dismissive of the international desire for a negotiated re-division of Jerusalem that it believes it will get away with whatever it wants, regardless of Palestinian aspirations? It would appear that beneath the bravado of the "eternal, undivided capital", recent Israeli governments have been well aware that the negotiated division of Jerusalem and the notion of two cities for two peoples are inevitabilities. Indeed, *Haaretz* reports that as recently as September 2008, Ehud Olmert was ready to give up Israeli sovereignty over the Holy Basin area of Jerusalem, implying a willingness to cede sovereignty over the Old City, Temple Mount and the Mount of Olives.[34] And although Netanyahu continues to insist that all of Jerusalem will forever remain under Israeli control, his recent, albeit reluctant, reference to a potential Palestinian state shows he is capable of major policy U turns, whilst Lieberman's recognition that the Netanyahu government is bound by the Road Map[35], which paves the way for "a negotiated resolution on the status of Jerusalem"[36], suggests that even the current Prime Minister is aware that he too might have to divide Jerusalem.

So why does Israel continue to place its citizens in areas that it knows it may be forced to give up? Could it be that instead of believing that Israeli-settled districts of East Jerusalem will remain forever Israel, they are instead demonstrating the same cynicism with which they placed Israeli citizens in Homesh and Gaza and in Yamit before that, only to remove them like political pawns when the time was right? It would appear that not only is the government playing a grand game of Supermarket Sweep, trying to secure as much of the city before the time runs out, but they may also be using its citizens as bargaining chips, ready to be exchanged in return for land and security concessions, when the time comes. In this way, quite impressively, Israel is knowingly and simultaneously screwing both the Palestinians and its own citizens, the former by placing Israeli settlers deep inside Palestinian residential areas of East Jerusalem in contravention of the Road Map, and the latter by doing the very same thing, knowing that their Road Map commitments will inevitably one day compel them to force the settlers out again, thus creating an unstable future for both sides and provoking international consternation along the way.

Such international opposition to the demolition of Palestinian houses extends of course to the grass roots activist level, and when we visit the house of one of the families under order of eviction, we find an organised team of International Solidarity Movement (ISM) activists on site, ready to protect the family when the Israeli forces come to evacuate the tenants. The front room of the house is packed with activists as team leaders organise a rota of volunteers to serves as lookouts, people to chain themselves to the walls of the house, those who will be "arrestable" by being on the front line of confrontation with the police and soldiers, and those who will stay inside and protect the family whose grateful members wander around the living room doling out tea and biscuits.

Not all the activists are foreign however and there are a number of Israeli volunteers amongst the ranks of dreadlocked travellers and *keffiya*-clad leftists; some members of ISM, some of other organisations and others here as independent protesters against what they see as a clear violation of human rights by their government. Amongst them is a young man named Josh Weiner, who has recently returned from a spell of reserve duty with the IDF in the recent Gaza war, and who now stands smoking *nargile* [a shared tobacco pipe] with young Palestinian adults under order of eviction from the homes of their birth.

As the evening draws on and the soldiers don't arrive, those who have not been assigned a role in the front line defence of the house retire to their rooms to sleep, unsure whether the eviction will come – as they often do – in the dead of night. One Montenegrin woman, a member of the International Women's Peace Service who has been in the country for a couple of weeks, rails against the "arrogance" of Israeli settlers, whom she sees "swaggering around as if they own the joint", working in cooperation with the army as they laugh at the Palestinians. "I'm all about peace," she says, "but I can understand the Palestinians who throw stones. If I was them – and someone was taking your land and humiliating you – I'd be hurling huge rocks."

Traces of that anger can be found on the faces of the Palestinians on the streets of Silwan the following day, as we walk through the city to another, larger protest tent in Bustan, another East Jerusalem Palestinian neighbourhood, all 88 houses of which are planned for demolition to make way for a proposed archaeological park, which critics say is yet another ploy by the municipality to drive Arab residents from Jerusalem and augment the city's Jewish identity. In a remarkable demonstration of sophistry, Jerusalem Mayor Nir Berkat has compared the as yet unbuilt city park to New York's Central Park, claiming that the Jerusalem site is "much more important" than its utterly inequivalent American counterpart.

"We are talking about a small group who built homes on a park in an open area," the *Jerusalem Post* quotes the mayor as saying. "I would like to see what [New York Mayor Michael] Bloomberg would say about illegal building in Central Park. Would he give up Central Park because there is illegal building there?"[37] Given that many of the Bustan homes were built prior to the Israeli occupation of Silwan in 1967, the mayor's claims that the as yet unestablished park outranks and indeed outdates the Palestinian neighbourhood show a remarkable knack for Orwellian rhetoric.

Needless to say, if Jerusalem is indeed an undivided capital, then the mayor ought to look after the needs of his Palestinian residents too, given that the Palestinian appointed governor, Adnan Al-Husseini, has no real power in the city, but as we wander around the potholed streets past mounds of rubble that mark recent demolition sites, gagging on the stench of burning rubbish piles that provide the answer to the district's lack of municipal services, the contrast with Israeli West Jerusalem couldn't be more distinct. That just 5-10% of Jerusalem's municipal budget is spent on Palestinian areas, despite the fact that Arab residents make up over a third of the city's population[38], is abundantly clear, with the region boasting little of the public transport, services or commercial investment of its West Jerusalem equivalents.

Old men on the streets are angry at the way they are being treated; outraged at the prospect of yet more demolitions, but there is a sense of resignation too. A sense that they know there have no credible way of preventing the state from doing what it wants to do. "There will be another Intifada" if things continue like this, we are told repeatedly, with a weariness at the prospect of the violence that such a flagrant disregard for human and national dignity is liable to provoke.

Amongst the cluttered houses, which reach haphazardly upwards and outwards to accommodate growing families, in contravention of unobservable construction laws, the odd Israeli flag flutters in the breeze, proudly flying in the face of the Palestinians residents forced to watch the ongoing appropriation of their home city. The flags mark the solitary houses of Israeli settlers tucked away amongst the Palestinian homes of Silwan, and fly atop the sentry boxes of the soldiers tasked with their protection. We are told by Palestinians on the street that these settlers are neither rude nor cordial to their neighbours – in fact there are no relations at all, as they drive to their homes in their SUVs, ensconce themselves within the fortified gates of their solitary homes and play no further part in community life, safe in the knowledge that their presence in the neighbourhood is part of Israel's gradual takeover of the Palestinian district. We try to talk to settlers in these houses, but we can't get past the private security guards who sit at the gates of their homes, handsomely expanded with full permission from the municipality. Even when we manage to speak to a Silwan resident over the phone she refuses to be interviewed, so insular is this small, isolated settler group.

However, used to flying their flags proudly, the Israeli municipality seems recently to have misjudged the level of flagrancy with which their takeover of Palestinian neighbourhoods can occur, and by bringing out the bulldozers to demolish two Silwan homes on the occasion of Hilary Clinton's visit to the capital in March, Israel found itself at last igniting the tinderbox that it had spent years constructing. Clinton responded by calling the demolitions "unhelpful" and a violation of Israel's Road Map commitments[39] sparking a significant diplomatic disagreement between the new Israeli administration and the new government in Washington. After much hyperbole from the mayor in dismissal of the American claims, including reportedly calling Clinton's comments "air", *Haaretz* reported on 29th June 2009 that Jerusalem has performed an unexpected about turn, announcing that they will be freezing demolition orders on around 70% of unauthorised buildings in East Jerusalem. The paper reports that the houses will become "grey houses"; still illegal, although no longer subject to legal action. It is a major development and one that follows swiftly on from the mayor's unveiling of what he has called the city's first "master plan" in fifty years, whereby he intends to pave the way for 23,500 new housing units in East Jerusalem to deal with the Palestinian housing shortage. Whilst such a provision is long overdue, it is also a long way away, with the plans intended for implementation some time before 2030. Furthermore, critics fear that it will simply consolidate Israel's annexation of East Jerusalem, with Al Husseini telling Reuters that it will "cement Israel's grip on the city and will force more [Palestinian] people out"[40], while writing for the Ir Amim blog in the *Huffington Post*, Palestinian lawyer and land planning specialist Sami Ershied claims that "the East Jerusalem presented in the plan will consist of whatever shreds of Palestinian population centers will remain after most Palestinian lands have been expropriated, and after the possibilities for Palestinian urban jurisdiction have been thwarted... [Jerusalem 2020] is ultimately designed to serve a political purpose that marginalizes one of the populations most in need of a master plan"[41].

Where such plans leave Sheikh Jarrah and the 88 homes in Silwan is unclear. For the two families facing imminent eviction, whose floors have been the sporadic resting place for hordes of international activists over the last few months, 19th July 2009 was the new judgement day; the date by which the families' eviction was planned to have taken place.

As for the longer term future, things remain just as uncertain; whether the Jerusalem 2020 plan will improve the living conditions of East Jerusalem's Palestinians, whether this will come at the price of even greater augmentation of Israel's annexation, or whether Israel will once again find itself clashing with an American administration bent on holding the state to its road map commitments remains to be seen. In the meantime however, settlers continue to take hold of solitary fortified homes within the crumbling streets of pitifully underserviced Palestinian neighbourhoods and the Palestinians of East Jerusalem are as far as they've ever been from having a city they can call their own.

Jerusalem may be undivided, but it remains very much a city of two sides.

From the right[42]

"No leftwinger would dare come on this tour," laughs Reuven, as the smug faces of his acolytes smiles in agreement. The day out, in the summer of 2007, was organised by the shadowy Jerusalem Capital Development Fund (JCDF) – a group, in its own words, "dedicated to reclaiming and strengthening the Jewish presence in eastern (historic) Jerusalem, greater Jerusalem and parts of Yesha". In simpler terms, they are the antithesis of rapprochement with their Palestinian neighbours, seeking instead to force them out of their towns and conquer more and more of their land in the interest of the Jewish people. Reuven and his co-conspirators are precisely those accused of being repsonsible for East Jerusalem's 'Judaisation' by the Palestinians of Sheikh Jarrah; the JCDF are the other side of the coin in the perpetual struggle between the two groups of nationalists laying claim to East Jerusalem.

We meet in the plush lobby of the Inbal Hotel in West Jerusalem, where we are able to size up our fellow attendees. All-American, all religious, all secure in their conviction that the cause of the Jewish people trumps all other hands in the Middle East game of poker.

As we listen to Reuven's introduction, it becomes apparent that the JCDF and its supporters feel hard done by and marginalised by the mainstream society, and Reuven's rhetoric smacks of John Nichols' rants in *Bowling for Columbine*, or the angst of self-anointed martyrs such as Daniella Weiss and Nadia Matar, whom we met in 2007. "If you read the propaganda – I mean news – in Israel," he begins, "you'll see how all our fearless leaders care about is giving away our land", subtly working his audience into a mood of contempt for the powers that be.

Our first stop, once we boarded the bus, is Rachel's Tomb – a holy Jewish site on the outskirts of Bethlehem."Does it make any sense at all that Rachel's Tomb is outside the Jerusalem city limits?" asks Reuven as we drive through the security wall encircling Bethlehem. Everyone shakes their heads in sympathy with his message, clucking sadly as Reuven assures us that "Bethlehem gets less and less safe all the time".

JCDF owns the house adjoining the tomb: the group aims to get planning permission to turn it into an $8m batmitzvah centre, where girls can celebrate their coming of age ceremony in style. But it's not altruistic motives that spur them on – the centre's erection would serve the purpose of artificially inflating Jewish tourist numbers to the area, in a bid to convince the authorities to annex the tomb to Jerusalem and eat into even more of the Palestinian territories.

"How many Arabs are too many?" asks Reuven rhetorically. "Any that you can count are too many," he gleefully declares, his crisp white shirt and knitted *kippah* no giveaway as to the vitriol within. "If you need your car repaired," chortles Reuven as we drive through the Wadi Joz neighbourhood, "come here, because the very part that was stolen from you can be bought back on the cheap here".

As I watch the faces of the others on the bus crease up with laughter, I wonder what they'd say if I hit them with a joke about "cripples" or "queers". No doubt they'd all be up in arms, telling me there's no need for that kind of prejudice – all the while blind to their own hatred that is somehow acceptable because it is only the Arabs they are talking about.

What makes it worse is the "sinister grandma" angle, a phrase we coined in the army to describe the little old ladies who used to come to Rachel's Tomb and advocate all kinds of slaughter against our enemies when trying to show us soldiers their support. On the tour itself the seemingly benign Christian couple from Tennessee who'd joined us out of "solidarity for God's people", are actually the worst of the lot. As we stand on the Mount of Olives, listening to Reuven's tall tales about yet more Arab aggression, the wife of the Tennessee ex-marine whispers that "if you ever need any help blowing up that dome [the Dome of the Rock], ask my husband – he's worked with explosives and he'd love to help".

I corner the couple during a break in proceedings and, all the while keeping up my rightwing cover, gently ask them if they meant it when they said earlier "we support the Jewish people, whatever they do". "Yes, of course," says the woman. "But what if Israel did something illegal or immoral?" I probe. "Well, I don't believe they ever would," she maintains. "OK, but let's say they did, then what?" I go on. Her face contorts in confusion and she replies, "Maybe I'd stop supporting them then but, like I said, that just won't happen."

The rest of the trip is spent listening to snide little digs about the Palestinians and barefaced lies about the political situation of the country, all the while touring the villages in which the JCDF hope to purchase yet more property. Reuven asserts that "Arabs just grab people's land and settle on it, flooding the place with their friends and family" – how he says that deadpan, given his day job, is extraordinary.

He describes wholly Arab villages as "not gentrified ... yet", but assures us that a Jewish presence would help them embrace modernity and respectability. We are told that "some of the so-called refugee camps they reside in have nicer houses than we live in ourselves", and that "Arabs can always find money to outbid us [JCDF] for property when they need to".

As we drive to the village of Abu-Tor, Reuven speaks of his grand plan for "solving the Arab problem". His use of phrases is already disturbingly close to the rhetoric of a certain group of Europeans in the 1930s, all the more so when he advocates "putting all the Arabs on trains and sending them to Jordan".

One of the more astute passengers on the bus points out to Reuven that "we have to buy them out, surely – we can't just ship them out on trains, because that would be like the Shoah". No, replies Reuven, "we'll tell them 'you're no longer welcome in this country', and then let Jordan or Egypt deal with them".

The ultra-nationalist streak so central to his, and JCDF's, manifesto is staggeringly blunt – not to mention alarming. To paraphrase Niemoller's famous poem, "first they came for the Palestinians, and I didn't speak out ..."

***

Slumped on a cheap plastic chair in the protest tent that has become his second home, in the East Jerusalem village of Silwan, Jawad's eyes blaze momentarily as he vents his rage. "Just because we're Palestinian, does that mean we have to believe their lies?" he spits, when asked how he felt about the claim that Jerusalem was now a "united" city.

"Everything's become worse [since the occupation]," he continues. "We pay almost 50% of the municipality's budget, and get less than 2% of the services in return [the official figure, according to the EU, is estimated at closer to 5%]. Our families are scared to visit us in Silwan, ever since the settlers set up home here; the settlers have stolen all of our trade by encouraging the tourists to only buy from them; they're trying to turn the whole of our village Jewish – and there's every likelihood that they'll succeed."

Jawad, a veteran activist who has been taking on the settlers in his home town for years, is in no mood to join in the celebrations that have engulfed the Jewish population of Jerusalem. Yards from where he is sitting, hundreds of jubilant partygoers have swarmed in to the grounds of Ir David (the settler-managed archaeological site of the ancient City of David), where a free concert is in full flow to mark Yom Yerushalayim, the anniversary of Jerusalem's unification during the Six Day War of 1967.

"I call it 'Occupation Day'", mutters Jawad bitterly. "I am very pessimistic about the future; I don't see a peaceful solution whilst the settlers have all the power."

Those same settlers are making their presence fully felt with the sound and light show they have put on in the middle of the predominantly Arab district of Silwan. Sponsored by Irving Moskowitz, the event has attracted an enormous audience, including Women in Green head Nadia Matar.

"What does unification mean to me? [Ultimately], from the Nile to the Euphrates," she declares. Her sentiments are shared by almost everyone we meet inside the venue, many of whom are utterly unconcerned with the side-effects of their fervent nationalism.

"I don't feel guilty at all about capturing their territory," said a wiry man sprawled on the grass listening intently to the music blaring out from the sound system. "If they don't like it, they can leave."

"Life's tough," shrugs Rabbi Pesach Lerner, an associate of Moskowitz who has flown in from New York for the show. "They kicked us out of here first, so now we're taking back what's ours," he booms, warming to his theme and brushing away any dissenting opinion espoused by those of us challenging his rhetoric.

We then fall into conversation with a young religious man who has been tasked with interviewing members of the audience for a promotional film commissioned by the organisers. He quickly realises his mistake in seeking our opinion and, once he turns off his camera, it is our turn to quiz him on his reasons for celebrating the event in such a brazen and provocative fashion in the midst of a Palestinian village.

Pointing at the scores of Arab houses with a front row view of the open-air concert, I ask "Is this event a hand reaching out in peace to our fellow residents of Jerusalem?" "I'm not sure," comes the man's hesitant reply. "You have to understand, this is an event for Zionism; not an event for world peace..."

That much is clear; as Jawad and his peers sit listlessly in their protest tent over the road, listening to the jubilation and joy with which their neighbours celebrate the conquest of the Arab half of the city, his anger is matched only by his sad air of defeat. The sheer number of celebrants he watches stream in and out of Ir David only serves to convince him how futile his struggle is to bring justice to the village of Silwan, as well as to the Palestinian people at large.

"There are the ideological settlers, of course," he says. "But [compounding the problem] is the majority of the Israeli population. Either they are naïve and have no idea what is being carried out in their name, or they simply don't care about the Palestinians' suffering. We try our best to educate the Israeli public about what is going on, but we have less than one percent of the funds that the settler groups have with which to publicise the reality."

The contrast between the unrestrained delight on one side of the street and the despair and resignation on the other is stark: the Jewish joy is the Palestinians' pain. The streets are filled with buoyant, buccaneering gangs of Jewish youths proudly waving outsized Israeli flags as they march round the Old City, as well as the occasional Palestinian walking past with head bowed, hoping to avoid bearing witness to the carnival of conquest.

If this is the unity that the authorities spoke of when promoting Yom Yerushalayim, then clearly they were lacking etymological prowess, tact or simple understanding of the reality of life for the non-Jewish half of Jerusalem that had been forced to become part of the "unified" city.

For Jawad and his peers in Silwan, there is no question that the event is just another chance for the settler-supporting nationalists to kick them while they are down – and, it seems, those doing the kicking weren't denying it either. "Life's tough"; "I don't feel guilty..."; "From the Nile to the Euphrates"; phrases that ring out far louder than the music emanating from the stage, and sentiments that show the true colours of those championing the cause of conquest and capture for another year.

The residents of Silwan, who have suffered constantly at the hands of an indifferent municipality that pays little attention to the basic sanitary and social needs of

251

the village, have their situation made worse by the growing number of settlers who have set up camp in their midst.

Not content with embedding themselves in buildings all over the town and provocatively draping Israeli flags from the rooftops, the settlers have also been busy conducting archaeological excavations throughout the area, in search of Biblical relics that will reinforce their claims that the district should be recognised as belonging to the Jews. Many ancient tunnels have been uncovered, which – since they are made of stone – haven't caused any damage to the buildings above, but recently local settlers, along with archaeologists they have hired, have begun digging a new series of cruder, flimsier tunnels that have had a serious impact on many homes belonging to Silwan's Arab populace.

Although the locals are bringing a case to the courts to demand a halt to the excavations, the settlers have ploughed on regardless and, since the authorities have proved reluctant to step in, Silwan's residents have decided to take to the streets to garner support for their cause. Setting up yet more tents in a parking lot in one of the main streets of the town, scores have come to protest the settlers' actions and call for intervention by the authorities.

Huge banners are prominently displayed on lampposts: "Tunnels are not more important than lives!" read one; "No new Nakba![43]" another. "The more they dig out the earth, the more they damage our houses," says Jawad. "The settlers say they will start work on the tunnels again this week, and we'll be here to stop them – physically, if we have to."

Their numbers are swelled by a dozen or so Jewish Israelis who have come to support the Silwan residents, demonstrating a solidarity that spans ethnic divisions. However, the overriding image of the situation in Silwan is of a group of marauding settlers with equal disregard for both the law and their Arab neighbours, whose selfish endeavours threaten to overshadow any efforts made by Jews and Arabs to get along with one another.

At least, that is the view of the Palestinian cab driver who drives us back to West Jerusalem when the demonstration is over. "Those with the money have the power," he says, referring to the seemingly bottomless pit of funds made available to the settlers by the Elad organisation (which runs the City of David centre, and – according to *Haaretz* – promotes the 'Judaisation' of East Jerusalem) to carry out their work. "We have none, so we can do nothing," he continues dejectedly.

"But," he goes on, glancing at us in the rear view mirror, as he wags his finger forcefully, "it's all a cycle – one day we'll have the power, and then we'll do to them what they do to us now. As we say, every dog has its day."

Further proof of the insidious actions taken by Elad and the Jerusalem municipality comes to the fore on an archaeological tour of Silwan a fortnight later. In the two weeks since we first met the protesters, several had been arrested on trumped up charges of violence against the settlers, before being released without charge – but having been made fully aware that their objections to the digging were not going to be tolerated.

"The collusion of the police, the army and the settlers is more pronounced in Silwan than anywhere else in the country," one demonstrator tells us. "The policemen tell the settlers 'kol hakavod' [all our respect] for buying up Arab homes, and they do nothing when we present evidence of the settlers attacking us." The protest tent in the centre of town is still going strong, well-attended by both local Arab residents and sympathetic Israelis who come to show their support for the cause.

Against this backdrop, it seems apposite to go on a self-styled "alternative tour" of Silwan's ancient sites, run by a Tel Aviv university professor of archaeology who makes no bones about where his sympathies lie in the dispute. He spends two hours walking our thirty-strong group around the town, castigating the work of Elad – the settler organisation who, he claims, "have a stranglehold over the entire area". Elad has been handed responsibility for excavations in the area, and use their position to prevent Arab construction, claiming that all open space is off limits to anyone but archaeologists.

Of course, when it suits Elad, they overrule their own regulations and build new settler houses, as we witness on our walk through Silwan. However, the worst part about Elad's grip over Silwan's antiquities is that it is their narrative alone that is told to most of the half a million tourists who visit the area every year. "They train all the guides in how to present the facts," says Professor Greenberg, "who in turn pass on this version of events to the thousands of people who go on their trips."

The IDF send all their soldiers on Elad tours, he says, where they are fed the line that Silwan has always had a Jewish presence, and by doing so Elad justify their reasons for "Judaising" the area in the present day. Whilst Elad assure anyone who will listen that Ir David has been the site of a constant Jewish presence ever since Bible times, other archaeologists assert that there is insufficient evidence to prove Jewish settlement in the area before the ninth century, and that if there was such a presence, it was a far smaller, unfortified encampment than Elad claim. Elad make no bones about their intention to flood the village with Jews with no regard for the Arab populace since, in their eyes, Silwan is the rightful inheritance of the Jewish descendants of their Biblical ancestors.

Midway through the tour, I notice one participant scowling at the guide and seemingly having a hard time keeping his thoughts to himself, and as I watch him I had a faint recollection of having met him before. As we wander off down the road to the next site, I pull him to one side and ask if something was wrong, to which he replies "this is a far left, extremist tour – just listen to his language, and how all he cares about is the Palestinians". Casting a furtive look to check that none of the other participants are listening, he whispers to me that "I'm here undercover – I actually run my own tours of east Jerusalem, but they're very different to this one".

The penny drops – I am face to face with Reuven, de facto head of JCDF and part-time tour guide, whose inimitable brand of sectarianism I'd witnessed first-hand recently. He clearly has no recollection of me when we meet again, and decides to unload his burden on me and tell me just where the professor is leading us astray with his "suicidal" language. "There were never Palestinians living here before '67," he tells me firmly. "In fact, there were no such people as Palestinians before '67."

He tells me that he has sneaked onto this tour to check out his opposition for himself, and that he hopes I won't give him away to our guide. I ask him if he ever worries that left wingers have played the same trick on him, but he just shakes his head and laughs, telling me "I'd spot them in an instant if they did". He says that his main interest is "raising enough funds to move Jews back into these areas", and that the Palestinians "should just learn to live alongside us". He doesn't care about trying to educate the left to see his point, he says, "since all we need is money – and there are enough right-wing supporters to provide that".

In his eyes, settlers have as much right to move into Palestinian areas "as blacks did when they moved into white areas in the 1970s", painting a ridiculously skewed picture of the settlers having to struggle for their rights in the wake of Palestinian oppression. In the case of Silwan, he tells me, "the Palestinians came to live here after '67 – but even now they refuse to recognise the country they've chosen to live in. It's like me putting up a tent in your front yard, then refusing to recognise that it's your front yard at all".

Despite having heard it all from him before, it is shocking to hear the way he so adamantly insists that the settlers are the injured party in all this. Whilst the likes of Reuven and Elad still insist that black is white, and whilst they are still able to skew the facts so brazenly in order to keep their coffers full, all the peaceful protests in the world won't make any difference locally. The settlement juggernaut will continue to thunder through the heart of Silwan and other Arab villages, as the noise of its engine drowns out any voices that try to speak up against the injustice.

According to Angela Godfrey-Goldstein, a veteran activist and advocacy officer for the Israeli Committe Against House Demolitions (ICAHD), the views of groups such as Elad are far more mainstream than would appear at first glance. She believes the settlers' policies have a great deal in common with Zionism as a whole. Echoing the self-professed tactics of Daniella and Ariyeh back in Kedumim she tells us that "Zionism is about putting down dots and then filling them in", as she takes us on a private tour of East Jerusalem, countering all of the claims made to us during the JCDF tour and our Yom Yerushalayim experience. She points to various mini-settlements scattered across our line of vision, up on the hills of Silwan and beyond, as proof of her theory. The settlers' homes stand out intentionally, thanks to the mammoth Israeli flags either flying from their rooftops, or draping their walls as though wrapping for outsized birthday presents. Thanks to a seemingly bottomless well of funds available to the settler groups, coupled with a certain level of support of the settlers' actions taken by the Jerusalem authorities, the rash of settler-acquired properties grows by the month, she tells us sadly.

ICAHD are about far more than preventing the demolition of Palestinian houses. They operate as a direct action group dedicated to exposing the many "shameful policies" in which Israel's politicians and military are engaged across the Occupied Territories. ICAHD's head, Professor Jeff Halper, has previously told me that "settlements are a proactive claim to land". Their existence, it appears, has nothing to do with security – they are merely a means to grab as much of the disputed land as possible before diplomatic pressure from abroad puts the brakes on.

Angela speaks of many diplomats she has met who complain that their role in the conflict is akin to "watching a car crash in slow motion that they're powerless to prevent". The implication is that concerned citizens of the world should lobby their own leaders to call Israel to heel, though she doesn't hold out a great deal of hope.

We drive through Palestinian communities in various states of disrepair, communities that fall under the jurisdiction of the Jerusalem municipality, but that are underfunded and ignored. Even simple amenities such as rubbish collection are barely operational in these parts, and no one on Israel's side appears in the least concerned. According to Angela, it is all part of the "quiet transfer", the gradual wearing down of the Palestinians to the point that they throw their hands up in despair, quit the area, and head east.

Housing permits are also part of the quiet transfer, she says. Much of East Jerusalem has been declared an "open green zone", preventing houses being constructed, which in turn leads to a severe housing shortage in the region. Fewer houses than people means that the cost of property soars, pricing the locals out of the market and forcing them to seek cheaper accommodation on the other side of the security wall. Once they leave, they rescind their rights to Jerusalem ID papers, destroying any hopes of employment in Israel proper – effectively keeping them caged in the poverty of the West Bank for ever.

Meanwhile, green lights are given to settler construction left, right, and centre – a blatant case of double standards, Angela points out. She takes us to the site of the Nof Zion development: a state-of-the-art housing project with stunning views over the Old City, located on the edge of Silwan and, of course, meant for Jewish buyers only. "Phase one [of the development] has already been completed," she tells us, "and the plans are for the project to eventually cover the whole of this hill." There will also be a similar neighbourhood constructed on the next hill along, she continues, where two settler houses already stand, Israeli flags flying proudly atop their roofs, alongside the towering slabs of the security wall which runs through East Jerusalem, irreversibly cutting off villagers from their former neighbours.

Moving on to the Mount of Olives, Angela points out the Ma'aleh Zeitim settlement, funded by Irving Moskovitz, "who is breaking US tax laws by funding a politically motivated project", she informs us. "But he says it is a commercial project rather than a philanthropic endeavour," she notes, although its contentious location and his previous form when it comes to settlements makes his assertion ring somewhat hollow. "Over fifty of the units are occupied, and they are building another sixty," she informs us.

When we get to Ir David, we are surrounded by shiny, happy tourists who swarm the ramparts engrossed in their historical tourism: septuagenarian Americans rubbing shoulders with Israeli schoolchildren, whilst Ir David staff (mostly young employees from settler backgrounds) shepherd them around the exhibits. However, Ir David's aims are far from benign, Angela tells us – and, she explains, the phenomenon of "overseas money steering Israeli policy" spreads far beyond the perimeter of Ir David itself. According to Angela, settlements throughout the West Bank benefit from oligarchs' patronage – such as Roman Abramovich, Lev Leviev, and Arcadi Gaydamak, and with such high-profile and high-rolling support, the Israeli government have found useful partners in their quest to cement Israeli claims to land and property across the Occupied Territories. The more political backing and private bankrolling the settlers receive, the more JCDF's vision of "reclaiming" the area once and for all looks like being borne out in the not too distant future.

Straddling the divide

Inside the walls of the Old City, however, lives a young Jewish man with an altogether different political motivation than that of the mammoth right wing groups. Having met at the demonstration in Sheikh Jarrah, we visit Josh Weiner at his home in the narrow market streets of the Palestinian quarter of the ancient holy city to discover how he reconciles his reserve army duty in Gaza with his opposition to Palestinian house demolitions; how he distinguishes between himself and the settlers who also live in this Palestinian neighbourhood. How, in short, he manages to forge his position as a "left wing Zionist".

Set back from the stacked spice stalls and cavernous alleys of the old city *shuk*, a small courtyard lies in shadow, pierced intermittently by the fresh spring sunshine. At the side a doorway opens onto a staircase leading up to Josh's apartment, which lies nestled amongst the walls and roofs of buildings on all sides, an integral block in this organic mess of crumbling housing. At a table beside an open window looking out over a clutter of rooftops and steeples, we drink Arabic coffee and eat garinim as Josh talks about how his return to Israel at the age of seventeen, after having left the country for London as a child, has influenced his political outlook.

Having been raised a Zionist and used to supporting Israel in England, Josh's time in the army and his life in Israel since then have opened his eyes to some of the country's faults, causing him to become more left wing, although he has been "unable to reject" his Zionist values, firmly believing that the Jewish homeland should be here. As yet, he claims that he hasn't "found a way to put the two together."

Instead of professing an overarching ideology then, Josh simply does what he can to work to improve relations between Jews and Palestinians on a one-to-one level. Hence why we found Josh in Sheikh Jarrah. "I am not an activist," he explains, but when he went to the neighbourhood and heard the stories in the protest tent, he thought that "the injustice was so sickening" that he wanted to help. And as an IDF reservist, Josh believes that he has help to give.

"I know what the soldiers think," he claims. "They don't hate, they're just doing their job... but they might go over the top. There's lots of fear about going into Palestinian houses; you're always afraid that there might be something there... There's a dehumanising of Palestinians in the army."

So by speaking directly to the soldiers himself, Josh believes that he might be able to make them act differently.

Josh is adamant that the way to improve Israeli-Palestinian relations is not by criticising from afar, like certain activists who, he claims, "see things in black and white", but rather by "being a part of things". Instead of refusing to serve in the army, which he regards an essential Israeli institution, Josh believes he can have more of an effect on behaviour and beliefs within the army's ranks by talking to people on the inside and perhaps refusing specific orders to make a point. Hence his service with IDF during the Gaza war, but his insistence that he would refuse to defend settlement outposts in the West Bank.

"I am not against serving in the army," he insists, "but guarding a settlement has nothing to do with Israel's security. The opposite."

Josh leads us up to his roof where a stunning view over the Esher-esque jumble of domed roofs inside gardens, and washing lines across walkways displays the old city in all its cluttered confusion. Bell towers and minarets poke through the moss covered walls, between solar panels and satellite dishes, and if you stand on tip toes you can just make out a slither of the golden Dome of the Rock above the apartment roof. Josh leans over the wall and points to one house jostling for space amidst the mess of buildings, an Israeli flag flying proud beside a porta-cabin lookout. This, he says, is the home of former Prime Minister Ariel Sharon.

Other Israeli flags fly amongst the crooked aerials and flapping washing, prompting Josh to comment that he is "embarrassed of the settlers who are moving in" around him. The obvious question, however, is as an Israeli Jew, how does he perceive himself to be different from other Israelis moving into this Palestinian neighbourhood?

"I don't change any policy around here," comes his reply. "No one is stopped on the street because of me. I have no state funded security on my roof or in the street and I don't affect people's lives. I just pay rent."

Nevertheless, Josh's presence in this area remains contentious, with people outside his immediate vicinity suspicious of him, whispering "yehud" [Jew] behind his back as he walks the streets, and even his own landlord has refused to put him on the lease, for fear of his own safety – and has asked Josh not to bring Israeli friends over to the house for fear of Josh's. Josh can understand his concern, due to the behaviour of the settlers who live in the neighbourhood, who carry guns and "sometimes run through the streets shouting and spraying graffiti reading 'Mohammed is a pig' and 'death to the Arabs'."

This, then, is the face of the Israeli citizen that the Palestinians in this neighbourhood are used to and Josh does his best to counter that image with positive every-day encounters.

"People who don't know me don't differentiate between me and a settler," he says. "And for lots of Palestinians I'm the first Jew they've spoken to other than soldiers... but the more I'm seen as a person, the more I'm accepted."

Slowly, Josh has been able to overcome some of the suspicions that persist towards Jews and relations between him and his neighbours have developed to the point that families bring food to his house every night of Ramadan while a neighbour who only has a West Bank ID, and is therefore in the city illegally, asks Josh to run errands for him when he is going into West Jerusalem. He has even started to give one of his neighbour's daughters Hebrew lessons.

"Part of why I'm here is to show the Palestinians – and the settlers – a different kind of Jew. So that when they hear things about 'the Jews', people like the girl I teach Hebrew to can say 'well Josh is a Jew too.'"

Respectively, living here has also changed Josh's attitude towards Palestinians. Where once he believed that they all hated Israelis, he now believes that like most people they don't care too much about politics. "They care about rights. They want to be free. Unimpeded... Most of them don't support Fatah or Hamas, they just want to be free to do their own thing."

Tensions do of course persist, however, and Josh felt unable to tell his neighbours where he was during the Gaza war, so palpable was the anger and frustration in the neighbourhood, and on the few nights when he came home to his flat, he would buy an Arabic newspaper and tuck it under his arm, abstaining from speaking Hebrew as he walked through the *shuk*. In general though, Josh feels that in his own small way he is doing his bit for the coexistence of these divided nations in this most contentious of cities. It is that more than anything which sets him apart from the settlers, who remain fortified within their lonely castles.

As we pass back down the steps and out into the teeming market streets, Josh points to a growing pile of rubbish by the wall outside his building. "They don't provide any proper rubbish collection around here," he states. "Apart from for the settlers."

And he drops his bag of litter onto the pile, before disappearing into the throng.

Chapter Nine
Modi'in Ilit and Bil'in:
Two sides of the wall[44]

The archipelago of settlements to the east of Highway 443 is a constant thorn in the side of the neighbouring Palestinian villages, especially in the wake of the construction of Israel's security fence (or separation wall, depending on who's describing it – a difference of opinion further confounded by the fact that the barrier is in some places a concrete wall, in others a wire fence). Modi'in Ilit is, ostensibly, a satellite suburb of Modi'in – a thriving town between Jerusalem and Tel Aviv – yet whilst Modi'in itself is the 'right' side of the Green Line, Modi'in Ilit most certainly isn't, and the ramifications of its location are widely felt.

Unusually for a West Bank settlement, which are predominantly national religious or quality of life settlements, Modi'in Ilit is an Ultra-Orthodox *yeshuv*, home to over 40,000 residents; with an annual growth rate of 18%, the *yeshuv* is growing too large for its borders, requiring a constant process of expansion and construction. The entire population is religious, and cars are forbidden from the streets on Shabbat, whilst worshippers flock to the eighty synagogues within the city limits. However, the religiosity of the residents is not connected to ultra-nationalism, as it is with the *dati leumi* of many other *yeshuvim*: those dwelling in Modi'in Ilit are mainly *Haredi* Jews.

However, following a terror attack in the *yeshuv* at the end of 2008, anti-Arab graffiti has begun to appear in Modi'in Ilit, particularly in locations where Arabs work. Most of the graffiti urges employers not to hire Arabs, since the attack vindicated the sentiments of many residents, who had long feared the presence of hundreds of

Arab workers in the town. Following the incident Mayor Gutterman decided to ban Palestinians from entering Modi'in Illit, even those with work permits. Israeli Arabs, however, cannot be withheld entry, and thus many continue to work inside the town, despite the protestations of many residents.

The farmland belonging to residents of the Palestinian village of Bil'in borders Modi'in Ilit's perimeter, and it is for this reason that the Israeli authorities decided to construct the security fence through Bil'in's fields, annexing much of the Palestinians' olive groves in the process. Whilst similar expropriations have taken place along much of the route of the wall, Bil'in has become the focal point of local and international activists alike, and their weekly protests against the wall's construction have garnered huge media attention, both within Israel and worldwide.

Two years earlier, we'd attended a demonstration marking the second anniversary of the residents' struggle against the army's encroachment on their land; there was blood, sweat and teargas spilt, as had been the case during every week of their battle with the IDF.

When I return to Bil'in's olive groves in 2009, the village is holding a demonstration to commemorate the fourth year of their fight for justice. Despite court rulings in the townsfolks' favour that demand the route of the wall be shifted away from their farmland, nothing has changed. The wall still stands, the olive trees are still uprooted, and the border police still meet every protest with volley after volley of teargas, rubber and live bullets.

The *shabab* [protesting Palestinian youth] still hurl rocks and other projectiles at the soldiers, the protestors still chant defiantly in the name of freedom, their flags still wave proudly in the stiff winter breeze – but, when the march is over for another week, their village is in as dire a predicament as ever.

Meanwhile, beyond the phalanx of Hummers and military jeeps, the nearby settlements of Modi'in Ilit and

Hashmonaim loom above the fields. The likelihood of a respite for Bil'in from the Israeli authorities recedes with every foundation stone laid in the neighbouring settlements; at the same time, the likelihood of rapprochement between the Israeli and Palestinian people grows slimmer.

Modi'in Ilit

I take shelter from the clouds of gas fired at the crowd in a village backstreet. A gaggle of teenaged boys appear, eager to quiz the stranger in their midst. One rolls up his trouser leg to reveal a week-old bullet hole just above the ankle, while his seven-year old cousin gazes from his perch on a wall. International politics and governmental posturing mean little to him: he is absorbed by the wound a gunman from the Israeli side of the border has inflicted on his relative.

Winning hearts and minds is not one of Israel's top priorities when it comes to the Palestinians, but it seems like it ought to be. For every child who witnesses the violence meted out against their people firsthand, there is a freedom fighter in the making – easily persuaded to

265

graduate from the school of *shabab* rock-slingers to fully-fledged militant so long as he feels there is no other way to protect his people's freedom.

As we talk, the protestors' voices are carried towards us on the wind blowing from the front line, along with plumes of gas that make our eyes stream and our throats raw. The crack of gunfire and scream of canisters arcing through the sky soon drowns out the demonstrators' shouting as people begin fleeing the scene.

The army's final flourish is a choreographed shower of scores of gas grenades – as perfectly staged as an Olympic fireworks display. All that is missing is a neon sign flashing "Happy anniversary, Bil'in". The soldiers are under no illusion that an occasion such as this merits a special show of force from their side.

The tragedy of Bil'in, as well as of so many other villages and towns throughout the West Bank, is that the people the protestors really need to reach with their flags and banners are miles away in Israel's cities – for whom the Palestinians' plight is out of sight, and out of mind. The settlers and the soldiers who witness the demonstrations couldn't care less about the trauma they cause; the only hope is that those moderates left in Israel one day take up the Palestinians' cause.

But as Israel ushers in another set of hardline leaders, those trapped behind the wall know that there is little hope of salvation in the short or medium term. Generation after generation sees no glimmer of hope. What many assumed was a temporary occupation has embedded itself so deeply into the fabric of the region as to be virtually impossible to uproot.

I return to Bil'in again, after the death of villager Bassem Abu Rahma at the hands of Israeli border police during the protest a week earlier. Both sides clash once more seven days later – with predictably bloody consequences.

The march is the first since Abu Rahma's death, and brings down the curtain on the week-long Bil'in Conference on Grassroots Popular Resistance, during which luminaries such as the EU vice-president Luisa Morgantini and Palestinan Prime Minister Salam Fayad addressed those gathered for the demonstration. Billed as a way to "strengthen the relationship with the international solidarity movements, and to find new ways to strengthen and support the popular struggle", the event makes much of the supposedly "non-violent" nature of the villagers' resistance, despite ample evidence to the contrary.

The protest I attend is a case in point: as usual, the majority of the demonstrators find themselves pronounced guilty by association, in the eyes of the border police, thanks to the dedicated core of violent marchers embedded in their midst. The sentence is handed down swiftly and sharply; the standard barrage of stun grenades, sound bombs, tear gas and rubber bullets meted out indiscriminately against all of those gathered near the perimeter fence.

I stand well back, watching the drama unfold with a depressing familiarity. The tension has been ratcheted up several notches in the wake of Abu Rahma's killing, with much of the crowd decked out in T-shirts bearing his face, and waving posters in his honour, but the underlying issue is the same as ever. Namely, the continued annexation of the villagers' land by the Israeli authorities, and the complete refusal of the army to comply with court orders demanding the route of the separation wall be altered to give Bil'in's residents back their fields.

There is no doubt that the villagers of Bil'in are entirely right to challenge the injustices being perpetrated against them; likewise all their Israeli and international supporters deserve credit for championing Bil'in's cause and showing solidarity with the victim's of Israel's aggression. However, just because their cause is just, does not mean that every course of action they take in the name of resistance ought to be unquestioningly applauded as well.

According to international law, it is entirely legitimate for the occupied to violently resist – on their land – the army of the occupiers, but legitimate does not necessarily equate to productive in achieving one's goals. Four years of weekly protests in Bil'in prove that point.

For all the media attention and the mutual back-slapping of the international solidarity crowd and the Bil'in locals, the net result of their actions has been next to nothing, in terms of ridding the village of the separation wall. The toll in lives lost has, of course, been far higher and the violent tactics in which many of the demonstrators engage has played straight into the hands of the hardline Israelis looking for any pretext to justify the wall's existence at all.

But to speak out against the methods of the protesters is to walk straight into a minefield. I encounter such sentiments when speaking to demonstrators walking in the direction of the border police in Bil'in. "It's their right to throw rocks," one man tells me, "and who are you – or anyone else – to deny them that right? We're Palestinian led, so it's not for us to dictate how they vent their anger at the situation."

Ergo, if the Palestinians say "jump", those marching in solidarity simply reply "how high?"

The Palestinians are stuck between (throwing) a rock and a hard place when it comes to taking on the might of the Israeli military machine. They know they haven't a hope in hell of winning via an armed struggle, yet are equally and painfully aware that the odds are stacked heavily against them while the likes of the EU and US back Israel in diplomatic circles.

However that doesn't mean that, in the absence of a plausible strategy, they ought to resort to the methods that have failed them in the past. Israel needs violence from the Palestinian side to justify both the occupation in its entirety, and the separation wall in particular, therefore every rock hurled at a border policeman is music to the IDF top brass. As far as certain Palestinians can see, they are left with no choice but to attack the soldiers in the process of expropriating their land.

***

One group of activists seeking alternative ways to assist Bil'in's residents are the Israeli-led organisation Rabbis for Human Rights (RHR). When I accompany them to the village there again seems a sense of futility about the mission, given the level of military and judicial pressure being brought to bear on the village. This time, however, the tactic is not to antagonise the army, but rather to show solidarity with the local farmers and assure them that they are not alone in their struggle for justice.

RHR has brought the group to help plant a few dozen olive trees in the fields next to Modi'in Ilit, in response to a recent attempt by the settlers to build a synagogue right in the middle of a Palestinian olive grove. When the farmers tried to block the invasion, the incident had turned violent, with one Palestinian hospitalised after being beaten by the settlers.

A few minutes after we arrive to get the planting underway, a group of ten settlers roll up in cars and jeeps, apparently to take part in a *sulha* [reconciliation] with the farmers. They sit and drank coffee in the "peace tent" that has been erected in the field, as they earnestly discuss the situation with their Palestinian counterparts. However, many present are sceptical of the settlers' intentions, suggesting that they timed their visit to impress the RHR activists rather than out of a real desire to make peace with their neighbours.

Mohammed, the head of the village committee, explains that for his part, "I have to deal with them as humans, even though they're part of the occupation". He insists that he isn't against them "because they're Jews", only "because their presence here means that our land is stolen from us". He tells the settlers that there is a simple way to resolve the conflict between them and the villagers once and for all – "just *leave*" – but, unsurprisingly, his suggestion isn't warmly received by his visitors.

While they continue thrashing out their differences around the warmth of an open fire, the rest of the group heads off to the fields to plant the seedlings. Watching the proceedings, it is clear that the farmers don't need the group's amateur tree-planting skills, but rather that it is all about the emotional support provided that makes the trip worthwhile. In Judaism, visiting the sick is supposed to alleviate a sixtieth of the patient's pain – and so it is here.

The farmers and villagers of Bil'in are, thanks to the ongoing occupation and expropriation of their land, suffering constantly at the hands of the Israeli authorities – so every comforting gesture from groups such as RHR is much-needed and warmly received. Of the fifteen-strong group, a third are foreign activists, and the rest native Israelis sympathetic to the Palestinian cause.

According to Mohammed, it is "more important that Israelis come to events such as this, rather than foreigners, since it is the Israelis who can elect the leaders of tomorrow". Rabbi Yehiel Grenimann, one of RHR's leaders, agrees: "We're trying to show [Israeli Jews] that there is a different religious approach to the conflict; a way to do something positive rather than just create another national ghetto".

However, one strident Israeli boy present has a different opinion. "I'm not sure it's worth us doing this at all, since I've seen so many meetings between Arabs and Israelis and it's all just symbolic bullshit," he says. His sentiments echo those I have heard in Ramallah from Palestinians fed up of playing nice with their neighbours while nothing changes on a political level – but Mohammed disagrees with this approach.

"We *must* work with Israelis who have the ability to act against the occupation, like these people here," he states. In his opinion, the only way forward is to physically bring together like-minded peace activists on both sides, if only to counter the pervading sense of pessimism that hangs over both peoples.

After the trees are planted, we return to the peace tent to break bread with the farmers, where Rabbi Grenimann explains why RHR's work is just as vital to Israelis as it is to the Palestinians. "I've had people stop me in the street and say 'you've saved my relationship with Judaism thanks to your work'", he says proudly. "Whether Orthodox, conservative, or reform, we come together to promote a universalist approach to Judaism."

How long the trees they planted will remain in the ground before being uprooted by either army bulldozers or settler hands is anyone's guess. Likewise the fragile truce that appeared to have been agreed on by the farmers and settlers during their brief encounter earlier in the day. But, regardless of how the situation plays itself out, it is enough that the farmers know that there are at least some Israelis who care sufficiently to brave the cold and rain to give a bit of emotional and practical support.

Back in Modi'in Ilit, behind the razor wire and perimeter fence, it is business as usual in the build-up to Shabbat. Last minute shoppers cram the supermarkets and bakeries; women and children rushing round buying food for the 25 hours of rest that lie ahead of them and their menfolk: the mood is one of stress mixed with excited anticipation of the respite the Sabbath brings. Standing in the city centre, one can be forgiven for seeing the *yeshuv* as anything other than a rural incarnation of Ultra-Orthodox neighbourhoods around the world: whether Bnei Brak or Meah Shearim in Israel, Stamford Hill in London, or Crown Heights in New York. But a cursory glance to the horizon – past the towering apartment blocks and between the gaps in the trees – is enough to remind the observer quite how contentious and contested is the site of this particular *Haredi* stronghold. With construction continuing apace at the settlement's edge, as Modi'in Ilit keeps expanding to accomodate its swelling population, the tension will only be ratcheted up further in the neighbouring Palestinian villages. At the same time, the likelihood increases of reprisal attacks, as already witnessed here a few months earlier, which threaten to shatter the veneer of peace and tranquility under which the residents of the city currently dwell. Whether by accident or design, this is the fate of all settlements in the region, thanks to the irredentist policies that go hand in hand with their construction – and without a clear policy of rapprochement on the part of the Israeli and Palestinian authorities, the grass roots work of Israeli activists is insufficient to prevent the cycle of violence and counter-violence repeating itself here ad infinitum.

Chapter Ten
Hebron: Doing davka[45]

Despite Kiryat Arba's somewhat unsavoury reputation for spawning ultra-fanatical settlers, our new friend Elitzur is adamant that his *yeshuv* is simply a victim of media misrepresentation. "There's trouble in every place," he says with a shrug – as in, Kiryat Arba is no better or worse than anywhere else we care to mention. We don't argue, preferring to carry on chatting amicably to Elitzur rather than engage him in political swordplay. He had befriended us as soon as we sat down for a drink in the local café; whilst the woman behind the counter prepared viscous Turkish coffee in plastic cups, Elitzur had bounded over and introduced himself. Within a minute of meeting us, he was pulling down his shirt top to reveal thick, matted dreadlocked chest hair, by way of proving his age to us: an unexpected move on the part of such a religious man, but an icebreaker nonetheless.

Black eyes dancing in a face framed by a huge greying beard and bisected by a blonde-streaked whiskered moustache, Elitzur goes straight on the offensive, trying to discover the origin of the strangers who've come to town. When he hears that we are London-born, he launches into an anti-Diaspora tirade, listing all the myriad reasons why Israel's a better place for Jews to live than anywhere else on Earth. He tells Seth that since he's from a religious family, he'll excuse the fact that he sports an earring – in fact, he says, he sees Seth as a potential *shidduch* [match] for an Orthodox girl in Jerusalem who's looking for a husband; he presses her number into Seth's hand and urges him to call her next time he's in town.

When we eventually disentangle ourselves from his clutches, we ask two boys at a bus stop to point us towards Hebron's Old City, having planned to journey the last half mile on foot. A tall, shaven headed man clad in reflective Raybans overhears our question, and orders us in flat, authoritative tones to wait for a lift in someone's car instead: "It's too dangerous for you to walk". A pair of security guards standing nearby nod their heads in agreement, their mini-Uzis waggling their concurrence as well from their shoulder straps. The man in the Raybans works for the electricity company; the guards are always with him when he goes out on a job, "because the Arabs aren't sympathetic round here".

We eventually get picked up by a minibus ferrying a few *yeshiva* students to the Cave of Machpela – one of the holiest sites in Judaism, where several of the patriarchs and matriarchs are buried, and situated in the heart of the Old City. Since Islam and Judaism have many antecedents in common, the Cave is holy to Muslims too, hence the authorities have divided the structure in two, to accommodate both a synagogue and a mosque. The fact that Machpela makes Hebron one of Judaism's four holy cities is what attracts so many fundamentalist settlers to live in the city; religious fervour the fuel that drives them onwards in their quest not only to keep a Jewish presence in Hebron, but – ideally – cleanse the city of its Arab residents once and for all. A mammoth task, given that over 150,000 Palestinians reside in Hebron, compared with around 1,000 Jewish settlers. The city is unique in the sense that settlers live in and amongst the Palestinians, rather than there being a clear demarcation of territory as in the rest of the West Bank, where settlements are fenced off from neighbouring Palestinian towns and villages. Josh's phone alludes to the proximity when it switches to the Paltel network upon entering Hebron ("*Marhaba*! Smell the jasmine and taste the olives. Jammal welcomes you to Palestine" reads the upbeat message on his screen). Whilst we'd seen similar technological overlaps earlier in our trip, such as when Seth's laptop tried to connect to the 'Abdalla Rafat wireless network' when passing through Elkana, the physical division of the settlers and the nearby Palestinians was far more stark and total than the equivalent set-up in Hebron.

The perennial clash between the settlers and their Arab neighbours has resulted in much of old Hebron resembling a ghost town: boarded-up houses and barricaded shops line the streets like gravestones; the only people on the street are heavily-armed soldiers looking bored as they languidly patrol the deserted, dusty main road. Crude stars of David have been sprayed onto most of the welded-shut metal doors of the closed-down stores, resembling provocative BNP graffiti sprayed onto immigrants' businesses in inner-city London; a stark reminder of the sectarian division coursing through the city's veins.

As we wander away from the Cave, we pass thick clumps of wild grass; weeds creeping over the rusty skeletons of former market stalls that haven't been used for years. Adorning a cracked wall is a memorial to a couple killed by terrorists in 2003, their faces staring out of the photo and across Shuafat Street to the Muslim cemetery opposite. Flags fly in support of Likud extremist Moshe Feiglin, as young settler children stroll past in the afternoon sunshine. We arrive at Bet Hadassa, a former clinic for Jews and Arabs, which was abandoned after the 1929 riots in which 67 Jewish residents were massacred by local Arab gangs. The compound now houses settler families, as well as a museum in memory of those slaughtered during the pre-state attack; when we arrive, a group of reservist soldiers are being shown around by an army educator, and they allow us to join them for the duration of the tour.

Their guide is far younger than her group: she is still in her stint of compulsory service, yet commands the attention of the other soldiers – unless their mobile phones ring, in which case they duck outside and take the call; reservists being bound by far less strict behavioural code than those doing their initial spell of national service. The *madricha* relays the history of Hebron to the troops, utilising in full the visual aids all around: photographs of injured victims with missing limbs, brains showing through cracked skulls, and swathed in bandages as they peer forlornly at the camera. The grisly exhibits leave a profound impression on the soldiers, as is the intention; this platoon are serving in nearby Gush Etzion, and requested from their commanders a visit to Hebron to "better understand the situation", according to one soldier to whom we speak.

Leaflets are liberally scattered around the museum, intended for consumption by curious tourists, troops or any other visitors passing through the complex. "Inequality and Discrimination in Hebron," reads one pamphlet in bold red letters. "In contrast to the false, anti-Jewish, and anti-Israeli propaganda," it continues, "here are the real facts..."

The text is predictably incendiary: "If the Jewish people has undeniable rights anywhere on Earth, it is in Hebron... [but today] Jews are only allowed to enter three percent of the municipal area... the Palestinian Authority deliberately operates and is establishing institutions in this area for the express purpose of 'strangling' the Jewish community... A Jew who enters [Arab] areas risks his or her life... the Jews are almost totally deprived of their property rights... while the Arabs build massively in Hebron, the right to build is almost totally denied to Jews... Law enforcement: zealous against Jews, lax against Arabs." Accompanying the charges of pro-Palestinian bias are various photos showing rioting Arabs, and Israeli troops arresting settlers, carefully selected to give the impression that even the Israeli government is happy to throw the settlers to the Palestinian wolves – despite clear evidence to the contrary emerging on an almost daily basis in the media. A notorious video released by human rights group B'Tselem recently showed the true extent of the harassment of Palestinians by settler families (including footage of a settler mother viciously baiting a Palestinian woman of similar age, settler children throwing rocks at Palestinian adults under the benevolent gaze of Israeli soldiers, and a settler guard shooting an unarmed Palestinian man in the chest at close range with a rubber bullet). Watching such footage in Kedumim, even fellow settlers Ariyeh and Yehudit were quick to condemn the actions of the Hebron extremists, who have been held up in every settlement we have visited as amongst the most extreme of all, with soldiers who served here even telling us that the Israeli settlers cause far more trouble for the Israeli army than the Palestinians.

We walk up the hill towards the Tel Rumeida settlement – home to infamous settler leader Baruch Marzel – which is situated at the top of a steep road with mini-checkpoints at either end. At one of the roadblocks, a blue-jacketed TIPH (Temporary International Presence in Hebron) observer stands remonstrating with a soldier on behalf of a Palestinian youth standing to one side of the road. TIPH's raison d'etre is to "monitor the situation in Hebron and record breaches of international law." In essence, they are stationed in the city to bear witness to the almost daily violent incidents that erupt between the Jewish settlers of Hebron and their Palestinian neighbours. Established in the wake of settler Baruch Goldstein's murderous rampage in the Machpela mosque – in which he gunned down 29 worshippers during a prayer service – TIPH's presence is enshrined in the Oslo agreements which govern the way Hebron is run by both the Israeli and Palestinian authorities.

Seth had spent time with TIPH on his last research trip to the city, patrolling with Sibyll and Mortens, respectively Swiss and Danish TIPH workers, who were old hands at dealing with the explosive situation using the limited tools at their disposal. During that tour the first incident was fairly mundane by comparison with what would come later – a youth protesting to the pair that every time Palestinian Authority workmen came to try and fix a sewage blockage in the *shuk*, Israeli soldiers ordered them to leave the area without allowing them to carry out their repairs.

"This is the third time we've heard this story in four days," said Sibyll, as she noted down the boy's complaint in her notebook. "All we can do is to try and get our liaison officers to try to intervene with the army and the PA, and attempt to get permits for them to complete their work [unimpeded]." Mortens concurred with her plan of action: "It won't happen overnight, though – we have to

write a report, contact the DCO [District Coordination Office, an outpost of Israeli officialdom in charge of affairs in the West Bank], and hope that they can achieve results." And in the meantime, the stench of raw sewage hung over the market and added to the sense of discomfort that the shopkeepers were forced to endure.

There had been reports that it was the settlers who had blocked up the sewage system, causing the problem, although that was hard for the team to verify. However, the next incident they were called to appeared far more clear cut. In a busy street underneath a barred window of one of the settlement buildings, a couple of tin cans with unidentifiable viscous liquid oozing from them lay on the edge of the pavement. "They tried to light it before hurling it at us," declared a middle-aged Palestinian man breathlessly, pointing up in the direction of the offenders' homes.

"They were 16 or 17," he continued, "not small kids at all." Hanging from the bars of the windows were sandbags filled with stones, which Sibyll said, "are prepared by the children, who then throw the rocks down at the Palestinians. The IDF come, but always deny that anything has happened." All that TIPH can do in such circumstances is pull out their notebooks, log a record of the incident, and then file the report with the DCO, which does little to placate the injured parties or to reassure them that anything tangible is being done to protect them.

"There's a feeling of real frustration amongst us," said Ghassan, a Swedish member of TIPH. "We can't intervene in a situation; all we can do is turn up and take photos." He explained that this causes inevitable resentment on the part of the Palestinians, while others on the Palestinian side "don't like us because they're convinced we work for the Israelis."

As they continued along the route of the patrol, they came across a gaggle of teenagers surrounding a dishevelled-looking man sitting askew in a wheelchair. His T-shirt badly ripped from shoulder to shoulder and covered in bloodstains, he shook as he turned plaintively to Mortens and Sibyll and pleaded for their help. "The army did this," he began. "They beat me, and there are fifteen of them still in my house now – you've got to go and do something."

After taking photos of his injuries to use as evidence, they hurried off in the direction of his house in the company of one of the boys who was acting as guide. However, their way was obstructed by a shaven-headed Russian IDF soldier who ordered them to take a far longer, circuitous route, since the Palestinian boy was banned from walking past the Cave of Machpela. When they eventually got to the raided house, the operation was still in full flow, with heavily-armed soldiers milling around on every floor of the building as the children of the house nervously looked on.

Thanks to the terms of their mandate, TIPH members are unimpeded in their monitoring work, thus the soldiers had to let them photograph the ongoing search and interview the commander once he'd declared the building safe. "There were rocks being thrown from the roof," he stated flatly when questioned. "I didn't see anyone in a wheelchair," he went on, looking to his charges for confirmation, "and if there had been, I promise you he'd still be here with us."

"It's a bit fishy that he managed to get out of the house and all the way down the road in a wheelchair in the middle of a raid." He proposed that the man's injuries might instead be a result of him jumping off the roof and trying to escape arrest, implying that the wheelchair was merely a prop used to garner sympathy from the TIPH team. Once the soldiers had left, the team entered the house and interviewed the wounded man's children, who assured them that he had been beaten by the troops.

However, they also admitted that their younger brother had been throwing rocks at the army, and refused to stop when his older siblings and father remonstrated with him. At the same time, they couldn't give a convincing explanation for how their apparently wheelchair-bound father had made it up the impossibly narrow stairs onto the roof to chastise their brother. This prompted Sibyll to complain that the hardest part of her job was trying to decide who was being honest and who just wanted to apportion all the blame to the other side.

The commander's parting words had been "We were just doing our job – no one should have rocks thrown at them, should they?" While entirely right, his concern seemed pretty ironic given the complete ambivalence the army showed earlier when Mortens and Sibyll tried to report the missile attacks on the Palestinians. That the IDF runs the whole show in the city, and TIPH can do little more than meekly complain from the sidelines is the heart of the problem when it comes to policing the area fairly.

Of course, Israel is hardly likely to agree to arm the likes of TIPH, just as they have all but repealed the authority's mandate to be in charge of keeping order in the Palestinian half of the city. However, given that a large part of TIPH's purpose is to try and afford the same level of protection and security to the Palestinians that the settlers enjoy, it is clear that there is no balance whatsoever at present.

Well-meaning but ultimately impotent foreigners wielding notebooks and pens are no match for M16-toting soldiers when it comes to delivering justice to the city's residents. Therefore it is no surprise that, despite what TIPH was set up to deliver, the Palestinians feel no better looked after now than they did before 1994. And that is no more likely to assuage their frustration and fears than any other half-hearted internationally-led initiative – meaning that their ongoing feeling of abandonment is entirely understandable while the best they've got is TIPH.

The settlers, on the other hand, see TIPH as being entirely in the pockets of the Palestinians: according to the leaflet we'd picked up in Bet Hadassa, TIPH are in league with "groups of anti-Semitic Christians [who] encourage terrorism and endanger the lives of soldiers and civilians alike...", as well as "pro-Palestinian Arab organisation[s]" and "Israeli leftist organisations", "even though TIPH is supposed to be objective and to refrain from provocations". Under a photo of "TIPH observers cooperating with left-wing anarchists", the text goes on to condemn those it deems to "breach and trample the Jewish citizens' rights to life and safety", underlying the rank hostility the settlers feel towards any of the human rights groups operating in the area.

The soldiers are somewhat more amenable to TIPH, thanks to the official ties that link them to one another, and the resulting code of practice the troops have to follow when dealing with TIPH on a professional basis. At the top of the hill, the female TIPH team member, who is still talking with the soldier, clucks like a dinner lady in the school playground sorting out two naughty pupils, as she intervenes between the soldier and the youth. The stand-off ends calmly, and the Palestinian boy goes on his way with a smile for both the woman and the soldier; the woman follows suit, ducking into the TIPH jeep along with her partner, before speeding off down the road to continue their patrol, the group's logo boldly displayed on all sides of the vehicle to announce their presence to settlers, Palestinians and soldiers alike.

We get chatting to the sergeant who'd been involved in the incident, who appears grateful to have some more people to talk to in order to relieve the boredom of his latest shift of guard duty. Standing with him at the checkpoint is a twelve-year old boy clad in religious garb, who is from the settlement of Alon Shevut and has come to Hebron with his family "to look around". He listens in insouciantly to our conversation, entirely at home around semi-automatic weapons and gun turrets, despite his youth. The sergeant checks out our credentials via a series of probing questions, then – when he establishes that Seth too has served in the IDF – warms considerably and is happy to answer our questions about Hebron.

He tells us that there is usually no trouble in the immediate vicinity: "the Palestinians never stone us, but sometimes the settlers do", before leaning in conspiratorially and out of earshot of the twelve-year old mascot. "Between you and me, the settlers are often even worse – they get together at *shul*, and because they're in a crowd they work themselves up even more and go off to attack the Palestinians". But he is just as quick to sneeringly deride TIPH as "*smolanim* [leftists] – they're here to work against us. [They] only help the Palestinians", he says, echoing the sentiments of the Bet Hadassa propagandists. "God forbid we should raise a hand to a Palestinian kid, then TIPH take photos and send them to all the world's media," he complains.

He can't wait to finish his national service, he tells us – he wants to move to Tel Aviv ("the best city in the world; a city that truly never sleeps"), and is apathetic about the future of the settlements, unsure whether they're a help or hindrance to Israel's security. He tells us that he spent most of his service fighting in Gaza, including during the recent Operation Cast Lead, and "won't miss the violence" at all when he finally demobs.

He tries to secure us an interview with his platoon commander, radioing in a request to HQ, which is situated next to the settlers' caravans in Tel Rumeida. The radio operator replies that we can come up to the base, but that we'll need to explain ourselves to the guard on the front gate before being admitted. We climb the hill, only to be told by the commander that we need to get authorised by the Spokesman's Unit first, so we thank him and head back down again, whilst we're eyed suspiciously by robe-swathed settler women from their doorsteps and windows. We notice a settler with a pickaxe heading up steps towards a sign reading "The Nahalat Shlema neighbourhood will be built here", and we follow him up to a hilltop covered in razor wire, scrubby grass, and an olive tree with a huge, gnarled trunk and massive, knobbled roots – clearly ancient, and clearly doomed as well it would seem, from the planned building about to take place.

We wander back towards the Cave of Machpela, stopping for refreshment at the cafe in the Gutnick Center – a mini-shopping mall funded by right-wing Jewish philanthropist Joseph Gutnick of Australia, who is one of many mega-rich donors buying up land and buildings on the settlers' behalf throughout the West Bank. At the cafe, a clever marketing gimmick is in play: "Adopt a soldier", visitors are urged from posters and leaflets adorning the walls. "Buy a coupon in the cafeteria for a family sized pizza and bottle of drink for just 65 shekels, and give the coupon to a soldier". Photos of well-fed and watered troops bordered the signs: "On behalf of the soldiers, we thank you", ended the message – and on behalf of the cafe's shrewd owners too, no doubt – capitalism and nationalism cleverly harnessed to the same wagon in order to satisfy the needs of soldiers, tourists and shopkeepers alike in one fell swoop.

We then head into the Cave itself, past the two tight rows of security checks, and then past two enthusiastic *yeshiva* students singing Hebrew songs by Jacob's Tomb. Fellow-worshippers are whispering prayers, studying religious texts and soaking up the highly-charged atmosphere of the site, the eye of the storm proving the calmest place to be, by comparison to the rest of the city. When we leave, we stroll up towards Bet Shalom, the cynically named "House of Peace" taken over by settlers in 2007, who were then forcibly evicted by the army a year later after a court ruling declaring that the settlers were illegally occupying the building, which rightly belonged to a local Palestinian family. The evacuation was the culmination of a tense stand-off between settlers and the Israeli authorities, which pitted Jew against Jew in a small scale version of the 2005 Disengagement. After Bet Shalom was successfully cleared by the security forces, the settlers responded by rampaging through the Palestinian side of Hebron, taking out their anger by setting Arab homes and cars alight and attacking innocent bystanders who they encountered during their riot. Next to the now-empty house stands a mosque daubed in a fresh coat of paint, which has been applied to cover up the racist graffiti daubed on the place of worship by settlers during the occupation of Bet Shalom.

On our way back to the bus stop near the Cave, we encounter Yossi Baumol, head of the pro-settler Hebron Fund, who Seth last met when he went on one of his group's tours of the city. He holds the "politically incorrect tour" as often as demand requires, hoping to spread his message to as many potential donors as possible in order to solicit funds with which to support Hebron's settler community.

"The Muslims have ethnically cleansed the Christians from Bethlehem and the rest of the West Bank," he'd told our group during that trip, with a mournful shake of his head. Clearly the irony of his statement was lost on the others on the bus – even though he had just advocated a programme of "urban renewal" in Hebron, his phrase for kicking out the Arab residents and replacing them with thousands of religious Jews. Curiously absent from his monologue were the frequent and vicious attacks by Jewish settlers on Arab residents of the city, but then – as he'd so gleefully informed us at the beginning – this "isn't gonna be a politically correct trip, and I make no apologies for that". The rest of the group didn't seem too perturbed – the bulk of them were New Yorkers who'd flown in for a family wedding, and had decided to make use of Yossi's oratory skills as a way to teach their children the "real" history of Hebron.

The presence of such impressionable infants was the worst part of the trip, though I was hardly surprised that their parents saw fit to bring them along. After all, the Jesuit motto of "Give me a child until he is seven and I will give you the man" works just as well when trying to indoctrinate Jewish kids to see the Arabs as our eternal enemy.

Towards the end of the tour, I'd cornered Yossi and asked him to expand on how the "Hebron problem" could be solved once and for all. "Look, maybe we need to do to them what they did to us in 1929," suggested Yossi. "I don't like to see people get hurt," he assured me, "but I don't see another way at the moment. The only way to stop Arabs running after you is to run after them, and then to keep them on the run." He went on to detail the ultimate goal of Islam, as he understood it: world domination, with everyone bowing down to the altar of

Muhammad. As he saw it, it is a case of "us or them – and we can't allow the choice to be made for us."

"We have to smash them conclusively," he said, growing animated and clenching his fists in rage. "I know it sounds extreme, but Hiroshima and Nagasaki were actually good for both sides in the long term: they saved American lives, of course, but also countless Japanese lives as well, by bringing the war to an end and showing them who was in charge".

"We have to collapse the PA and retake control of the Palestinians," he told me. "Aren't you worried that that would affect the Jewish majority in Israel?" my friend had asked innocently. "Not in the slightest – we just won't give them the vote," said Yossi decisively.

"Listen," he went on, "the average Arab mum with 55 children is no demographic threat, since she herself has no interest in democracy. If we don't give them the vote, they won't care – they're used to being ruled by others, so why should it be any different here?"

His plans for retaking the "Greater Israel" of Bible times made complete sense to the others, who lapped up Yossi's next offering. "It's all part of God's plan," he declared. "Why do you think that those countries that should be ours are also the same countries with such unstable governments?" He let that sink in briefly, before expanding on the theme.

"Egypt and Jordan – they're not meant to be ours, so they have strong leaders and domestic calm," he said, ignoring reality in favour of knocking square pegs into round holes. "Whereas Lebanon and the PA territories – all of which should be part of Israel, and will be – are collapsing around their populations' ears." The rest of the group adored that rationale; after all, whenever "God's plan" was mentioned, they found it unnecessary to apply logic, and just let their starry-eyed wonderment take over.

The religious lunacy of Yossi had seemed as beyond the pale as that of the Islamic groups who believe that Israel must be obliterated in order to fulfil the will of Muhammad. But, just because these groups live on the edges of reality, it doesn't mean they don't play an enormous part in the destabilisation of this region, with their vast financial and human resources, and their willingness to stop at nothing to achieve their aims.

When we encounter Yossi this time, he has lost none of his fire-and-brimstone *shtick*. He tries to convince us that his line of reasoning is no different from that of Thomas Jefferson, "who said 'The tree of liberty must sometimes be watered with blood' – he said it, not me," Yossi continues, hands raised defensively, despite us not having challenged him on the point. He tells us that the current government, headed by Benyamin Netanyahu, is "just as bad" as the previous, Olmert-led coalition, and displays all the paranoia and anti-state acid that he had the last time Seth had seen him in full flow. A brochure we pick up as we leave the Jewish side of the city carries a three-page spread on the Hebron Fund's recent 'Gala Anniversary Dinner' in America, which was attended by 700 supporters: "more guests than last year... despite the economic situation in the US and the political challenges in Israel".

However, The Hebron Fund's donors, according to Palestinian activist and former presidential candidate Mustafa Barghouti, "are actually fund-raising for illegality. Americans are paying money for things which are considered to be criminal acts by international law. I don't know if they are really aware of the consequences of what they are doing."

On several occasions during our walk around the crumbling houses and narrow lanes of the Palestinian streets of the old city, we see groups of Palestinian children throwing handfuls of stones at each other, at pedestrians... even at us. With pockets full of pebbles the unaccompanied children run around the streets playing their bored games, stepping almost unconsciously into stereotypical roles, as bored groups of Israeli soldiers a

287

few years their senior play their part and pull the children aside, shaking them down for projectiles, and threatening to arrest them before letting the children run off to their laughing friends. On these occasions, it appears to be a cyclical, unsettling game, but one gets the sense that this is an emulation of a far graver reality, continually bubbling under the surface and ever ready to return to the city streets.

We cross the checkpoint into the Palestinian section of Hebron, an area strictly off limits to Israeli Jews, and consequently free of the presence of Israeli soldiers as well. The *shuk* is well-stocked, but with few shoppers browsing the displays; we are clawed at and harassed the moment we set foot in the market, by stallholders and shopkeepers desperate to peddle us their wares. The Old City of Hebron is the least salubrious neighbourhood of Palestinian Hebron – the only residents left living there are the poorest and most sidelined of the community, we are told by a Palestinian acquaintance who lives in a more salubrious part of the city.

When we reach the city centre, the streets are as heaving as downtown Jerusalem, Ramallah, Tel Aviv, or any other well-to-do urban centre in Israel or the Occupied Territories, and the lack of bored, stone-throwing teens testifies to how far removed this neighbourhood is from the Old City. Indeed, it is easy to forget that the Old City section of Hebron – which is the only part of town constantly in the news – is a mere fraction of the entire city's sprawling confines. The daily reality for the vast majority of Hebron's Palestinian residents is far more mundane and upbeat than that experienced by their unfortunately-located neighbours residing amongst the settlers near Machpela. Western shops and products line the busy streets, gleaming bank buildings nestle alongside upmarket restaurants and cafés, and it is hard to believe that just a mile away occur some of the most hostile and hate-fuelled clashes that the region experiences.

Just as many Palestinians' only experience of Israelis is their contact with gun-toting settlers and military personnel, so too are many Israelis' views of Palestinians shaped by images of rock-throwing teenagers and suicide bombers via the local media. If those on either side could see how the man on the street lives – behind the front lines, and far from the madding crowd, it might be possible to overcome the stereotypes and prejudices that so dominate each side's impressions of the other. But such thinking is merely wishful at present: for now, in places such as Hebron, the headlines are doomed to be dominated by the clashes rather than the calm, and so it will doubtless continue for many years to come.

Chapter Eleven
The South Hebron Hills: Above the law

According to the Israeli human rights organisation B'Tselem, settler attacks against Palestinians in the Occupied Territories "have become routine" over the last few years.[46] Increasingly segregated from their Palestinian neighbours, many settler communities in the West Bank have raised a native generation of highly nationalistic youth that views the Palestinians as invaders of its territory and a natural enemy of the Jewish people. Such a climate of intolerance, mixed with the mistrust generated by the years of two bloody Intifadas, spawns frequent aggression towards Palestinian residents, sometimes in random retaliation for Palestinian attacks, sometimes as part of a pro-claimed 'price tag policy', which meets every outpost evacuation with violence against their Palestinian neighbours, and often with no discernible trigger at all.

Attacks reported in the Israeli and international media include stoning cars and pedestrians, torching houses, destroying crops and trees, beating villagers, opening fire in residential areas and chasing shepherds from their farm land. In December 2008, the Israeli authorities' evacuation of the aforementioned Hebron 'House of Peace' led to a rampage of settlers through Palestinian parts of the city in what the then Prime Minister Ehud Olmert termed a "pogrom" against the Palestinian population. Two men were shot at close range; cars and olive groves were set alight and, in one reported incident, a group of settlers torched a home in which a large family cowered, as private security guards looked on. Whilst such violence might be perpetrated by a minority of extremists, the nationalistic settler communities and the governments which have facilitated their expansion over the years share the responsibility, due to the impunity with which the attacks are committed and the fostering of a general climate of enmity and racism.

Thanks to the recent "Shooting Back" initiative by B'Tselem which provides West Bank Palestinians with video cameras to document such violence, irrefutable evidence of attacks is now widely available on the internet and a quick YouTube search brings to light a number of instances of extremist settler brutality, amongst them the notorious footage of the beating of an elderly Palestinian shepherd along with his wife and nephew by a group of four masked settler youths, armed with baseball bats, in fields near the Hebron region settlement of Susia. However, despite the international press attention gained by the award winning B'Tselem project, settlers are rarely brought to justice, with neither the Susia attack nor the Hebron shootings resulting in successful prosecution.

According to B'Tselem, "The Israeli authorities employ an undeclared policy of leniency and compromise toward Israeli civilians who harm Palestinians. The authorities show little interest in uncovering the substantial violence that Israeli civilians commit against Palestinians in the Occupied Territories, and discriminate between Israelis and Palestinians in enforcing the law"[47]. Overall, according to Yesh Din data of July 2008, only 10% of all reports of settler attacks against Palestinians result in an indictment being filed, with the Israeli NGO identifying "recurring patterns of defects and failures in investigations" of this kind conducted by the Samaria and Judea District Police.[48]

Perhaps the most infamous region of the West Bank for such confrontations is the South Hebron Hills, where local settlers have gained a reputation for belligerent antagonism towards the local Palestinian population, and where, as in other areas, the establishment of settlement outposts have intruded on private Palestinian land and resulted in the closure of access roads and large agricultural areas in this Israeli-administered 'area C' district. In the face of attacks, and the problem of land appropriation in general, Palestinian villagers of the area have organised a programme of non-violent resistance, which sees residents come together to farm land close to settlement outposts, remove arbitrary unmanned roadblocks and reclaim buildings and fields that they have lost to the settlements' expansion. At the centre of this campaign is the village of At-Tuwani, where members of international aid group the Christian Peacemaker Team (CPT) have taken up permanent residence. Along with representatives from Italian non-denominational organisation Operation Dove, the CPT members augment the Palestinians' non-violent tactics and monitor acts of aggression against the villagers by residents of the nearby Israeli settlement Ma'on and its illegal outpost Havat Ma'on, as well as other surrounding settlements.

In a rudimentary building on the edge of the small village of stone houses scattered across the hillside, we sit with Hafez Hereni, representative of the Tuwani popular committee, and Chris and Joy of CPT, to discuss the methods and efficacy of the non-violent campaign. Over teeth-rottingly sweet tea, flavoured with sage leaves picked from the surrounding mountains, Hafez describes how the quiet village of Tuwani was once home to around seven hundred people, but that the establishment of Ma'on in 1981 and the subsequent arrival of Israeli settlers the following year forced Palestinians out of the villages in the area, because of harassment and the appropriation of agricultural land essential for the harvesting and grazing on which the community survives. Moreover, the passing of demolition orders on village houses, including on buildings constructed prior to the establishment of the state of Israel, led Hafez to believe that the expulsion of Palestinians from the region is the settlers' intent; that the villagers' departure was not simply the inadvertent result of the antisocial actions of a few extremists, but rather the "deliberate, combined effort of the army and settlers to push the Palestinians from area C."

B'Tselem's research supports Hafez's appraisal of the collaboration between the settlers and the Israeli authorities:

"For years, Israeli authorities have both barred Palestinian access to rings of land surrounding settlements, and have not acted to eliminate settlers' piratical closing of lands adjacent to settlements and blocking of Palestinian access to them.

(...)

The authorities entrusted with enforcing the law not only fail to take sufficient action to end the violence and prosecute lawbreakers, they join them and block Palestinian access themselves. Soldiers regularly expel Palestinians from their farmland, often under the direction of settlers. Israel has also established a physical system of barriers – barbed-wire fences, patrol roads, illumination and electronic sensory devices – far from the homes at the edge of the settlements, in effect annexing large swathes of land to the settlements."[49]

Behind Hafez's head, a colourful new Arabic map of the world is displayed on the wall, in which the state of Israel does not feature. Such a picture would appear to support Israeli suspicions that Palestinians will never accept the state of Israel and that their demands for a state in the West Bank are only the first step towards taking over the Jewish state too. However, as we sit and listen to Hafez's description of an *actual* land grab, rather than a theoretical one; of the loss of the last remaining patches of land by those who are already stateless, considerations of the hypothetical challenge to the territory of a prosperous and well armed first world power seem not only academic, but, frankly, hypocritical. Of course Israel has the right to a secure state, but when support of this right is used to justify the

At-Tuwani

continued occupation and expropriation of Palestinian land, it feels wildly out of place.

According to international law, all Israeli settlements are illegal, as provided by the Fourth Geneva Convention which forbids the transfer of a civilian population into occupied territory. However, Israel and the settlers themselves claim that because the West Bank was unilaterally occupied by Jordan following the 1949 armistice, and was taken from Jordan by Israel in 1967, the land is not technically occupied as no internationally recognised state borders ever existed. This, they claim, means that the settlement of Israeli civilians in the land is not illegal. However, Gershom Gorenberg demonstrates clearly that the Israeli government itself was, even in September 1967, fully aware of the illegality of the transfer of civilian populations to the West Bank and deliberately overlooked the evidence. Quoting a top secret letter to Prime Minister Eshkol from Foreign Ministry legal counsel Theodore Meron, Gorenberg writes that "Eshkol knew that settling civilians in occupied land, including the West Bank, violated international law."

"Moreover," claims Gorenberg, "Israel's own actions in the West Bank showed recognition of that status. The army command in the West Bank had already issued a legal proclamation stating that 'military courts will fulfil the Geneva provisions' and that when a military decree contradicted it, the Geneva Convention took precedence."[50]

Eshkol and the government, Gorenberg argues, kept Meron's advice secret and pursued their policy of settlement. Nevertheless, the fact that current governments continue to ignore, or choose to overlook, the illegality of civilian settlement does not mean that they weren't fully aware of the legal ramifications of their actions when they were first begun. Moreover, a top secret comprehensive government database of all of Israel's settlements obtained by *Haaretz* in February 2009 reveals that the current government is fully aware of the extent of illegal construction within the settlements, as well as the scale of building on private Palestinian land, contravening the 1907 Hague Convention on War which prohibits the confiscation of private property. According to the newspaper:

"An analysis of the data reveals that, in the vast majority of the settlements – about 75 percent – construction, sometimes on a large scale, has been carried out without the appropriate permits or contrary to the permits that were issued. The database also shows that, in more than 30 settlements, extensive construction of buildings and infrastructure (roads, schools, synagogues, yeshivas and even police stations) has been carried out on private lands belonging to Palestinian West Bank residents."[51]

Buildings in Ma'on itself are shown by the report to have been built without permission, whilst the Israeli NGO Peace Now uses Civil Administration data to show that 15.47% of the settlement is built on private mostly Palestinian land. Similarly, the outpost of Havat Ma'on, which is illegal even according to Israeli law, is not only built without permission, but also extends onto private Palestinian land. According to Israel's road map commitments, the outpost is supposed to have been demolished, and yet it continues to be supplied with water, electricity and defence by the Israeli authorities. Moreover, even if the government was inclined to evacuate the outpost as it is committed to do, evacuations in the past have simply resulted in the transfer of the population to other West Bank settlements in the Occupied Territories. For example, just as many Gaza residents were relocated to settlements in the West Bank, so will the settlers of the illegal Migron outpost be relocated to fifty of the planned 1500 new housing units that will constitute an entire new neighbourhood in the settlement of Geva Binyamin, east of the separation barrier. Unsurprisingly, a significant 23.87% of Geva Binyamin itself is built on private land, according to the 2006 data compiled by the Civil Administration and obtained by the Peace Now – private land the vast majority of which is Palestinian, according to the Israeli NGO.[52]

Against this backdrop, it is sobering to hear the description of how the continued sustenance of Ma'on and its outpost impact on the Palestinian locals who, according to international and Israeli law should be protected from such an intrusion. Calm and manifestly focussed, CPT member Chris, who has been living and working in Tuwani for three years, explains how by erecting the outpost of Havat Ma'on in 2001 settlers have cut off the only access road that connects Tuwani to the nearby village of Tooba. Sandwiched between Ma'on and its outpost, the road became a hotspot for attacks by settlers who would ambush the Tooba schoolchildren who used the road to walk to school in Tuwani, chasing them away with rocks and verbal abuse, so that eventually the children were forced to take the circuitous and considerably more arduous mountain route. As a result of CPT pressure, Chris explains, the IDF was drafted in to provide safe passage for the schoolchildren from the Havat Ma'on residents, but when the settlers erected a gate, illegally blocking off one stretch of the road, the army refused to accompany the children along the road's full length, meaning that the children are still subjected to sporadic attacks, as are shepherds and other residents who attempt to farm their own land around the settlement.

Attacks are not reserved exclusively for the Palestinian farmers, however. Joy describes how in 2005, whilst escorting observers from Amnesty International around Palestinian land near the settlement, two American CPT members were assaulted by residents of Havat Ma'on armed with clubs and chains. One member, Kim Lambert, suffered a broken arm and knee, while her colleague Chris Brown sustained a punctured lung and multiple bruising. And whilst this attack was more brutal than many – and provoked more media attention than others on account of its international victims – it is far from a lone case. Indeed Chris informs us that on the very morning of our arrival a group of settlers had attacked a local farmer and chased him from his field.

Chris is surprisingly measured in his estimation of the reasoning behind such attacks, recognising the difference between the extremists of Havat Ma'on and the economic settlers of cities like Ariel, suggesting that the hardliners are motivated by a "nationalist religious ideology which wants the Palestinians off the land". Chris seems resigned to this assessment and as a veteran Christian Peacemaker he realises the limitations of trying to reconcile what are, essentially, two diametrically opposed groups of people. Moreover, beyond reasoning with settlers, security guards and the army when it becomes necessary, Chris emphasises that dialogue is not the purpose of his presence. Instead he is there to facilitate the Palestinians' non-violent resistance to harassment and the appropriation of their land.

Hafez, who has been searching through files on a laptop on the table in front of him, looks up, and one gets a sense of his tenacity when, with a permanent frown etched onto his weather-beaten face, he insists that the "harder the settlers try to take our land, the more determined we are to stay". He turns the screen towards us, eager to demonstrate how that determination is manifested, before the limited electricity supply, which is powered by a generator, cuts out for the day and the house is consumed by the darkness of the surrounding hillsides. (Despite the fact that the neighbouring illegal outpost of Havat Ma'on is fully powered, the Israeli administration, which has full control over the area, has neglected to provide Tuwani with electricity or running water.)

On the screen is a video of a slightly younger Hafez, in 2006, engaged in the same actions in which he is employed today, as he resists arrest by IDF troops and border police following a peaceful demonstration against the erection of a wall on village land – a wall which the Israeli courts later declared illegal and ordered to be removed. Such demonstrations form the backbone of Hafez's work, as he and other villagers campaign against the various measures used by the IDF to facilitate the settlements' expansion, and physically remove unmanned road barriers which restrict their movement around the West Bank. Such physical obstructions, which are often simply huge mounds of rubble, are in addition to the many manned and unmanned roadblocks, permanent and temporary, that exist throughout the West Bank and although Israel insists they are an important tool in the prevention of terrorist activities against Israel, B'Tselem claims this is only part of the story:

"One of the main purposes of the policy to restrict Palestinian movement is to protect Israeli settlers. Given that the settlements are illegal, the policy only aggravates the situation: it comprehensively and disproportionately impedes the freedom of movement of an entire population in order to perpetuate an illegal enterprise."[53]

In June 2009 Israeli newspaper *Haaretz* reported "a dramatic change in Israel's roadblock policy in the West

Bank", highlighting the Israeli defence establishment's reduction of manned roadblocks on West Bank roads from 35 to ten in the course of eighteen months. "However," the article continues, "the UN's Office for the Coordination of Humanitarian Affairs says its data shows there are 630 different obstacles and roadblocks in place throughout the West Bank."[54] Furthermore, B'Tselem highlights the fact that the number of permanent physical obstructions – as opposed to manned checkpoints – is on the rise, the monthly average having risen steadily from 410 in 2005 to 541 in March 2009.[55] The organisation outlines the specific problems that such physical obstructions present when it claims that "unlike staffed checkpoints, physical obstructions leave no room for flexibility in permitting crossing, as there is no one present to remove the obstruction in cases of emergency".

In response to such tactics, Hafez regularly organises groups of villagers equipped with shovels to approach the roadblocks and remove them. This is just one aspect of the Tuwani villagers' resistance which also sees them farm land within illegal buffer zones that settlers have established around settlements and outposts, and resist the steady appropriation of their agricultural and private land. Such resistance is having an effect and although the obstacles keep coming, Hafez can point to houses and villages that they have reclaimed from the settlers, and is proud of having recently ploughed a new patch of land that had previously been under the violent guard of the Havat Ma'on extremists. On the back of these successes, Hafez claims that the population of the village is rising once again, having dropped off rapidly prior to the start of the campaign in 2000.

Watching the video of Hafez's arrest on his laptop, it is striking to observe the patience with which he repeatedly tries to shrug off the soldiers and border police, lying down as they attempt to drag him away from the peaceful protest and hurl other demonstrators, including elderly women, from their path. Even when one soldier boots Hafez as he lies on the ground, he does not fight back. This is the essence of the region's campaign of resistance – to subvert and obstruct the means of the occupation without ever resorting to violence, thus "not giving the authorities an excuse to fight back".

This is no small detail. For Israeli society, traumatised by waves of indiscriminate suicide bombings and murderous attacks, it is easy to justify all IDF actions in the Occupied Territories as security measures, specifically designed to overcome a Palestinian enemy perceived as invariably violent. However, by championing non-violent means Hafez not only highlights the latent oppressive nature of the roadblocks and restrictions, designed to aid illegal settlement expansion, but subverts the dominant Israeli stereotype of Palestinians as violent troublemakers. According to Hafez the message is slowly getting through and he claims a number of Israeli activist groups and individuals amongst the supporters of his work, but insists that it will take longer for the wider Israeli society to understand the nature of his campaign.

"People in Israel and around the world have no idea of the struggle and I want to explain it to them more and more... I have just been in Italy – thirteen cities in fifteen days, talking about our work. Now I want to go to the US, Canada and Scotland to keep raising awareness."

Hafez, Joy and Chris intend to use the arrival of Middle East Quartet envoy Tony Blair in Tuwani a few days after our visit to highlight the settlers' aggression and to draw attention to the Tuwani villagers' non-violent resistance, which has already gained enough attention to invoke the interest of the former British Prime Minister.

***

A farming village, Tuwani is early to rise and early to bed and once Hafez has gone we use the last half hour of electricity to charge our phones; brush our teeth using a small jug of water that Hafez has brought us from the well, and bed down under thick blankets against the cold night, just as the lights throughout the village cut out. Darkness reclaims the village, but the persistent barking of dogs reverberating across the hills won't allow it to go quietly. After just a few hours the dogs wake the cockerel, who wakes the donkeys, which wake the Muezzin, who wakes us at approximately 4.30am, and not long after that we are up and out into the dim morning gloom to the stone walled courtyard of the house where four CPT and three Operation Dove volunteers share a dormitory.

We shake the shadows from our eyes and set off across the mountain with Sandra and Irita, two Italian Doves, to meet the children and escort them back to Tuwani for their weekend football match. There are no lessons today Soon the dull light begins to glow and before long the mountains are awash with sunlight, which, along with the pace of the walk, compels us to remove our jackets. Through clusters of pungent lemon herbs the village peters out as the last house crumbles into a landscape of littered rocks from which all of Tuwani has been constructed. The village edge stands a stone's throw from a glade of trees to our left, which conceals the numerous caravans of Havat Ma'on. As we pass, Sandra and Irita keep an eye out for early rising residents who may pose a problem on our return, but we round the wood without trouble and enter an open expanse of rolling hills, startling a herd of gazelles as we come.

Walking along the swollen hump of the hill, Irita points out the small patch of land – little bigger than a five-a-side pitch – that the villagers have recently reclaimed and planted after ten years of settler obstruction. Having successfully regained this patch, they have now taken the struggle to other patches of land.

Soon the dome of the hill dips down and a deep valley spreads before us, with Tooba lying on the other side of the steep hill opposite. We begin our descent, leaning into the hillside to avoid slipping, until a figure in the distance grows large, revealing itself to be an elderly Palestinian man on a donkey, mounting an infeasibly steep path up the hillside. This is Omar, the Tooba village leader, whom Irita and Sandra know well. When we eventually arrive in Tooba, it is Omar's family that greets us.

The village itself is just a small bunch of caves on a rocky hilltop terrace; the odd donkey tied to a post; chickens pecking at grain and a handful of children who have ceased to kick their football to stare curiously, hands against the sun, at the new arrivals. We walk across the dusty land, past the barking dogs and a home-made pigeon feeder towards a cluster of man-made walls where stone awnings conceal entranceways that step down into the hillside and extend into dark, cavernous recesses, serving both as grain stores and capacious family homes.

Omar's wife invites us into her home and we stoop to pass through the entrance, pausing for our eyes to get used to the utter darkness, before we slowly begin to make out a large living quarter, with grain stacked in bags at the back and natural shelves to the side covered with mats and blankets, apparently serving as the sleeping area. Sectioned off to one side is the kitchen and Omar's wife disappears behind the screen as her son implores us to sit on the mat towards the front of the cave until sweet sage tea and a plate of hot, home-baked flatbread appears, along with a small tin tureen of olive oil, one of a sour home-made yoghurt and, somewhat less appetisingly, one of lard. Abstaining from the latter, and from conversation on account of the hour, we sit and eat generous hunks of bread and yoghurt, as Omar's children run around pulling on jumpers and tying shoelaces in between joining their mother in entreating us to eat more.

Once the children are ready we leave the village with three young boys and head back the way we came; this not being a school day the army are not providing escort, so Irita and Sandra advise that we cannot travel along the road between the villages for fear that the settlers will be waiting. The boys skip ahead, well used to the

302

journey, as the adults stumble somewhat less competently behind and eventually Sandra and Irita deliver their charges safely in Tuwani without incident, at which point we rejoin Joy who is heading back into the hills with a pair of binoculars to keep a watch over the shepherds in case of attack; today is Shabbat and as such, we are rather disturbingly informed, is a day when the unoccupied settlers tend to conduct more of their assaults.

Such attacks are not limited to physical attacks on pedestrians, nor to the firing of guns at passers-by as one unsettling CPT video shows us, but also extend to acts of agricultural sabotage such as the destruction of Palestinian crops and, reportedly, the slaughter of villagers' donkeys. As we walk Joy explains that the villagers of Tuwani are only just getting over their economically crippling reputation for selling bad milk, which, according to the *Independent* newspaper in April 2005, was the result of "highly toxic chemicals... spread on Palestinian sheep pastures in what villagers believe is an escalation of a campaign of harassment against them by Jewish West Bank settlers."[56] According to Joy, the act of sabotage compelled the villagers to survive for over a year almost entirely on selling the craft products of the Women's Cooperative to charitably minded international volunteers.

Joy leads us up the hill over which we passed this morning, from where we have a good view of Havat Ma'on. All is quiet. We look past the outpost, along the hilltops on the horizon, and gain a clear perspective of a long string of settlements – Maon, Havat Maon, the Maon cowsheds, Carmel, Avigail and others – a perforated continuum demonstrative of the shoelace mechanics of settlement expansion that Michael in Efrat had described to us back in 2007, whereby settlements are staggered along adjacent hilltops, creating extensive strings of settlement with enforced buffer zones between each one which are then filled in and padded out over the years. From the Palestinian side the effects of such a strategy are clear to see and whilst Daniella boasted of the expansive effects of the technique for the settlements, the loss is correspondingly great for the Palestinian villagers as more and more of their land is taken away. As we have seen in Ramat Gilad and countless other outposts, once hilltops are settled they are soon defended by the army which refuses to abandon its compatriots. To facilitate this, 'defensive' rings are imposed around the settlement into which Palestinians are forbidden to enter, resulting in a land grab which is generally exploited by settlers who farm and build on the land, which in turn creates new 'buffer zones' around the old buffers. In this case such tactics have resulted in the closure of the road from Tooba to Tuwani and although the beating of the international volunteers motivated the army to provide safe escort to the children, traffic can no longer make the fifteen minute journey from village to village, forced instead to take the hour long circuitous route around the outpost.

Despite the success in gaining the army escort, Joy describes the everyday struggle of dealing with the IDF, whose purported role is to protect all those who live in the territory, but who, as in Hebron, frequently end up favouring their compatriots in their disputes with the Palestinians. This despite the fact that the army themselves have frequently come under attack by violent settlers, including, according to reports in the *Jerusalem Post*, having been stoned by residents of Ma'on itself.[57] Because of this lack of transparency and the arbitrary nature of the IDF's response to the Palestinian shepherds' grievances, CPT volunteers carry maps and copies of IDF and court edicts with them as they accompany the Palestinians, to make sure that if the army are present as arbiters in a dispute with settlers, they don't impulsively end up siding with the Israelis. Nevertheless, Joy claims, these legal documents often have little impact and international observers have been arrested by the army for trespassing, only for the courts to say that there are no grounds for arrest, and time and again the army show themselves to be indifferent to the Palestinians' legal rights. In one particularly disheartening incident, two soldiers were filmed mooning Palestinians and international observers in response to a complaint of unjustified removal of Palestinians from their land, showing just how seriously some soldiers take their job of protecting the citizens whose land they occupy. Joy sums it up with the observation that "some of the army are settlers themselves. Some listen to us and take us seriously. Others don't. Some observe IDF edicts and act according to the law, while others simply ignore us and take our maps which show where the official military zones are and rip them up in front of us."

Such fluctuation in official Israeli action, dependent on whether the Palestinians encounter a conscientious soldier like Elad from Efrat, or an expansionist settler soldier like the guard at Ramat Gilad, means that Palestinians have no independent law enforcer on which to rely. According to Ehud Krinis of the Villages Group, an Israeli organisation that works with Palestinian villagers to improve their daily lives, Palestinians are prevented from taking their complaints to the police, too:

"First, the police stations are inside the settlements which means that the Palestinians are often denied access to them. At the same time, complainants are often subject to persecution for having dared to file a report: they find themselves denied permits to work in Israel, and so on."

All of which explains the Palestinians' dependence on international observers to film and document settler attacks and support the villagers' struggle, ensuring that they are not simply forgotten about.

On the Israeli side, however, international activists are often mistrusted, accused of instinctively siding with the Palestinians over Israel, reducing a complex situation to black and white and in fact antagonising the conflict. Writing in *Haaretz*, prominent settler spokesman Israel Harel supports his friend's claim that left wing activists are "agitators... Israeli and foreign 'peace activists' who incite the Arabs... When the Palestinians and their abettors approach the boundaries of settlements without IDF security, clashes erupt, which are then reported by a media eager to accuse the settlers."[58]

However, regardless of the veracity of Harel's argument in the specific cases to which he refers, it cannot extend to the actions of the villagers and international activists in Tuwani, where protests are non violent, and where attacks happen frequently in the absence of any non-Palestinian "agitators". Furthermore, activists not only lend weight to Palestinian protests, but according to Hafez their cameras have the effect of causing IDF troops and policemen to behave more civilly towards the Palestinians than they would otherwise. In this light, Harel's argument looks to be simply a convenient way of smearing legitimate protesters in an effort to paint the settlers' actions in a better light.

Needless to say, the international activists have similarly low regard for the settlers against whom they often find themselves in confrontation. There is no trouble during our time in the fields of Tuwani, although plenty of video evidence of such attacks is available on YouTube and the CPT website, but there are moments of concern as Joy and her colleagues sweep the hillsides with their binoculars, reacting with alarm to the sight of cars driving on the roads to and from Ma'on. As Joy herself observes, the settlers could quite simply "be going for a nice day in the hills, or for a nice picnic", but her experiences with the settlers mean that she instinctively adds the addendum "or they could be looking for someone to attack." For Joy it is not the settlements that need the protection of a buffer zone.

In a further subversion of stereotypes, CPT activists' reports that settlers frequently bring their children to confrontations with Palestinian farmers prompts Joy to despair that "what the settlers do to their children is terrible – the way they raise them to hate". Having heard this charge levelled against Palestinians time and again throughout the West Bank, it is interesting to hear it being made against the settlers themselves. Indeed in an area where Palestinian children are raised to see their parents engaged in non-violent protests while the children of Havat Ma'on witness their parents' violent activities, the traditional apportion of blame by Israelis and settlers alike as to who is responsible for the absence of peace would appear in this case to be misplaced.

Almost every Israeli settler we have spoken to derides such abuse as that meted out by the Havat Ma'on extremists, insisting that such behaviour is not representative of the vast majority of settlers, and is confined instead to a small contingent of hardliners. And yet this offers little reassurance to the Palestinians who have to suffer the duel ignominy of humiliating attacks along with the steady loss of their land. For them, the handfuls of extremists – who live and work alongside the other settlers – are fully backed by the wider settler community who do little to prevent such attacks, and ultimately support them by facilitating the expansion of the outposts which perpetuate such actions. Just as many Israelis, particularly in the West Bank, refuse to discern between Palestinians, writing them all off as the enemy, so does the distinction between good settlers and bad mean very little to the Palestinian villagers of Tuwani. As far as they are concerned, they are all on their land and with no independent arbiter, it is left to people like Hafez to do what he can to stop their land disappearing altogether.

***

On the other side of the buffer zone, we feel the settlers' suspicion of international activists for ourselves, when we visit Ma'on to hear the settlers' side of this particular story. After having hitched a lift with a man who complained of the internationals who come "inside Ma'on to cause trouble with the locals", we are stopped by three different people in the space of five minutes as we walk through the well-kept streets of the small, ordered settlement, who demand to know who we are and what we are doing here. The third such inquiry comes from the Ma'on private security guard who confirms our suspicions of the residents' wariness of outside interference when he admits having stopped us because we "look a bit like the international left wingers who cause trouble around Ma'on".

We get talking with the security guard, a Ma'on resident for 22 years, originally hailing from "the colonies" of South Africa, and he offers to give us a lift around the settlement. Josh climbs into the front seat, the barrel of the guard's rifle resting against his leg, as we head along the well paved roads, the faded orange ribbon on the rearview mirror flapping in the wind from the open window.

"I'm the bad guy," jokes the guard as he shows us the Palestinian village of Tuwani from a new perspective. "They see me in the Jeep and the kids come and chat and laugh around me – and the internationals just stand there and film it all: I'm the bad guy with the gun, surely I'll do something bad."

According to the guard, activists such as those from CPT exaggerate the conflict between the settlers and the local Palestinians and "stir up trouble" of their own, especially on Shabbat, a day on which both sides seem to agree as being one of increased confrontation. He finds it bemusing that CPT send missions to Iraq, Kosovo and Darfur and then to Israel "as if we're one of these hotspots," arguing that the activists instinctively take the Palestinians' side in a conflict that is not nearly of the scale that "the media" make out.

However, according to Irita, the Italian Doves make a point of working with both sides in conflict situations, but they have found it hard to find placements with Israeli victims of the conflict, due to the pervasive suspicion that international activists instinctively side with the Palestinians.

From the guard's perspective, Palestinians have a chance to have "a good economic situation in Israel", by which he means the West Bank too, "if only they'll give up violence", but he blames Hamas and other extremists for creating a conflict situation, leaving Israel with the only option of "beating the S.H.I.T. out of them until they stop". Confusingly, however, he admits that the Palestinians of Tuwani and the surrounding villages are not violent and that they are trying to achieve their aims through non-violent means. Yet he also states that he enforces a buffer zone around Ma'on and Havat Ma'on, calling the army to escort the Palestinians away from the settlements when they farm too close to the border – the expulsion of Palestinians by soldiers "under the direction of settlers" that B'Tselom describes. "It is not in our interests to have them so close," says the guard, thus undermining his claim that Palestinians' economic position would improve if they give up violence.

As we pull off the ordered roads and head up the rougher tracks, across the closed Tooba-Tuwani road, to the attached outpost of Havat Ma'on, which we had last seen enshrouded in trees from the edge of Tuwani, our guide admits that despite the lack of violence on the part of the local Palestinians, there have been attacks by settlers on Palestinians, claiming that "there is a basis to the news stories, although they are exaggerated."

These attacks, he claims, are the work of "extremists" in Havat Ma'on, who do their own security rounds "with an iron fist" and who have been responsible for "some serious attacks [resulting in] people being hospitalised." Indicative of the decentralised and unaccountable nature of Israeli rule in the Occupied Territories, the Ma'on security guard is able to pass the buck onto indeterminate others, who are dismissed as being an exception. In this way he avoids accepting collective responsibility for a culture of racism and hatred endemic in many nationalistic settlements that fosters the extremist climate that spawns such attacks, and which even endorses the principle of such confrontation by supporting continued expansion at any cost.

"The Palestinians know not to get too close to the people from Havat Ma'on without the internationals around," he continues, contradicting his earlier claim, and the common settler argument expounded by Harel, that the internationals are the trouble makers. Furthermore, although the Ma'on security guard describes himself as a mediator between the extremists of Havat Ma'on on the one hand and the Palestinians and the international activists on the other, it is clear which side he is on when he drives through a flying checkpoint on the road outside Ma'on. As we are waved straight through the checkpoint with a friendly hello, the elderly Palestinian man in a chequered keffiya driving the van to our right is asked for his identification while a group of soldiers inspect the sacks of grain that form his cargo. Not only is the guard an Israeli civilian, free to travel without restriction on the West Bank roads, but he himself is a settler, a resident of Ma'on whose job is to keep the Palestinians off their own land, and who claims to have "good relations" with the "extremists" of Havat Ma'on who send their children to school in the main settlement.

Despite his claims to keep the peace, the guard's allegiances are indisputable and just as he mistrusts the international activists of CPT and the Doves, it would seem that the Palestinians and activists are right to claim they have no one to whom they can turn for justice in their own land.

Instead they remain stuck between extremist settlers, arbitrary soldiers and indifferent security guards as the buffer zones grow and their land is slowly pulled from beneath their feet.

Chapter Twelve
Facing facts:
One man's war
on the settlements

In a small, smoky office in the shadow of the IDF General Staff Headquarters in Tel Aviv, we meet with Benny Raz, a stocky middle-aged man with an exemplary career of service in the Israeli military. Former soldier in the elite anti-guerilla unit, Sayeret Eguz; head bodyguard for IDF Chief of Staff David Elazar; El Al security guard repelling attack from Carlos The Jackal; stints in both the Mossad and Shin Bet Security Agencies as well as the Prime Minister's Office... and resident of West Bank settlement Karnei Shomron since 1992, Benny Raz's CV reads like that of the most dedicated Israeli patriot. But Benny is no ordinary settler.

Having come to Karnei Shomron for the quality of life, Benny claims that he was led to believe that his large and affordable new house was built on land to be shared peacefully with the Palestinians. However, the assassination of Yitzhak Rabin and the events of the Second Intifada changed his political outlook, so that when, in the spring of 2005, he realised that the West Bank barrier was in the process of sealing Karnei Shomron on the Palestinian side of a de facto international border, Benny decided he wanted out of the West Bank. Having witnessed the forced evacuation of Gaza's Israeli residents, Benny was unwilling to sit and wait for the government to come and pull him out of his house when they decided it was time. Instead he wanted to sell up and leave immediately, but he had a problem: its location outside the fence meant that his house had plummeted to little over a third of its value. Benny was stranded; unable to afford to move back inside the Green Line, but unwilling to stay. And so the career military man began a new war – this time with the government of Israel itself.

Benny began to ask around and realised that he was not the only person who thought like him. Many more, he claims, wanted to get out of the West Bank immediately, rather than wait for a compulsory evacuation under a future peace agreement, but they couldn't afford to leave. Benny soon realised that the only way for people like him to move back into Israel was for the government to begin compensating settlers who wanted to leave the West Bank. To that end, with the help of the then Meretz MK Avshalom Vilan, Benny established the Bayit Ehad movement, dedicated to pressuring the government to pass a law of Voluntary Evacuation Compensation to reabsorb all West Bank settlers willing to move back into Israel.

It has not been easy work. Having once had the Parliamentary lobbying powers of both Vilan and former Labour MK Collette Avital, leaving him free to canvas other West Bank settlers, Benny now describes himself as an "orphan", alone with his Bayit Ehad movement, following the loss of both Vilan's and Avital's Knesset seats in the 2009 election. His workload tripled, Benny has remained tireless in his campaign both to influence the Knesset to pass the Voluntary Evacuation Compensation Bill, and to build grass roots interest in the Occupied Territories, as well as to raise funds. For Benny this is no longer about simply selling his house. His campaign is to force the government to take responsibility for decades of promoting settlement in the territories and compensate all those who now find themselves outside the assumed future Israeli border, willing but unable to leave. According to Benny there are 73 such settlements outside the fence, with a combined population of roughly 100,000 people and, as he demonstrates by waving a thick wad of collected names and addresses over the solitary desk in his poky back office, thousands of them have signed up with Bayit Ehad already. In Benny's estimation, there are tens of thousands more where they came from.

"At least 70% [of the 100,000 outside the fence] want to leave." He insists, his broad fingers fanning through the pages excitedly. "Or even 80%. They'll tell you that if you gave them a cheque for their house tomorrow they'd go."

Moreover, Benny believes that this figure would rise on the back of growing momentum, claiming that if the compensation money materialised there would be 200,000 people ready to move immediately. These figures sound exorbitantly high, however, given the number of settlers we have spoken to over the last two years, but Benny claims that he is not exaggerating. Rather he argues that it is for fear of retribution that they don't speak out. Jealously guarding the rights of Jews to settle in the West Bank, many settlers fear the potential damage that Benny's movement could do to the settlement enterprise and have made their disapproval abundantly clear. Within two weeks of speaking up in favour of enabling settlers to leave the territories, Benny learnt what he was up against when the head of the council fired him from his job in transportation.

"He said 'sir, you are a traitor for returning the territories...You are basically working for the Arabs. You are a fascist, you are a German' and so on," recalls Benny, angrily beating his hand on the table to punctuate the charges. "I swallowed it all and shut up."

Others, though, are less willing to suffer such punishment and it is for this reason that Benny collects his names in the utmost secrecy, travelling from family home to family home to meet with interested parties, making sure to respect each signatory's requests for their particular degree of privacy. Certain names he puts in touch with the press to publicise their cause. Others, which include families from even the most extreme settlements like Kiryat Arba and Itzhar, are kept far from the public eye and serve only to create a groundswell of support for

Benny Raz (right) and Moshe Katz

Bayit Ehad and its compensation proposals. According to Benny they are right to be fearful.

"[People talk about] two states for two peoples. We already have two states. There is the state of Israel and there is the dictatorial state in the territories. Twenty per cent of the ideologists – the rabbis, the synagogues – they rule in Judea and Shomron... For example I put up a sign saying 'don't leave Israelis behind the fence'. A guy from the *yeshiva* came, ran up and pulled it down. I asked him why – 'did you read what it said?' He said 'no.' 'So why did you take it down?' He said 'the Rabbi told me to'."

Benny has been the victim of several threats of physical violence, including a confrontation following a Bayit Ehad meeting in nearby religious settlement Shavei Shomron, when an angry mob of settlers surrounded his car, with him and his son inside, and tried to overturn it, before the army had to come and escort him to safety. Perhaps the most unsettling incident though was when a man threatened to kill Benny, "not here and now, but when there's no one else around". Benny took the threat seriously enough to go to the police – something it is hard to imagine that this former elite soldier would have done if there wasn't genuine cause for concern. Little wonder then that Benny now claims to be "more afraid of the Jews than the Arabs".

However, Benny's determination only seems to have been bolstered by such confrontation. Claiming to have "thrown away his work for his politics", Benny is now consumed by his campaign, which even takes precedence over his home life. With a wife who works in Karnei Shomron's nursery and is unwilling to leave her home, Benny's battles extend to within his own four walls, going so far as to claim that he and his wife "would even divorce, if it became necessary. I live this so strongly... I said that even if I have to eat bread and water I'll fight for what I believe in."

Such a separation of love and principles is apparent in Benny's attitude towards the state itself. On the one hand he insists that he is "crazy about the state of Israel" but on the other hand he feels that he has dedicated enough of his life to serving the state and is no longer prepared to watch as the settlement policies of successive Israeli governments continue, in his view, to damage Israel's international standing. On this matter Benny is typically vociferous.

"We need to lower our tone a bit throughout the world. We make the biggest noise. We're a state like a small dot that... I'd say it's like a cancer sending secondaries throughout the world. On the one hand I'm proud of my

315

state that has succeeded in sixty years to achieve what we have achieved. But we will destroy everything if we don't open our eyes and see how we're living. Enough. We're no longer the heroes that we once were."

And Benny himself has had enough of playing the hero role. Having served his country militarily for the majority of his adult life, he is now tired of being on the front line. If, as many advocates of Israel's settlement policy argue, Israel's retention of the West Bank is a means of keeping the war with the Palestinians away from the major cities like Tel Aviv and Jerusalem, then let the army serve that function, he argues, not him. As for those who point to the example of Gaza as a reason not to evacuate the West Bank, Benny is just as dismissive.

"The rockets will come if I'm there or not there... Like with Gush Katif. The army were in Gaza and the rockets reached Ashkelon and Beer Sheva and all these places... Why do I need to be there? I'm not a conquering army. I'm a citizen of Israel. There is an army that conquered in 67. The IDF conquered the place. And the army will guard the place. The army must be the shield of the state of Israel. Not Benny."

At this point it becomes apparent that Benny is no longer simply advocating that the government helps him to leave the Occupied Territories, just as it helped him to settle there; he is in fact advocating a major shift in Israel's general political outlook. The one time right wing Mossadnik now expounds the Palestinian cause with the fluency of the most hardened left wing activist.

"All the time, they'd taught me in the army that you have to kill the Arabs, be against the Arabs, in security too and in Mossad and everywhere but suddenly I started to see things from the other side... [The Palestinian's] life is no life... He has no economy, he has no security... Soldiers come to the house and take him out... for interrogation... He can't go from this village to that village to visit his son. He can't even cross the road... to water his trees – he needs permission from the army. I realised that these are deprived people."

It is no surprise then that Benny finds himself at the centre of such heated arguments in the settlements – the gradual entrenchment of divisions between Jewish and Palestinian communities over the course of the occupation means that such humanising empathy with the enemy is an anathema to those on the right of the settler communities. Benny, however, goes further still, citing the history of the Jewish people's drive for nationhood as a precedent for the legitimacy of the Palestinians' own aspirations.

"I am against terror... but I understand their way. Why? Because I don't forget where we came from. I'll give you an example. Who detonated the world's biggest bomb since the Second World War? Menahem Begin. He even killed seventeen Jews. And he was our Prime Minister... We too came from Germany and Europe, the Germans did terrible things to us. My parents fled Iraq. People fled Yemen. Morocco made things difficult for Jews. We came in search of land. We came in search of a land for ourselves. But I understand that the other side too wants a state like me."

The only way for Israel to undermine popular Palestinian support for terror campaigns, then, according to Benny, is to negotiate a two state solution and the return of the West Bank and he highlights the hypocrisy of such a government that on the one hand funded and supported Hamas as opposition to Arafat, but refuses to engage with them now that they have ceased to do their masters' bidding. "The whole world has changed," claims Benny. "The Soviet Union has broken up. The Berlin Wall fell. Ireland... Cyprus... We too want to change. We can't live by the sword all our lives... Against terror there is only diplomacy."

Benny believes that his proposals fit perfectly into such a diplomatic process.

"Any PM would be stupid not to take this law... I'm saying come and take me – here I am. You have the road map. I am your road map."

However, Benny despairs that the chance for a swift diplomatic resolution has receded, following Netanyahu's return to power, claiming that Bibi and the "racist" Lieberman have "set us back twenty years".

"Netanyahu is a dangerous man," asserts Benny, his fist returning to the tabletop as he bangs out his frustration. "You can write that ten times. Bibi Netanyahu is a danger to the state of Israel."

Another politician's rise to premiership, however, has given Benny far more cause for optimism. Barack Obama, he believes, will be more forceful with Israel in the pursuit of a two state solution than his predecessor. Meanwhile, Benny is encouraged by the EU's involvement, and in particular that of President Sarkozy of France. Sarkozy is reported to share Benny's negative view of Israel's Foreign Minister and according to *Haaretz* he even called on Netanyahu in June 2009 to remove Lieberman from his position.[59] And in June 2008, in an address to the Israeli Knesset, the French President amazed Benny by endorsing the Voluntary Evacuation Compensation Bill as a means of expediting peace between Israel and the Palestinians. Such publicity is essential to Benny's cause, for it keeps the prospect of the bill alive in the chambers of power and influence.

And yet, once the French President has gone home and the debate turns to more pressing matters, it is just Benni alone in his stuffy office with his telephone and his relentless tenacity. With no sponsors, no more Knesset members representing his cause and diminishing funds threatening to cripple Bayit Ehad within a matter of months, Benny's future is far from secure. It is no wonder then that in the here and now this "orphan", surrounded by enemies and even contemplating divorce spends so much time building up his list of names. For now they're all he has.

***

A few days later we get a call from Benny inviting us to the agricultural settlement of Hamra, in the Jordan Valley, to speak to an old couple that wish to sell up and move out of the West Bank. They want to speak to us; to get their story heard.

We climb into Benny's car and begin the crawl out of a mild Tel Aviv, up into the creamy mountains north of Mitzpeh Yeriho, where minarets and watchtowers puncture the horizon, and back down the other side, where the expansive valley floor shimmers in heat below us. Singing along quietly to the Beatles playing on the radio, Benny drums his giant hands on the wheel in between fielding calls from various settlers eager to meet with him and explain their particular predicament. Four days previously, two Israeli policemen were shot dead in their car in a terror attack in the valley and Benny takes the opportunity to point out potential escape routes along mountain paths, explaining how easy it would be for terrorists to attack our car, shoot us and run away again. By the time we reach Hamra, we are glad to be off the road.

A pocket of colour fenced in barbed wire from the hazy desert floor, Hamra is an agricultural *moshav* and part of the original Allon plan, which intended to create Israeli settlements along the relatively uninhabited border with Jordan, in order to create a buffer zone between the two then warring countries. However, the plan was largely unimplemented, the allure of settling all over the West Bank eventually proving too strong, so that the harsher and more remote landscapes of the Jordan Valley remain mostly unsettled to this day. Despite its beauty – modest white houses nestle between thick lawns scattered with yellow mustard flowers and ruby red hibiscus – Hamra has the feel of a community that has been all but forgotten. The agriculture on which the *moshav* depends has dried up, the secular community unable to demand the same government investment that the politically influential residents of the larger mountain settlements receive. The younger generations have moved out and the lack of

319

new industry in the region, which is far beyond the realm of the Separation Barrier, suggests that the government has given up on Hamra and is simply waiting for its elderly residents to die off.

Drinking bitter-sweet Arabic coffee and eating dates on the sofas of his cool, wood-panelled living room at the edge of the tiny settlement, hard of hearing Moshe Katz shouts his way through an explanation of why he wants to leave, soon prompting his quiet, patient wife Yafa to get up and move to another room. Having been tempted to come to the Valley by a government that asked people to strengthen Israel's borders following the ignominious outcome of the Yom Kippur War, Moshe says he has been "betrayed" by successive governments who have failed to deliver on their promise to make Hamra and the sur-rounding areas a prosperous Israeli city in the Jordan Valley. Without even a doctor or a shop in the settlement, Moshe and Yafa must drive a long distance to get provi-sions and go even further through various checkpoints along unsafe roads to reach the nearest town. The many cameras incongruously perched amongst the trees and bushes of the blooming *yeshuv* make Moshe feel like he is "in a ghetto", while the sense of abandonment by the state makes him want to leave now. But of course the fact that no one wants to move here means he can't sell his house, hence why he got in touch with Benny.

"I'm a pawn in a game of chess for the state. I don't want to be moved whenever and however they want. I'm 67. I want to finish the game and leave now... I didn't come here for something like this. If this is how it's going to be, why waste money on building the [Separation] Fence? Let's just leave."

Moshe has no qualms talking like this. Unlike many of the religious settlers on Benny's list who are reluctant to give voice to their views for fear of retribution from their neighbours, Moshe insists that for a secular man like himself, in a non-ideological farming region like the Jordan Valley, telling people you want to leave is simply not an issue. On the contrary, Moshe is adamant that 80% of the area's residents would leave immediately if they could. Drawing a distinction between the religious ideological settlers and those like himself, he highlights the difference between Benny's relationship with his neighbours and his own. "Benny has a problem," he barks, in his ageing, gravelly voice. "I don't."

"What's the difference between me and a settler?" asks Moshe rhetorically, gesticulating wildly with a subversive sparkle in his eye. "The settler says 'God gave me this land'. I say 'what, the land told you so? What are you talking about?!' I came here to strengthen the land so that there would be a strong state... But now we don't need to rule over the Arabs, over a people that don't need us. We can't... Why can't they have their own state? I'm not apprehensive about that."

It is impossible to say whether things would have been different if the government had made good on their pledge to fill the valley with Jews and give Moshe the city he came here for. Certainly it is the lack of such a provision that has made him tired of his situation and it is a sense of betrayal by the government he once so strongly supported that now makes him want to leave, rather than any particular political ideology. In this respect, too, Moshe is different to Benny. However, Moshe is a farmer and a pragmatist and just as he moved to the region because it made sense to him, he now wants to leave for the same reason. The world is changing, he insists, and it seems that the world has changed Moshe too, over time. He might not share the same ideals as Benny, but both ageing men have invested a great deal in the state and they are now both determined to work together to make back their investment. The state owes them, they believe, and must welcome them back into the heart of Israeli society.

Moshe rises and takes an old ornamental cutlass from its place on the wall, weighing it inquisitively, before unsheathing it and handing it to Benny, with a tale of how the blade came into his possession. Meeting a Bedouin sheikh in Santa Katerina whilst fighting in Sinai during the Yom Kippur War, Moshe had revealed that he had been born in Romania, at which point the sheikh revealed that his tribe, too, were originally from Romania, having migrated south centuries earlier. The sword was given by the sheikh as a memento of their meeting, recalls Moshe smiling, as Benny turns the dulled metal object over in his hands, absorbed by his friend's tale.

The two ageing *sabras* stand exchanging war stories; the broad, weather beaten Romanian, with the thick, calloused skin, and the burly Iraqi, dark and balding, laughing and joking like age old friends. The Ashkenazi's eyes glisten as he belts out his teasing tales and the Sephardi responds with warm smiles and laid-back sincerity; two old generals, left out in the field long after the battle is over. Two soldiers that the state forgot.

Moshe leads us back out into the thick fragrant air of the Hamra garden, scooping up a handful of eggs from his chicken coop on his way and forcing them on Benny to take home.

And then we are back on the road. Benny lights a cigarette and contemplates his next meeting – a new family in the extreme right wing settlement of Itamar who insist on meeting in the Israeli city of Holon, for fear of being spotted with Benny and ostracised from their community.

Arriving in Tel Aviv, Benny reminds us that he still has no funds, "so if we can think of anyone who can help..." And then he heads off to Holon, "to explain the law... and try to give the family a sense of confidence and optimism".

Quite where he finds his own is anyone's guess.

***

Back in Karnei Shomron, the disparity between Benny's optimism and the facts on the ground is made patently clear. In the red-roofed settlement it is business as usual, as Benny gets a brisk dismissal from our host Tova, middle-aged mother of six and one of the first people to build in Karnei Shomron. She insists that, contrary to his claims of 70-80%, Benny represents only twenty to thirty families of the 1300 in the settlement – and that all are in the secular Ginot Shomron district. And while she agrees that their house has lost value since the route of the Separation Barrier became clear, she insists that it's not a problem, because she wouldn't dream of selling anyway. Indeed Tova is adamant that the religious ideology of Karnei Shomron's residents means that none of them would leave the settlement voluntarily.

Perhaps the truth lies somewhere in the middle. Of the religious ideologists we have spoken to throughout our visits, many, certainly a greater percentage than Tova concedes, even amongst the most religious and ideological families, have admitted that if they were sure that they were leaving their homes for a certain and lasting peace agreement, they would go, providing they were adequately compensated. However, almost as many have passionately insisted that they would never leave willingly – and not just the Nadia Matars and Daniella Weisses, but regular family folk, belying the 80% figure to which Benny referred. However, this is of course a small survey of people and it is hard to predict just what the genuine spread would be, if the offer was actually on the table. Nevertheless, a far wider survey conducted on behalf of Peace Now in 2002 concluded that 68% of settlers would obey an evacuation decision, while only 6% would consider illegal means of disobeying the order.[60]

Meanwhile though, as we sit with Tova and her 28 year old son Dvir and chat over cake and juice, it is clear that the prospect of leaving the settlement willingly, prior to a potential forced evacuation, is unthinkable. What they do fear however is the advent of another Disengagement, such as the one carried out by Sharon in 2005. Just as the right wingers' hero performed a policy U-turn at his supporters' expense back then, so do people like Tova suspect that any Israeli government could perform such a manoeuvre at any time – even the right wing government of Bibi Netanyahu. This despite the fact that Tova voted for Habayit Hayehudi, whose Daniel Herschkowitz now serves as a government minister, and regardless of Moshe's earlier claim that the religious settlers wield significant political clout. Family members like Tova have lost their faith in government, sensing that withdrawal from the West Bank is becoming increasingly likely.

And whilst Tova might be a middle-aged mum, calm and relaxed and perhaps unlikely to physically stop such a process, she now has a son in one of three caravans in a remote hilltop outpost, and a daughter living amongst the extremely reclusive settler community in Silwan. Tova does not know exactly what form the resistance to a potential evacuation of these settlements would take, but she is sure there would be resistance: "It's their home. It's hard to know what they would do."

And, unlike Benny, Tova's archetypal religious family does not believe that a Palestinian state could exist in peace alongside Israel. Suspicion prevails, even for their youngest son Dvir, who has spent a lot of time living in the mixed Arab-Jewish neighbourhood of Jaffa, and who is perhaps one of the most laid-back people one could ever meet. "They don't want peace – their goal is that we won't be here at all," he states, flatly.

Perhaps it is because of this deep rooted belief, then, that Tova's family continues to live in Karnei Shomron and, despite the evidence that Obama's administration might take a tougher line on Israeli settlements, can't quite imagine an accord will be reached that would actually force them to leave their home. A building surveyor for the entire West Bank, Tova's husband Yair, a lanky, reserved man, is responsible for building throughout the West Bank. He insists that, in spite of a supposed freeze on settlement expansion as outlined in the 2002 Road

Map, growth of the settlements continues, which Obama's Middle East Envoy, George Mitchell, is refusing to let drop, putting him on a collision course with Netanyahu and his West Bank-residing Foreign Minister Lieberman. Yair affirms that he has more than enough work to keep him busy, although he claims that permission is harder to obtain than the settlers would wish.

Life, then, continues as normal. Dvir points at the boycott of West Bank goods to show that there is always pressure on West Bank settlers, but, he explains, his family and those like them can't let themselves be affected by the pressure of "a few crazy people shouting all the time."

"We can't live in fear of evacuation... of Obama... of a new Intifada..." says Tova calmly. "Life here is good. That's a sign that we're doing the right thing."

We leave Tova and Yair and get into Dvir's open backed van for a whistle-stop tour of Karnei Shomron and the surrounding area. We begin with a drive up the steep, hand-tarmacked path to the settlement's illegal hilltop outpost, Ramat Gilad, established in 2001 by the grandchildren of local land baron and legendary settler figure, Moshe Zar, an Israeli of Iranian origin, whose formidable home presides over all the surrounding land from a commanding hilltop nearby. A highly controversial figure as one of the settlement movement's key financiers, Moshe Zar (mentioned earlier) buys private land from Palestinians and, according to hundreds of Palestinian complaints, steals it too, for Jewish settlement throughout the West Bank. It was the murder of Zar's son Gilad by terrorists in Spring 2001 which prompted the settling of the eponymous outpost on which we now stand; an outpost which Peace Now emphasises ought to have been dismantled, according to Israel's Road Map commitment to dismantle all outposts established after 2001. The hilltop, however, is very much alive and is home to several young families who live in a variety of permanent and semi-permanent portacabins, arranged around a slapdash children's playground.

We crunch over the gravel of the windswept hill, knocking on doors, but no one is home. Passing a row of caravans on the hill's edge we take in the view of Tel Aviv to the West, couched in cloud on the horizon, until we come across one solitary man working on a small construction – but he is unwilling to talk to us. We head instead for the lone guard post that stands sentinel on the other side of the hill, overlooking Palestinian villages across the valley. There we meet the twenty-seven year old soldier charged with guarding the hilltop, one of four who bunk in a corrugated iron cabin and keep watch over the handful of families. The son of an Ashkenazi Jewish man who quite uncommonly traces his lineage back 150 years in Israel, and a woman whose parents survived the concentration camps, the soldier is consumed by fear of anti-Semitism and he responds to our rather innocuous opening query (and, presumably, our English accents), with a bitter spiel about the rampancy of anti-Semitism in England today. When he does finally get around to answering our question, he claims that the outposts are good for Israel, as they are a defence for cities like Tel Aviv – taking one step further the common argument that the settlements keep the war away from the centre, by claiming that outposts keep it further still. The guard, it turns out, is a product of a Rav Kook yeshiva, which imbibes its students with the philosophies of the late spiritual mentor of the settlement movement. He is also, himself, a settler.

Jealously claiming to be the country's true patriots, national religious settlers play a significant role in Israel's armed forces, supplying a disproportionately high 20% of the IDF's officers, a provision which led to internal friction during the 2005 Disengagement as many soldiers disobeyed orders. However, not all settler soldiers share the Ramat Gilad guard's view that outposts are a good thing for the state, with one IDF officer we spoke to in Elkana opposing the cavalier attitude of hilltop settlers who put the army at risk by demanding protection. "I would love for the army to leave them alone to fend for themselves," he had told us. "But that would never happen."

As we talk a car swings into the rough patch of land by the lookout post and out lurches an old man with a limp and crooked eye, who strolls over and warmly slaps the soldier on the back. Turning, the man takes a second to recognise Dvir, before his eyes suddenly light up and he grabs our embarrassed host's cheek as if he was a small child. This, it turns out, is Moshe Zar himself, whose name has been on everyone's lips since we began our visits to the settlements in 2007. The Marmite of West Bank settlers, some speak of him with utter adulation, while others, like Benny, decry him as little more than a common criminal. "Criminal" is rather an apt description – in 1984 Zar was tried and convicted by an Israeli court and sentenced to several months in prison, although his crime was far from common: he was the getaway driver for the Jewish Underground terror group in the 1980 bombing that caused Nablus Mayor Bassam Shak'a to lose both his legs.

As Zar pushes and slaps Dvir with avuncular familiarity, it becomes clear that he is the godfather around here, his cocky swagger and natural charm suggesting both the power and the grace of a big screen gangster. Indeed, it is not too far from the truth. Having survived an attack by Palestinian assailants who put an axe in his skull, Zar is described by Samantha M Shapiro in *The New York Times Magazine* as a "sort of... Wild West-style vigilante mayor of his stretch of the West Bank, inspiring awe among many of the Jews there and fear among the Palestinians."[61]

Zar turns to us and demands to know who we are. We explain and ask if he'd be interested in sharing a few words for the book. He fixes us with his one good eye, as if deciding our fate, before smiling genially and explaining in a hoarse voice that it's not really his thing. This is something of an understatement; according to the writer Robert Friedman, Zar threatened to open fire on him in the summer of 1985 when he drove up the hill to his house to request an interview. With that in mind we decide not to push the matter and leave Zar to stagger back to his car. And like that he is gone.

We leave Ramat Gilad and head along a shared Palestinian-Israeli road to an Israeli owned petrol station, run by a Palestinian man in his forties. The phone doesn't stop ringing and although the man seems willing to talk, he is unable. We decide to try elsewhere, but are granted a parting soundbyte for our troubles:

"There is no answer to the situation," says the man drily. "Only if two people don't get along, they have to divorce."

The young Palestinian climbing out of the souped up car on the petrol station forecourt is less measured in his analysis of the local settlers.

"They cause problems for everyone," he says with a shrug before disappearing into the shop.

This outlook is shared by the burly Palestinian gaffer of the nut and seed factory that we visit next. Walking past executive Mercedes with Palestinian plates to enter uninvited through the open factory door, we are spotted by the gaffer who asks us to join him and his colleagues for their sweet tea break. Part of a mixed Israeli Arab, Palestinian, Jewish and Bedouin workforce, the gaffer has worked in the factory for years and is chummy with all of his colleagues, the mechanics of daily interaction in the workplace far outweighing the segregation of political and national viewpoints. He describes conditions in the West Bank by making a distinction between Israelis and settlers:

"Israelis are good people," he says. "The Jews are generally a nice and decent people. But it is the settlers who cause the problems. They want the land for themselves. There is no solution."

The gaffer's Israeli friend wanders into the factory and slaps his boss on the back and begins to chat to us as the gaffer gets back to work. What is his perception of relations between the settlers and the Palestinians? There are no problems at all, he responds, as far as he can tell. The difference between the outlooks of the Israeli worker and his Palestinian colleague is striking and it seems that, as is often the case, only the one who experiences the problem directly is aware of its existence.

Meanwhile, Dvir stands patiently with us, listening to all that is said and reserving judgement. These are conversations he has had many times before, he tells us, as we drive out of the car park. As a settler who has integrated himself into the centre of Israel, complete with its tapestry of backgrounds, outlooks and political allegiances, Dvir is well used to having to deal with the politics of his situation, having to reconcile the fact that his siblings are amongst the "crazy settlers" to which the Palestinians refer, while he himself is one of the "good, decent Israelis" that the gaffer described.

However, despite their conviviality with the Palestinians around them, neither Dvir nor the Israeli factory worker share the Palestinians' concerns about the presence of West Bank settlements, so to expect those settlers who don't interact with Palestinians at all to see their side of the story is hopelessly naive.

Which is why Benny's community-based economic campaign makes sense. Benny appears to have realised that whilst politics guides people, economics rules them, which is presumably why rather than trying to evoke sympathy for the Palestinians, he focuses instead on the settlers' comfort. By highlighting the fact that it won't always be easy for settlers to live outside the fence – due to a fall in property values and a decline in security – Benny takes the armchair idealists out of their comfort zones and hopes to create enough of a pull to undermine the facts on the ground that Moshe Zar and members of the extreme right are busy creating.

Two extremists operate out of Karnei Shomron, then; two polar opposites: in the blue corner Moshe Zar. In the red corner, Benny Raz. Zar busies himself with creating the facts as Benny tries his best to undermine them. Zar uses money, giving hope and comfort to the settlers, telling them that their future is bright. Raz emphasises that the money is dwindling, along with the comfort and the hope; your future, he says to the settlers, is looking bleak. Zar does all he can to show that his facts make sense, but if Raz can show that the facts and stats no longer add up, there's a chance he could create enough of a groundswell to precipitate a mass exodus of Jews into Israel.

Crucially though, Zar's facts on the ground would be nothing without the continued government support that gives the settlers the comfort and security they require. Likewise, unless Raz gets the government endorsement he so desperately desires, his mission is likely to fail, and the facts on the ground will remain. After all, it was the government that created the settlements. And only the government can take them away.

Epilogue
The settlement freeze:
Settlers out in the cold?

"Bibi's inspectors keep out!" scream the banners draped over settlement entranceways throughout the West Bank. In their black body armour and helmets, one hundred policemen amass at the gates of Ma'aleh Levona, where hundreds of youths scream at them through the metal fence: "Go Home!" The police wait stoically behind the settlers' makeshift barricade of rocks and furniture, until the signal, when they hurl stun grenades at the crowd and scale the barrier, picking off the more demonstrative protesters as they march into the settlement. And behind the armed forces comes the focus of all the anger, the 'inspectors': Civil Administration officials charged with carrying out one of Israel's most controversial jobs of the year – delivering orders to cease construction in the settlements.

Such is the result of Israeli Prime Minister Benyamin Netanyahu's announcement of the so-called 'settlement freeze', a ten month moratorium on construction in West Bank settlements, following months of pressure from a US administration keen to placate a frustrated Palestinian Authority, which had refused to resume negotiations with Israel until settlement construction was suspended. The freeze represents a major policy shift on the part of the right wing Prime Minister and just as one-time settlers' man Ariel Sharon was perceived to stab his people in the back with his unilateral Disengagement from Gaza in 2005, so do many Jewish residents of the West Bank now feel betrayed by their other champion, Bibi, a long time supporter of the settlements and, until very recently, denier of the Palestinians' right to statehood.

The settlers are angry. And just as Sharon's Disengagement led to clashes between settlers and the state, the current animosity between the two sides threatens to spill over into violence once more. As the freeze moves into its second phase, the Israeli media report that a draft IDF document outlines the security forces' plans to deal robustly with any settlers violating the temporary building suspension. Including proposed powers to seal off any settlement in violation of the freeze while illegal buildings are razed, the document calls for the deployment of large units of security officers in order to meet violations with "paralysing force".[62] Whereas over the last forty years successive governments have had an ambivalent approach to illegal settlement construction, reminiscent of Nir's allusion back in Kfar Adumim that as the government prevents the settlers from building in theory, it allows them, with a wink, to continue to grow in practice, the IDF would now appear to have an unambiguous line vis à vis the settlers. Indeed one experienced IDF officer is reported in *Haaretz* as saying that "the political echelon has finally stopped winking. This is the first time we're receiving clear, detailed instructions on how to deal with building in the settlements."[63]

In the face of the security forces' firm line, many settlers are adopting a resolute stance of their own. "We're very angry; all of us here are very angry about the freeze," says Tova, whom we first interviewed in Karnei Shomron. "We want to grow; to build the *yeshuv*, to give our children somewhere to live, but we're not allowed to now. We won't let this happen in silence... If we thought it would help then we would let it happen, but since we don't, we won't. This is the *kav adom* [red line]."

Just how settlers intend to respond to the freeze varies from place to place, with residents of Efrat inviting the media to witness a symbolic laying of a concrete foundation, while Nadia Matar continues to lead her groups of right wing activists in settling new hilltops, in a show of defiance to the state. Other settler groups are planning to stage large scale acts of civil disobedience in Israeli towns within the Green Line while extremists resort to violent demonstrations against the security officials responsible for enforcing the freeze. Indeed, Rabbi Yosef Elitzur, one of the heads of a *yeshiva* in the extreme right wing settlement of Yitzhar is reported by *Haaretz* to have written "if there is no quiet for the Jews, there will be no quiet for the Arabs A Civil Administration base can serve as a target for a quick, precise infiltration... You destroy ours, we destroy yours!"[64]

Meanwhile, the 'price tag' policy of violence against the Palestinians continues, with rampages in Palestinians villages, including torched cars and tractors in the village of Einbus and a suspected settler attack on a Mosque in Yasuf near Nablus, with the building fire-bombed and books burnt. "Price tag – greetings from Effi," gloated the Hebrew graffiti discovered on the front of the Mosque, following the attack (Effi is an Israeli name). Whatever the measure, committed settlers are united in their opposition to the freeze and their message is clear: they do not intend to go down without a fight.

But has the government really "stopped winking"? To begin with, even the angriest settler would be hard pushed to accuse Netanyahu of being a left wing Prime Minister and quite clearly the freeze is not so much a decisive move towards the goal of withdrawing from the West Bank, but rather the result of months of pressure from a US administration displaying an unprecedented degree of coolness towards its old ally, Israel. Illustrating the Israeli government's lack of commitment to the idea of negotiating over the future of Israeli settlement in the West Bank, Angela Godfrey-Goldstein of

ICAHD points to the the recent cabinet decision to make certain settlements 'national priority zones'. The new status, which will be conferred on various settlements, including several remote communities far from the large settlement blocs, and which will affect some 110,000 West Bank Israelis, entitles the selected settlements to millions of dollars worth of funds by way of grants, tax benefits and other forms of aid. "OK, it's not for building," says Angela, "but it's for consolidating... I don't trust the freeze at all."

It would appear that the national priority zones are yet another example of the continuing practice of giving with one hand and taking with the other; a case of the Israeli government giving several spoonfuls of sugar to the settlers to help the medicine go down. Moreover, the medicine itself does not appear to be nearly as strong as it would first appear. Netanyahu's decision to exclude public buildings such as schools and synagogues from the freeze, along with some 3,000 private homes for which permits have already been granted, means that the freeze is far from the full settlement construction freeze that America sought, while the exclusion of East Jerusalem from the moratorium has provoked indignation from Palestinian President Mahmoud Abbas, who still refuses to resume negotiations with Israel. On the Palestinian side of the city, evictions continue. In Sheikh Jarrah, where grateful family members distributed tea and biscuits to international activists helping protest their planned eviction from their home of over fifty years, the family house now stands decked out in Israeli flags; its occupants now Israeli settlers; its Palestinian inhabitants forced out. Add to this the belligerent statement of Israeli Foreign Minister Avigdor Lieberman, himself a settler, that "it is clear to everyone that in ten months we will be building again in full force"[65], and the freeze begins to look very ambiguous indeed.

So is this freeze the first step en route to an eventual evacuation of more settlements, as many settlers fear, or is it simply another case of the Israeli government biding its time, giving too little to bring Abbas back to the table, but just enough to ensure that when building resumes in ten months' time, they can point to yet more 'painful concessions' and claim they did all they could, but unfortunately there was no partner for peace? It is difficult to know at this stage. Indeed, it is likely, given the broad nature of the current governing coalition, that a unified policy direction does not exist. It would not be the first time that the Israeli government's settlement policy has been simply to wing it. What is clear, however, is that the ongoing ambiguity towards the settlers – sending in troops of security forces to freeze building, but doling out tax breaks and aid, saying no to West Bank settlers, but yes to East Jerusalemites; using force against the settlers whilst the Prime Minister insists "these are our brothers... [the settlements] are parts of our homeland"[66] – is continuing a dangerous tradition that goes all the way back to Sebastia, wherein the government refuses to take a clear, firm line with the settlement enterprise.

Having established itself in opposition to the state, the leaders of the settlement enterprise thrive on confrontation, and the settlers' relationship with the government has always been one of paradox. Hence, after the Disengagement from Gaza and various West Bank settlements, the number of Israeli settlers in the Occupied Territory is higher than ever. Thriving on their self-image as victims of left wing conspiracies and state persecution, extreme settler groups use their perceived victim status to demand more and more concessions, in the way that the protesters in Jerusalem used the occasion of Tisha B'Av to point to successive Jewish tragedies as a reason to demand more land.

Israel's settlers embody countless paradoxes, from the anti-Zionists of the Ultra-Orthodox, through the American Christian funds for Jewish Israeli expansion, to the left wing settlers who, like most people, put their personal well being before abstract notions like politics and peace. Having continued to take an ambiguous line on settlement construction, successive Israeli governments have allowed these paradoxes to thrive, so that the idea of an achievable end to Israel's occupation now appears more unrealistic than ever, because the more complex the problem the becomes, the more complex is its solution.

The dismantlement of a few extremist outposts will no longer bring about an end to settlement growth, as it might have done during the time of Daniella's tents in Sebastia. Instead, outpost removal, or a partial, temporary freeze on construction, has little more effect than slapping someone in the face: it simply antagonises the settlers further. Like spoilt children, settler leaders are so used to getting their own way – with continuous expansion, subsidies and state protection for the most unlawful of enterprises – that when they are told that one of their toys might be taken from them, they react with disproportionate temper tantrums, as seen in the 'price tag' policy of retribution against their Palestinian neighbours. Their grievances – be it Disengagement or the freeze – are then used by extreme leaders to justify greater expansion and consolidation of the settlements. As long as the government continues to give with one hand and take with the other, the settler leaders will continue to be given everything they demand, whilst simultaneously revelling in their status as the unloved, much maligned victim; a volatile combination. Until the government adopts a uniform, unswerving approach to the settlements, extremist leaders will inevitably use their sense of righteous indignation, and the expectation that they can have whatever they want, to continue to expand, trampling over any remaining hope of a two state solution in their wake, leaving just two alternatives: a one state solution and an accompanying end to Israel and Palestine as we know them – or apartheid.

Of course, for the extremists of the settlement enterprise – those who conquer new hilltops for Israeli outposts – the freeze is largely irrelevant as such construction was already forbidden under Israeli law. Instead it is a good excuse to whip up indignation amongst the settler youth; to play on their sense of victimhood and demand that even more outposts are erected in the face of rampant state oppression. Doubtless the outposts will continue to go up as fast as the state can pull them down, and these cat-and-mouse tussles will continue to grab the headlines, these extremist elements being an easy target for the world's derision. However, whilst the radicalism of the hilltop youth is undoubtedly a problem for the local Palestinians, it distracts the world from the truth of Israel's settlements – that they are far from merely a bunch of religious extremists on a few hilltops, and are instead a full cross section of Israeli society living normal lives, in normalised, sanitised cities with far firmer foundations in the West Bank than a few tin shacks flapping in the wind.

The facts on the ground have steadily developed from wild assertions, to ambiguous statements to irrefutable truisms, all the while under the cover of a few hot headed extremists who continually move the goal posts rightwards. To continue to look at settlers simply as a bunch of religious fanatics is greatly to underestimate Israel's takeover of the West Bank. It is impossible to sum up or generalise Israel's settlers in a few paragraphs as they represent such diverse sections of Israeli society, but this inability to pin down the settlers into one group arguably says more about the settlements than anything else: the settlers' diversity and even their normality represents the sheer vastness of the settlement enterprise as it now stands.

Time and again our travels brought this point home – when answering people's questions as to what the settlers were like, repeatedly the answer was 'surprisingly normal'. It is easy to scapegoat the extremists, but as long as they keep pushing the boundaries of extremism and remaining the objects of the world's hate, the more they make the bulk of the settlers seem ordinary and acceptable. It was once an act of ultra nationalism to build in the West Bank; now that is the preserve of the young people up the hills with their guns, while to live somewhere like Ariel and Ma'ale Adumim is simply to improve your quality of life – indeed certain settlements can even be deemed national priority zones. Good behaviour and normalisation has the effect of legitimising the moderate settlements' existence in the eyes of the majority: the outposts are the extremists, the trouble makers; they're the ones who must be stopped. As for the settlement blocs, well they're not really settlers at all, are they? Appeasing the world by confronting the easily scapegoated extremists, successive Israeli governments have been able to consolidate the quieter, more acceptable – and considerably larger – settlements, to the point that the Israeli consensus seems to be that they will never be given back.

And so settlements in general, and the larger settlement blocs in particular, continue to consolidate in spite of the freeze and as they continue to entrench themselves in the West Bank, their segregation and isolation increases. No longer are the settler children exposed to their Palestinian neighbours like their parents before them; no more do they interact on anything resembling equal terms. Instead they are haunted by memories of Palestinian violence and corrupted by talk of enemies, hatred and war. The segregation of West Bank settlements is virtually complete and the enemy is kept at bay with fences, surveillance and guns. The resultant isolation puts an end to objectivity and moderation and leaves even the most 'normal' of settlements in a vacuum in which casual racism, mistrust and animosity are allowed to grow relatively unchecked.

That is not to say that all settlers are racist, but rather that the scales are tipped very much in favour of enmity and suspicion of the distant Palestinian other. Having met some wonderfully welcoming, hospitable and interesting individuals in our travels, and indeed noting that collectively the settlers' sense of community and duty is extremely strong, it is hard not to be struck by the fact that their severance from the outside world and the dependence of their very existence on the politics of their situation leaves them open collectively to a great deal of extreme and imbalanced judgement. Turning in on themselves, many settlements have developed a strong sense of isolationism and suspicion not only of the Palestinians, but of the rest of Israel and the world, too. The greater the mistrust, the less faith there will be in their leaders, not to mention the notion of peace or rapprochement with the other side.

However, in the face of such consolidation of the status quo, it is an international opinion increasingly impatient with Israeli intransigence that could have the strongest impact on Israel's settlement policy, just as the freeze would not have happened at all if it was not for American pressure. World leaders appear to be galvanising in their opposition to the Israeli occupation of the West Bank. With President Obama showing significantly less patience towards Israel's settlement programme than his predecessor, and with the European Union's new foreign affairs chief Catherine Ashton using her opening speech to deliver some stern words to Israel regarding its "occupation"[67], the tide would appear to be turning. Obama has made it a top international policy target to establish a Palestinian state alongside Israel. Meanwhile, the EU has angered the Israeli leadership by passing a resolution calling for Jerusalem to serve as the capital of both Israel and a future Palestinian state, ignoring Israel's unilateral claim to sovereignty over the whole city[68]. Israel, it would seem, is losing control of its traditional allies and is looking increasingly isolated in the international arena. This more than anything could transpire to be the greatest impetus for a sea change in the way that Israel conducts its settlement policy.

However, Israel is no stranger to international controversy and has survived such criticism before. How seriously, then, will Israel take the current international impatience over its own intransigence? It has been said that Netanyahu's government simply regards Obama's as a one-term administration; an inconvenience to be suffered until a Republican President returns to the White House and Israeli settlements in the West Bank cease to be such an important issue. The simple truth is that it is easier for each Israeli government to avoid having to deal with the problem of the settlements, and the larger the settlements become, the more that is the case. The mishandling of the Gaza Disengagement, along with the virulent abuse emanating from the extreme fringes of the settler movement even as a result of a partial construction freeze are sufficient to make any Israeli politician even contemplating another Disengagement think twice. Having failed to nip the settlements in the bud, the Israeli government is now faced with the prospect of having to uproot an almighty tree and attempt to replant it in the promised land within the green line. International condemnation is a minor inconvenience in comparison. It is far easier just to sit it out.

As for the settlers, they don't have nearly so long to wait. Ten months, in the context of forty-odd years is a very short time and settlement leaders are masters of Realpolitik. It is however important to note that the freeze, albeit partial, is an acknowledgement that perhaps the Israeli government, even a right wing one such as Netanyahu's, doesn't regard the settlements as permanent and it sets a precedent which makes such freezes easier to effect in the future. However, should the current freeze end after ten months as Lieberman promises, and building resume "in full force", past experience suggests that, despite complaints of being weakened and diminished; of being the victims of left wing conspiracies and aggression, the settlement enterprise will emerge from this temporary setback and begin the new decade just as strong, if not even stronger than it finished the last.

Endnotes

[1] Peace Now survey of 3,200 respondents conducted by Dr Michael Hopp in July 2002 http://www.peacenow.org.il/site/en/peace.asp?pi=62&docid=2175

[2] http://www.peacenow.org.il/data/SIP_STORAGE/files/6/2846.pdf

[3] The golden Dome of the Rock in the heart of Jerusalem's Old City, is situated on a site known to Jews as the Temple Mount and to Muslims as The Noble Sanctuary. Holy to both religions alike, this was the site of the Second Jewish Temple, destroyed by the Romans in 70CE and is also the point from which Muslims believe Mohammed ascended into heaven.

[4] Pen name of Asher Ginsberg, a 19th Century cultural Zionist who prioritised building a Jewish spiritual centre in Palestine, over Theodor Herzl's Political Zionism, which sought to expedite the establishment of a Jewish state.

[5] Religious girls can opt for this kind of work instead of serving in the army. Reut Feldman, one of the girls killed in the Kedumim car bomb, was on such a placement in this very camera room before she was killed.

[6] Jews and Arabs are more commonly reputed to be descendants of Isaac and Ismael respectively.

[7] Operation Shlomo was an IDF operation in May 1991, organised in the face of political unrest in Ethiopia that saw 14,400 Ethiopian Jews airlifted to Israel.

[8] Typically non-Jewish care workers.

[9] Though still in common usage, Marrano is the derogatory name given to forced converts who continued to practise their Judaism in secret. Less insulting is the term Hidden Jew.

[10] http://www.peacenow.org.il/data/SIP_STORAGE/files/6/2846.pdf

[11] http://www.fmep.org/reports/archive/vol.-17/no.-3/the-occupation-as-history-lessons-from-the-conquest-of-hebron

[12] A programme designed for nationalistic religious students that allows them to divide their army service with Torah study.

[13] A proposal by Israeli Deputy Prime Minister Yigal Allon in the aftermath of the Six Day War, to redraw Israel's borders with Jordan, establishing a string of Israeli settlements along the Jordan valley to create a security corridor between the two states, and creating enclaves of autonomous Arab regions in the more densely populated areas of the West Bank's mountainous regions.

[14] Gershom Gorenberg, *Occupied Territories: The Untold Story of Israel's Settlements* (London: Tauris, 2008) pp.100-120

[15] Despite receiving a greater share of the vote than expected, at 23.4%, Feiglin lost the 2007 Likud primary election to Benyamin Netanyahu, who received an overwhelming majority of the vote, with 73.2%. Feiglin went on to win the 20th place on Likud's Knesset list for the 2009 General Elections, but was demoted to 36th place by Netanyahu, who sought a means of curbing the influence of Feiglin's radical Jewish Leadership movement within Likud. Following the General Election, Likud's receipt of 27 Knesset seats meant that Feiglin was not elected as a member of the Knesset. His campaigns continue.

[16] Amalek was the ancestor of the Biblical tribe the Amalekites, who were enemies of the Israelites. The term Amalek has come to be used to describe any enemy of the Jewish people.

[17] Amos Oz, *In The Land of Israel* (Harcourt, 1993) p.256

[18] Yom Tov is the Hebrew term for a Jewish religious holiday.

[19] Interview conducted in March 2009

[20] Interview conducted by Josh; first person refers to him.

[21] http://news.bbc.co.uk/1/hi/world/middle_east/4804666.stm Tues 14th March 2006

[22] Gershom Gorenberg, *Occupied Territories: The Untold Story of Israel's Settlements* (London: Tauris, 2008) pp. 224-5

[23] http://www.guardian.co.uk/world/2009/mar/07/israel-palestine-eu-report-jerusalem

[24] http://unispal.un.org/unispal.nsf/99818751a6a4c9c6852560 690077ef61/2f8fb6437db17ca5852575a9004d7cb4?Open Document

[25] http://www.haaretz.com/hasen/spages/1096333.html

[26] http://www.icahd.org/eng/news.asp?menu=5&submenu= 1&item=675

[27] Ir Amim report: "Evictions and Settlement Plans in Sheikh Jarrah: The Case of Shimon HaTzadik". June 25th 2009

[28] Ibid

[29] Ibid

[30] http://www.haaretz.com/hasen/spages/949976.html

[31] http://www.guardian.co.uk/world/2009/mar/07/israel-palestine-eu-report-jerusalem

[32] Ibid

[33] Ir Amim, "Evictions and Settlement Plans in Sheikh Jarrah: The Case of Shimon HaTzadik". May 19th 2009

[34] http://www.haaretz.co.il/hasen/spages/1094882.html

[35] http://www.reuters.com/article/worldNews/idUSTRE52U4VH20090401

[36] The road map for peace, full text. http://news.bbc.co.uk/1/hi/world/middle east/2989783.stm

[37] http://www.jpost.com/Home/Article.aspx?id=136549

[38] http://www.guardian.co.uk/world/2009/mar/07/israel-palestine-eu-report-jerusalem

[39] http://www.haaretz.com/hasen/spages/1068546.html

[40] http://www.alertnet.org/thenews/newsdesk/L4625486.htm

[41] http://www.huffingtonpost.com/ir-amim/what-is-behind-jerusalems_b_222101.html

[42] Certain tours in this section were attended by Seth only; first person refers to him.

[43] *Nakba* – lit. 'catastrophe'. The term used by Palestinians for the 1948 war and the establishment of the state of Israel.

[44] Certain Bi'lin demonstrations were attended by Seth only; first person refers to him.

[45] Certain tours in this section were attended by Seth only; first person refers to him.

[46] http://www.btselem.org/english/Settler_Violence/Nature_of_the_Violence.asp

[47] http://www.btselem.org/english/Settler_Violence/Law_Enforcement.asp

[48] Yesh Din. Law Enforcement Upon Israeli Civilians in the OPT data sheet, July 2008

[49] http://www.btselem.org/english/Publications/Summaries/200809_Access_Denied.asp

[50] Gershom Gorenberg, *Occupied Territories: The Untold Story of Israel's Settlements* (London: Tauris, 2008) pp.99-102

[51] http://www.haaretz.com/hasen/spages/1060043.html

[52] http://www.peacenow.org.il/data/SIP_STORAGE/files/6/2846.pdf

[53] http://www.btselem.org/english/freedom_of_movement/Checkpoints_and_Forbidden_Roads.asp

[54] http://haaretz.com/hasen/spages/1095231.html

[55] http://www.btselem.org/English/Freedom_of_Movement/Statistics.asp

[56] http://www.independent.co.uk/news/world/middle-east/israeli-settlers-poisoning-our-sheep-say-west-bank-farmers-526329.html 27th April 2005

[57] http://www.jpost.com/Home/Article.aspx?id=12556

[58] http://www.haaretz.com/hasen/spages/1030568.html

[59] http://www.haarctz.com/hasen/spages/1096504.html

[60] Peace Now survey of 4,000 respondents, 3,200 of which were West Bank settlers; 8000 from Gaza. Conducted by Dr Michael Hopp in July 2002 http://www.peacenow.org.il/data/SIP_STORAGE/files/5/485.ppt

[61] "The Unsettlers", Samantha M Shapiro (*New York Times Magazine*, 16th Feb 2003)

[62] http://www.ynetnews.com/articles/0,7340,L-3822282,00.html

[63] http://www.haaretz.com/hasen/spages/1133308.html

[64] http://www.haaretz.com/hasen/spages/1133309.html

[65] http://www.haaretz.com/hasen/spages/1135852.html

[66] http://www.ynetnews.com/articles/0,7340,L-3815699,00.html

[67] http://www.haaretz.com/hasen/spages/1135787.html

[68] http://news.bbc.co.uk/1/hi/8401913.stm